NEURAL NETWORK MODELS IN ARTIFICIAL INTELLIGENCE

ELLIS HORWOOD SERIES IN ARTIFICIAL INTELLIGENCE

Joint Series Editors: Professor JOHN CAMPBELL, Department of Computer Science, University College London, and
Dr JEAN HAYES MICHIE, Director of Knowledgelink Limited; and The Turing Institute, Glasgow

*In preparation

NEURAL NETWORK MODELS IN ARTIFICIAL INTELLIGENCE

MATTHEW ZEIDENBERG, B.A., M.S.
Computer Sciences Department
University of Wisconsin, Madison, USA

ELLIS HORWOOD
NEW YORK   LONDON   TORONTO   SYDNEY   TOKYO   SINGAPORE

First published in 1990 by
ELLIS HORWOOD LIMITED
Market Cross House, Cooper Street,
Chichester, West Sussex, PO19 1EB, England
A division of
Simon & Schuster International Group

Printed and bound in Great Britain
by Hartnolls, Bodmin

British Library Cataloguing in Publication Data

Zeidenberg, Matthew
Neural network models in artificial intellience. —
(Ellis Horwood series in artificial intelligence)
1. Artificial intelligence
I. Title
006.3
ISBN 0–13–612185–3

Library of Congress Cataloging-in-Publication Data

Zeidenberg, Matthew
Neural network models in artificial intelligence /
Matthew Zeidenberg.
p. cm — (Ellis Horwood series in artificial intelligence)
ISBN 0–13–612185–3
1. Neural computers.   2. Artificial intelligence
I. Title.   II. Series
QA76.5.Z36   1989
006.3–dc20   89–24457
                                              CIP

Table of Contents

For my grandmother, Mrs. Toby Schwartz,
my parents, Rayna and Phillip,
and my sisters, Deborah and Lisa Beth

Preface

The purpose of this book is to serve as a relatively brief introduction to the field of neural networks and their uses in cognitive simulation. There is tremendous interest in this field, but, at this writing, there is no book that attempts to overview the field in a balanced and rigorous fashion. There has been an enormous amount of research done in this area in the past several years. I try to present some of the best and most representative research in the field; since the amount of research that has been done is so large, I have been unable to cover all of it. I have also provided a bibliography, which is referenced throughout. Each chapter begins with an overview of the work in a particular area (for example, natural language processing) and proceeds to a review of important and/or representative work in that area.

Chapter 1 overviews the field of neural networks, reviews some of their history, and discusses some of the basic conceptual and philosophical issues involved. Chapter 2 gets into the mathematical specifics of the various network models.

Chapters 1 and 2 are prerequisites for the remaining chapters in the book, which are each devoted to a particular area of artificial intelligence(AI). Chapter 3 is devoted to the area of production and expert systems. Chapter 4 is concerned with knowledge representation. Speech recognition and synthesis is the topic of Chapter 5. Chapter 6 concerns visual perception and pattern recognition. Chapter 7 covers language understanding. As may be observed by even a cursory examination of Chapters 2-7, there are few problems in AI that have not been explored using the connectionist paradigm. Any one of Chapters 2-7 can be read independently, although there are relationships between chapters, particularly between Chapters 4 and 7, since knowledge representation is necessary for language understanding, and between Chapters 5 & 6, which both deal with problems—vision and speech—in the domain of perception.

Acknowledgments

I would like to thank Sue Horwood for suggesting that I write this book, Sarah Teague, Allan Whittle, Mike Shardlow, Rosemary Harris, and Jane Willett of the Ellis Horwood staff for helping see it through to its completion, and Anne Coleman for competent typing assistance. This book would not have been possible without the work of the many researchers whose work it discusses; their example is inspirational for those of us who hope to make a career of research, and I am grateful to them. I would also like to thank Gregg Oden, Leonard Uhr, and Vasant Honavar for advice, discussions, and suggestions, M & M for California computing, and my family—my parents, Rayna and Phillip, my sisters Debbie and Lisa, and my grandmother Toby—and friends—especially Sandy, Ken, Duncan, and Igor—for moral support.

Madison, Wisconsin, 1989   Matt Zeidenberg

1

Issues in Neural Network Modeling

1.1. Introduction

The past five years or so have seen a substantial amount of work being done in the area of neural network modeling. This research attempts to build model neural networks that solve significant psychological problems, such as natural language understanding, visual processing, etc.

A neural network is a computational model that is a directed graph composed of nodes (sometimes referred to as units or neurons) and connections between the nodes. With each node is associated a number, referred to as the node's activation. Similarly, with each connection in the network, a number is also associated, called its weight. These are (very roughly) based on the firing rate of a biological neuron and the strength of a synapse (connection between two neurons) in the brain. There are usually some special nodes with their activations externally set, called the input nodes; there may be, in addition, some nodes that are distinguished as output nodes.

Each node's activation is based on the activations of the nodes that have connections directed at it, and the weights on those connections. A rule that updates the activations is typically called the *update rule*. Typically, all the activations would be updated simultaneously. Thus a neural network is a parallel model. Because of the lack of general availability of parallel computers, neural networks are typically simulated on conventional serial computers.

Learning in a neural network typically occurs by adjustment of the weights, via a *learning rule*. The network is typically trained to either complete an input pattern, classify an input pattern, or compute a function of its input. At the beginning of learning, with the weights all "wrong", the network performs badly at one of these tasks: at the end, with the weights adjusted, one hopes that it will perform well. Typically the update or learning rules do not change, only the weights. After learning, the weights are usually not changed further, unless something new must be learned.

Many network connection schemes, update rules, and learning rules have been invented: these are covered in gory detail in Chapter 2.

Neural network models, like AI itself, date back to the 1950s. At the beginning of the 1980s, many researchers, discouraged at the speed of progress in traditional, symbolic AI, turned back to neural network models. They felt that this line of research had been unjustly hurt by the publication, in 1969, of Minsky and Papert's book *Perceptrons*, which pointed up the limitations of a particular kind of neural model, the two-layer perceptron. In 1985, a special issue of *Cognitive Science* was devoted to the subject of "connectionism", which was a new name for the field of neural network modeling, and which emphasized the idea that it was the topology of the connections in a network that was critical to its behavior. In this book, I will use "neural network model", "connectionist model", and "connectionist network" interchangeably.

Another reason for the renewed popularity of connectionist models was the fact that parallel computers began to become available. Connectionist models are one important variety of parallel computational models.

In 1986, a two-volume set of books called *Parallel Distributed Processing: Explorations in the Microstructure of Cognition* was published which reported research done by a group of cognitive scientists at the University of California at San Diego, and led by David Rumelhart and Jay McClelland (1986b). The most important result in those volumes—although they contained many important ideas—was the report of the discovery of the error back-propagation algorithm for learning the weights in an associative network (see Chapter 2). Much of the connectionist literature since then has comprised studies of what can be done with networks that are trained using this algorithm.

Rumelhart, McClelland, and co-workers advocated a particular type of network model, a distributed model, in which a typical concept— such as a word— would be represented by a pattern of activation across a set of nodes. This is in contrast with local representation, in which a particular concept is represented by the activation of a single node. We discuss the relative advantages of local versus distributed representations in section 1.4.

1.2. The Statistical Nature of Connectionist Models

A critical fact about neural networks is that they are **statistical associative** models. A typical network model has a set of input patterns and a set of output patterns. The role of the network is to perform a function that associates each input pattern with an output pattern. A learning algorithm, such as back-propagation, uses the statistical properties of a set of input/output pairs— called the training set— to **generalize**, that is, generate outputs from novel inputs. Without the ability to generalize, neural network models would be like look-up tables, which are not very interesting. For a formal discussion of generalization in learning, see Valiant (1984).

It is important to recognize the difference between statistical and rule-based inference. Statistical inference allows for exceptions and randomness in the association between two variables, whereas rules are deterministic. In a neural network model, the history of the system—that is, what training it has seen—determines the system's response to a new stimulus. Often, rule-based systems are non-adaptive, that is, they do not respond to observed changes in the stimulus environment, although they can be made to be adaptive. Rule-based systems can be made to handle exceptions as well, at the expense of making the rules more complex.

Thus neural networks derive their inspiration from two distinct yet related fields—associationist psychology and neuroscience. Associationist psychology has a long history: behaviorism is one form of it, but the idea that human memory works associatively dates back at least to classical times. Neuroscience and associationist psychology have an uneasy alliance that comes from the simple observation that neurons synapse with one another, therefore the firing rates of such neurons are associated. If the brain is simply a web of such associations, perhaps the mind is as well.

As Touretzky (1988) points out, usually a connectionist system either classifies the input or performs some function of it. In either case the function computed tends to be a continuous one, with relatively similar outputs being assigned to similar inputs. There may be a certain number of discontinuities intrinsic to a classification task, since the outputs in such a task are a discrete set of symbols representing the sets in which the inputs are classified.

Some type of measurement of similarity between patterns is critical for a statistical process such as a neural network. In computing its output for a given input, a connectionist model computes some sort of correlation between its input and the set of stored weights associated with a given node in the layer above the input. Typically this correlation is a dot (scalar) product; if x_i and w_i are the ith components of the input and weight vectors respectively, then the dot product is given by

$$\sum_i w_i x_i$$

Yet there are many methods of forming statistical correlations between patterns. A review may be found in Kohonen (1988); a summary of that review follows:

Probably the best known measure of the distance between two vectors x and y is the Euclidean distance, given by

$$\sqrt{\sum_i (x_i - y_i)^2}$$

This generalizes to the Minkowski metric, given by

$$\left(\sum_i (x_i - y_i)^n \right)^{1/n}$$

which, when $n=1$, is sometimes referred to as the "Manhattan" distance (because in order to get between two points in Manhattan (New York City) one must move along a grid). When $n=2$, it is the Euclidean distance.

If what matters is not the magnitude of the vectors that are being compared, but their relative orientation θ, this is given by

$$\cos \theta = \frac{x \cdot y}{|x||y|}$$

$\cos\theta=1$ implies x and y are parallel (and thus as similar as possible); $\cos\theta=0$ implies x and y are orthogonal.

In fuzzy logic (Zadeh 1973), in one version presented by Kohonen, two scalars' similarity is given by

$$e(x,y) = max(min(x,y),min(1-x,1-y))$$

where x and y are drawn from the interval between 0 and 1 inclusive. x and y are variables that represent the degree of truth of two propositions, and e represents the degree to which they are equivalent. These differences, when they are taken between vector components, can be combined using the Minkowski metric above with some value of n (most typically $n=1$ or 2). Kohonen points out that this method is simpler to compute than a dot product, since the maximum and minimum functions are simpler to compute than the product function, and that, in forming the distance, this method counts weak signal data more than the dot product does.

All of the similarity measures mentioned so far deal with real-valued input vectors. For discrete-valued vectors, one similarity metric is the Hamming distance. This is simply the number of vector components in which two vectors x and y differ. Each element of each vector being compared is drawn from a finite set of symbols. In the case of binary vectors, the Hamming distance is given by the sum of the exclusive-or function (xor) across all components:

$$\sum_i xor(x_i,y_i)$$

Although most of the computations carried out in connectionist models involve the dot product of weights with input (often then composed with a functional, such as a sigmoid function), it is helpful to keep in mind that this is only one of the many similarity functions that could be used.

1.3. Relevance of the Brain

Research in neural networks stems from the idea that simulating, on a computer, the way that the brain processes information may prove useful in understanding thought processes. Neural network research dates from the 1940s. In 1943, McCulloch and Pitts published their classic paper "A Logical Calculus of the Ideas Immanent in Nervous Activity" (1943). McCulloch and Pitts's neurons were simple logic gates, the *and, or,* and *not* gates familiar to logic designers. McCulloch and Pitts proved that a computer built out of these "formal neurons" was Turing-equivalent, that is, equivalent to the most powerful class of computing devices known (Turing machines).

As Cowan and Sharp (1988) and many others (for example, see Shepherd 1989) have pointed out, actual neurons are much more complex than simple logic gates, and "their complexities can be accurately simulated only by intricate computer chips". These complexities have been elucidated only in recent years, since McCulloch and Pitts's work. Most neuron models that have been developed for neural network research are less complex than actual neurons. Neural network researchers argue that since their models are Turing-equivalent, they can simulate any computation at all, so there is no need to use more complex neuron models.

The brain consists of approximately 10^{11}-10^{12} neurons connected in a complex fashion. Neural network and brain researchers believe that the way that the neurons are connected to one another is critical to understanding the behavior of the brain as an information-processing system.

1.4. Distributed vs. Local Connectionism

The brain, like the rest of the body, is built of unreliable components. Neurons can wither and die. How is it possible that the brain continues to function fairly reliably over a long period, despite this? This was a question that interested John von Neumann, a mathematician who was one of the founders of computer science (Von Neumann 1956). He devised a neural network that utilized redundant neurons, using a "voting" protocol. In such a net, a set of neurons "vote" on whether or not another neuron should fire. If a majority of the inputting neurons fire, i.e. vote "yes", then the outputting neuron will fire (and possibly input into some other neurons). Thus if an outputting neuron starts out with a strong majority, the failure of some of the neurons inputting to it to fire will not affect its outputting, and thus performance will not be degraded. Redundancy has been the cornerstone of much work in reliable systems. Randell and his co-workers (1978) review work in this area.

Much of the debate among connectionists concerns the degree to which information should be localized in a single neuron (Barlow 1972), or distributed across many neurons. A distributed memory is the latter kind, one in which a symbol—for example, an ordinary word—is represented by a pattern of activation.

While studies of brain function have proved that different activities—for example, speech, vision, or motor control—are localized in various specialized parts of the brain, many people believe that single neurons do not represent high-level pieces of information. The argument goes as follows: if one had a neuron that represented, for example, one's grandmother, then there would be people running around who were perfectly normal except for their inability to recognize their grandmother (i.e. whose grandmother neurons had died). Since there are no such people (as far as we know), therefore there cannot be any grandmother neurons (or yellow Volkswagen neurons, etc.), or there must be many redundant copies of a grandmother neuron. Human memory appears to suffer from "uniform degradation"; instead of individual memories becoming lost, performance on recall of all memories becomes worse and worse (with age or injury).

Local representations are also subject to a combinatorial explosion, in which a node is needed for every concept. This is because there are an infinite number of concepts, because of the natural combinatorial nature of language, and each one would require an individual node. For example, in a local representation, one would have to have a "tall blond man" node, whereas in a distributed representation one would have nodes for "tall", "blond", and "man", all of which would be activated simultaneously to represent "tall blond man". These individual nodes are often referred to as microfeatures to emphasize the fact that individual concepts can be decomposed into them. Microfeatures are often chosen on the basis of a researcher's feeling that the chosen concepts are somehow basic to a complete semantics of the concepts being represented, but very few researchers have chosen their microfeatures in a principled way. For limits on how this might be done, see works on semantics such as those by Barwise & Perry (1983) and Jackendoff (1983).

One of the more active research centers, the University of Rochester, emphasizes the use of local representations in connectionist models (Feldman 1986). Feldman, Ballard, and their colleagues and students at Rochester have applied these types of models to problems in knowledge representation, vision, and language comprehension. For examples, see the reviews of the work of Shastri in Chapter 4, Sabbah in Chapter 6, and Fanty in

Chapter 7. The main advantage of local representations is they are relatively easy to understand and implement. The main disadvantage is the combinatorial explosion in the needed number of nodes.

In distributed representations, information is represented redundantly, but a single neuron may participate in the representation of several pieces of information. This idea is not new in psychology: for instance, Pribram (1971) proposed a "holographic" theory of memory, in which every memory was stored as a hologram. A small piece of a hologram may be used to reconstruct the entire image (at lower resolution), thus, the hologram contains redundancy. In the connectionist formulation, a distributed memory is typically viewed as a pattern of activation over a set of interconnected nodes in a neural network.

The relationship between local and distributed representations is analogous to that between unary and higher radix number systems. In a unary system, the number of symbols needed to represent a set of n numbers is proportional to n, whereas in a binary or higher radix system it is proportional to $log_r n$, where r is the radix. The radix of the system is, in a distributed model, equivalent to the number of states a given node can have. Normally there are two, activated or deactivated, although nodes may have anywhere from two to an infinite number of states.

One problem with a distributed memory is *crosstalk*. Consider three nodes A,B, and C, and three concepts 1,2, and 3. If concept 1 is represented by AB (i.e., nodes A and B activated), concept 2 by BC, and concept 3 by AC, then if any two of the concepts are activated, the third one will be as well, even if it is not there. This is crosstalk; the concept erroneously evoked is called a *ghost*.

One particular technique for constructing a distributed memory is known as *coarse-coding*. Coarse-coding is best understood as a way to represent a digitized image. Suppose there are two layers of neuron units, each of which is a two-dimensional array, so that the input layer represents an ordinary digitized image array, stored in the activations in the units. Suppose one output unit is associated with each of a square array of units in the input, say a 3x3 or a 4x4 array, then it responds when any of the units in that small array are active. The array of units that the output unit responds to is called its *receptive field*. Typically, in a coarse-coded memory, output units have overlapping receptive fields.

Figure 1.1 shows a coarse-coded memory with 16 input units (shown as white circles), 9 output units (shown as grey circles), and receptive fields of 4 units per output unit. The receptive fields overlap so that the left two units of one output unit's field compose the right two units of the receptive field of the output unit to the right of it, and similarly for the output units above and below each other. Coarse coding is a distributed memory technique because a single unit's activation in the input units corresponds to a pattern of activation in the output units. For instance, if unit (2,2) of the local input pattern is activated, then units (1,1), (1,2), (2,1), and (2,2) of the coarse-coded output units would be activated.

Coarse-coding is a useful method of reducing the number of units that is required to represent some stimulus. However, since a coarse-coded image reduces resolution, local detail is often lost. Distributed models in general require less units than local models; the more distributed the model, the fewer units.

Rosenfeld and Touretzky (1988) review techniques for coarse-coded or distributed memory representation. They use the phrases coarse-coded memory and distributed memory interchangeably. They define a coarse-coded symbol memory (CCSM) as: (1) a set of N units with binary-valued activations, (2) a set of α symbols and (3) a mapping of each of the symbols onto a bit pattern in the units. That is, a symbol is—as in most definitions of distributed memory—represented by a pattern of activation across a set of binary units. Each unit has a receptive field consisting of all the symbols in each unit for which it is activated. A *ghost* is a pattern in the memory that corresponds to a symbol that was not intended to be stored; it is the result of crosstalk. The failure rate of a CCSM is the rate at which ghosts emerge.

They define P_{ghost} as the probability that a ghost will emerge, given that the CCSM has stored a certain number of items k. They note that a local representation is one in which $k=N=\alpha$ and $P_{ghost}=0$, that is, one in which each symbol has one unit assigned to it. Aside from the terminology, there is no difference between a CCSM and a binary function on a finite set of symbols.

One CCSM that they explore is the random receptors model, in which each unit is assigned to each symbol with a probability s. They show that the probability of a ghost is minimized when

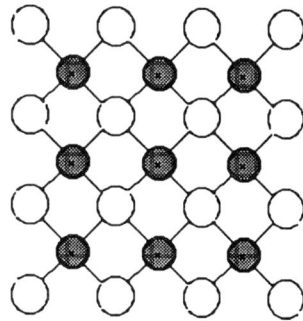

Figure 1.1. A Coarse-coded Symbol Memory.

$s=1/(k+1)$, where k is the number of items stored. They also show that, for this model, this implies that the number of symbols α in the alphabet can be related to P_{ghost}, the number of units N, and the number of symbols stored k (if k is large) by a function

$$\alpha(N,k,P_{ghost}) \cong P_{ghost}\, e^{0.368(N/k)}$$

They note that this implies that capacity (k) can be increased linearly by linearly increasing the number of units (N), because of the term N/k in the above formula. It also shows that the probability of representing a ghost symbol can be reduced by reducing the number of symbols to be represented, or increasing the number of units, which makes intuitive sense.

Rosenfeld and Touretzky go on to analyze the effects of dividing up a CCSM into two or more CCSMs. They conclude that, unless you have some information about which pairs of symbols will be stored at once, it does not pay to split the system.

They compare the coarse coding scheme used by Touretzky and Hinton in DUCS (see section 3.2 for a complete description) with the random receptors method. The DUCS memory uses randomness, but in a more structured way than purely random receptors. They note that the random receptors method gives a lower probability of getting a ghost for a given number of system units and patterns stored, but the DUCS system typically only needs slightly more units to achieve the same result. They conclude that DUCS needs more units than a random receptor model since there is more redundancy in representing a given symbol. In the random receptor model, the number of units in a receptive field of a unit is dependent on the number of symbols that are stored, in DUCS it is fixed. This leads to sub-optimal performance.

They consider another distributed representation, the wickelphone representation used by Rumelhart and McClelland (1986a) (see section 7.12) in their model of the learning of the past tense forms of English verbs, in which the phonemes of words are represented by the phoneme name and its left and right context phonemes (since a sound is different depending on its context). The name and context phonemes are each represented by a microfeature vector of 11 bits representing various phonetic features, such as voicing, place of articulation, etc. A wickelphone therefore requires 33 bits of information to describe it. They represent the wickelphones as wickelfeatures, in which one wickelfeature node represents a conjunction of three phonemes. A single wickelfeature node always is compatible with several or many actual wickelphones; for instance, it could be compatible with t,d, and k. Their main point in reviewing the wickelphone representation in the context of coarse coding is to illustrate that microfeature-based distributed representations and coarse-coding are not necessarily incompatible, but can complement one another.

Designing a distributed memory is equivalent to assigning receptive fields to the units in the system. They note that a stochastic method for generating receptive fields can cause unacceptable variation in the size of the fields, and affect the performance of the system. They have developed a method for generating optimal fixed sized receptive fields, the bounded overlap method, but this requires an exponential search, which is too expensive in the typical case of a few thousand units (Rosenfeld and Touretzky 1988).

They suggest a practical method for designing a distributed memory whereby each unit in the CCSM has its receptive field set to a consecutive set of F symbols, chosen cyclically and repeatedly, from the symbols in the symbol set in some order. The receptive fields are then shuffled randomly for some time, by exchanging a symbol between the receptive fields of units x and y that is in the receptive field of y but not x for one that is in the receptive field of x but not y. They note that the pattern size (the size of a pattern representing a symbol) is $L=NF/\alpha$, where α is the number of symbols, and the expected overlap O_E between two patterns

$$O_E = L(F-1)/(\alpha-1)$$

We want to minimize the degree to which the overlap $C(i,j)$ between the patterns for the ith and jth symbols differs from the expected overlap, as measured by the variance

$$V = \frac{1}{2} \sum_{i \neq j} [(C(i,j) - O_E]$$

After shuffling the receptive fields, they are shuffled some more, but each shuffling step is taken only if it reduces the variance. The algorithm stops when the variance is reduced to an acceptable level.

1.5. Distributed Models: A Critique

Oden (1988b) gives a useful discussion of distributed models. One of his main points is that a model that looks distributed is always local from another point of view. For instance, in the model of schemata presented by Rumelhart et al. (1986f), a bedroom is represented by a series of nodes representing the objects in it. The model is distributed with respect to the bedroom, but local with respect to the objects in it. Similarly, in the case of coarse-coding, when a stimulus is encoded in terms of the responses of detectors that have overlapping areas of sensitivity, the array of responses is distributed with respect to the stimuli, but is local with respect to the detectors.

Oden points out that distributivity is not a characteristic predominantly of connectionist models; even the ordinary binary encoding of a number is distributed, since each bit can participate in the representation of many numbers. Distributivity, according to Oden, is a question of degree and perspective.

Oden tackles the common claim of connectionists that the nodes in a network can be non-symbolic, that is, that they can have no semantic interpretation, especially in a distributed network. This claim is a resulting of misconstruing a complex, hard-to-make interpretation as no interpretation. Oden gives the rotation of a coordinate system as an example. A pair of coordinates that could be readily interpreted in terms of one system could not be as readily interpreted in terms of another, rotated, system. Yet all the original information is preserved.

To give another example: if I take a digitized picture of Lenin and run it through some invertible transformation so that the picture becomes unrecognizable, does this make the result non-symbolic of Lenin? I think not: all the information necessary to construct the picture of Lenin is still there (since the transformation is invertible).

The third property of connectionist models that Oden discusses is their continuousness. He notes that all models must deal with continuous data, since the real world is continuous, but models differ in the degree to which they transform these data to continuous or binary variables. Some connectionist models have neurons that fire "on" when their input exceeds a threshold, and "off" otherwise. These are discrete models; the non-linear sigmoid response curve and the linear response curve of other connectionist models are continuous models (see section 2.3). Oden notes that connectionist models provide for "the use of best-fit pattern matching, which in turn allows for the kinds of categorization, content-addressability, and automatic generalization that (they) are known for." Traditional cognitive models make discrete classifications based on necessary criteria or cutoffs; they do not allow for there to be degrees of fit to a set of possible concepts, as there is in a connectionist model, where a concept node may be more or less activated, or in fuzzy set theory, in which an element may have a degree of membership in a set that is any value intermediate between 0 and 1. An example of how a connectionist model may closely correspond to a particular symbolic, cognitive approach—the fuzzy propositional approach—is given in the following section.

1.6. Connectionist Models and the Fuzzy Propositional Approach

Oden (1988a) has worked out a relationship between his earlier work in symbolic cognitive science, in what he termed the fuzzy propositional approach, and connectionist models. In the fuzzy propositional model, each proposition A is assigned a truth value $t(A)$ between 0 and 1. One form of this model uses a multiplicative law for conjunction: $t(A \ and \ B)=t(A)*t(B)$.

The following rule is used for disjunction: $t(A \ or \ B)=(1-t(A))*(1-t(B))$ The result of amplifying a truth value $t(very \ A)$ is given by $t(A)^v$, where v is some constant. These formulas are borrowed from probability theory, although it is different to say that A is partly true than it is to say that A is has a certain probability of being true.

Starting with some experiments that Oden and Rueckl (1986) did on stimuli that vary continuously on two dimensions, Oden derives some response formulas.

Figure 1.2. Stimuli similar to those used in experiments. Reprinted by permission.

The exact stimuli were "eat" and "lot" (see Figure 1.2)— the difference between them is based on a continuous variation of the height of the loop in the "e" or the "l" (in their hand-written versions) and the depth of the dip in the line that connects the "a" or the "o" with the "t". If t is the truth value of the first letter being "l" and d is the truth value of the second letter being "a", this gives the formula

$$t(\text{"eat" relative-to "lot"}) = \frac{t(eat)}{(t(eat)+t(lot))} = \frac{(1-t)d}{(1-t)d+t(1-d)}$$

It there is a possibility of, for instance, the loop in the "l" being <u>very</u> tall, or any of the other features being amplified in this way, we have

$$t(\text{"eat" relative-to "lot"})= \frac{(1-t)^{w1}d^{w2}}{(1-t)^{w1}d^{w2}+t^{w3}(1-d)^{w4}}$$

Oden notes that the typical semi-linear, sigmoid response function of a neuron (see section 2.3) can be approximated by $f(x)=1/(1+e^{-x})$, where is the input to the neuron and f is the output. To map his scheme on to a connectionist network, he postulates that there are nodes whose activation corresponds to "short", "tall", "deep", and "flat", where the first two of these refer to the loop of the e/l, and the second two correspond to the dip between the a/o and the t. Thus, "short" and "deep" would be positively connected to the "eat" node, and "tall" and "fat" would be negatively connected to the "eat" node. The "lot" node would have opposite connections. Numerically,

$$a_{eat}=f(w_1a_s+w_2a_d-w_3a_t-w_4a_f)$$

where a_s is the activation of the "short" node, etc. Plugging this into the formula for the semi-linear response function, we get

$$a_{eat} = \frac{1}{1+e^{-(w_1a_s+w_2a_d-w_3a_t-w_4a_f)}} = \frac{(e^{a_s})^{w1}(e^{a_d})^{w2}}{(e^{a_s})^{w1}(e^{a_d})^{w2}+(e^{a_t})^{w3}(e^{a_f})^{w4}}$$

Beyond the fact that the activations are exponentiated, this is identical to the version given by the fuzzy propositional model. Under other conditions, however, Oden notes that the isomorphism between the two models does not hold. In any case, the two models are close.

Oden makes the case that a symbolic system, such as the fuzzy propositional model, can be used to understand connectionist systems, which otherwise would be collections of nodes that operate as if by magic. He argues that the symbolic and the neuronal levels are complementary, not in conflict. It is not sufficient to design a system that learns a task by adjustment of weights; one must be able to give a semantic interpretation of the system.

1.7. Philosophical Issues

Connectionism has stimulated vigorous discussion of its usefulness as a research strategy for cognitive science. To its detractors, it is a new form of associationism, and the debate on its merits simply a rehash of the late 1950s debate between behaviorists and cognitivists, which the cognitivists basically won, in that cognitivism became the prevailing school of thought. Of course, connectionism is explicitly representational, while behaviorism was anti-representational.

The best known philosophical arguments for connectionism, and against it, are, respectively, those of Smolensky (1988), and Fodor and Pylyshyn (1988). Smolensky was a contributor to the PDP books (Rumelhart et al. 1986b). Fodor and Pylyshyn are well known proponents of the symbol-manipulation approach to AI; for a sample of the earlier philosophical work, see Pylyshyn (1984) and Fodor (1981). The book edited by Graubard (1988) contains several articles concerned with the philosophical controversy around connectionism.

1.8. Smolensky's "Proper Treatment" of Connectionism

Smolensky (1988), in his controversial article "On the Proper Treatment of Connectionism" attempts to characterize the limitations and advantages of the connectionist approach, and to reconcile it to the traditional approach to AI. He characterizes connectionism as the "sub-symbolic" approach, as opposed to traditional AI as embodied in the Physical Symbol System Hypothesis (PSSH) of Newell (1980). He interprets the PSSH as stating that the "sub-symbols" in the connectionist paradigm are constituents of the symbols used by traditional AI. The two paradigms also have different levels on which they operate; the symbolic approach uses what Smolensky calls the conceptual level, and the connectionist approach uses what is called the sub-conceptual level.

Smolensky says that natural language has provided the major theoretical focus of the symbolic paradigm. Cultural knowledge about specific domains is typically embodied in language, and linguistic symbol lists, in the form of rules, are used in conjunction with some type of logic to create simulations of human action. The machine acts as a rule interpreter, which is a model of conscious rule application. In addition to this rule interpreter, Smolensky posits the existence of a second, unconscious processor, which acts on knowledge drawn from individual experience to perform tasks such as intuitive expert game playing, motor coordination, that is, almost all skilled action. He calls this processor the intuitive processor.

He considers the following possible assertions, all of which he will reject: that the intuitive processor deals with "linguistically formalized rules" which are applied sequentially, that the program of the intuitive processor is itself symbolic, and that these programs are similar to those of the conscious rule interpreter. He rejects these assertions, as most connectionists do, because—as yet—models of human performance that are based on them lead to too much brittleness and inflexibility, because the amounts of knowledge that would have to be embodied to make them workable is too large, and because they lead to few insights about how the brain works. (Fodor and Pylyshyn argue that there is no particular reason why they should lead to such insights; see the next section.)

After rejecting a symbolic approach to the intuitive processor Smolensky considers the opposite extreme; that the intuitive processor uses the same architecture as the brain does. The trouble with this hypothesis is that we don't know what the brain's architecture is. Instead of this hypothesis, Smolensky advances the hypothesis that the intuitive processor has a connectionist architecture. The version of connectionism that Smolensky advocates is what he calls the "connectionist dynamical system hypothesis". This hypothesis views a connectionist system as a parallel computer containing many processors, with each of which is associated a number (or possibly, a set of numbers). Thus the state of the system can be described by a vector, a state vector of activations. The system has an equation describing how the state vector evolves in time, which Smolensky calls the activation evolution equation. The state of the connections in the system (that is, the weights on them), can also be described by an equation, which Smolensky calls the connection evolution equation. Thus a connectionist system is, for Smolensky, a dynamical system such as that found in physics. Typically these are governed by differential equations.

Next, Smolensky considers the meaning of the activations in a connectionist system. Each of the activations does not constitute an entire symbol; rather a symbol (e.g., word) is represented as a distributed pattern of activation across the system, each unit is sub-symbolic and participates in the pattern for many symbols. He takes this to a (possibly new) extreme, by hypothesizing that the sub-symbolic behavior of a connectionist system is not explicable in terms of the conceptual level. This rejects the idea (see Fodor and Pylyshyn, next section) that connectionist models are implementations of symbolic processes. Smolensky believes that if connectionist modeling is an implementation theory, the connectionist research program is defeated. The mere fact that connectionist networks and Von Neumann machines (conventional serial computers) can simulate one another does not reduce connectionism to an implementation theory, because a Von Neumann simulation of a connectionist machine does not manipulate the kinds of linguistic-level symbols used in a typical rule-based system.

Smolensky reviews three methodologies for choosing features at the sub-conceptual level. This first is the borrowing of these features from previous symbolic models, such as was done in Rumelhart and McClelland's (1986a) model of the formation of the past tense, where phonetic features were used (see section 7.12) The second is the learning of the relevant features in hidden units using learning procedures such as back-propagation. The third method is to choose features in such a way so as to tune a system so that it matches human performance.

One technique that does this, according to Smolensky, is multi-dimensional scaling (Shepard 1962), which looks at the raw corpus of data and extracts vectors which can be used to represent the stimuli. Smolensky points out that, if we want to look to the brain for guidelines on how to derive features at the sub-conceptual level, we lack information. We have more information in vision than in any other domain—in a domain such as language processing the information given is virtually nil. Thus Smolensky points out (the protestations of some other connectionists to the contrary), that the semantics of the features at the sub-conceptual level are, at this point, more closely related to the semantics of concepts at the conceptual level than they are to the activations of neurons in the brain. Moreover, the actual activity of the brain is much more complex than is reflected in most current connectionist models. Yet, clearly, because of the rough correspondence between connectionist models' architecture and the brain, connectionist models are likely to operate under similar principles to the brain.

Smolensky concludes that connectionist models are at a level intermediate between that of symbolic models and the brain, and should not be seen as biological models themselves. He argues that a reduction will someday have to be made from successful connectionist models to neural circuits. The expression of neural circuits directly in models is made difficult by insufficient knowledge of the dynamic behavior of the brain, according to Smolensky. The degree to which a connectionist model can be approximated by a symbolic model depends on whether or not the process being modeled is one of conscious rule application or of intuition. Conscious rule application processes modeled on the connectionist level can be described "with reasonable precision" on the conceptual level, but intuitive processes can be described only roughly on the conceptual level. This is because the symbolic level relies strongly on its own implementation language for its functioning.

On the other hand, connectionist models can serve as an implementation language for conventional symbolic processes. However, the details of how this is done are not completely specified, although Touretzky and Hinton (1985) (see also Touretzky 1987) have done valuable work in this area. Smolensky divides knowledge that is useful in interpreting stimuli into two sets: P-knowledge (parallel knowledge) and S-knowledge (sequential knowledge). P-knowledge can be used in parallel; e.g., a listener attempting to understand a sentence can simultaneously use syntactic, phonetic, morphological and semantic knowledge. On the other hand, S-knowledge cannot be used in parallel; a player of a game has to execute a single rule before s/he can contemplate the execution of a second rule. According to Smolensky, P-knowledge is much more context dependent than S-knowledge, because it is necessary to know which aspects of the P-knowledge can operate in conjunction with one another.

Next, Smolensky attempts to characterize what it is about a model that makes it cognitive, and how connectionist models can be cognitive. He defines a cognitive system as one that maintains a large set of goal conditions under a variety of environmental conditions. A thermostat is not cognitive because it does not maintain a large set of environmental conditions. Thus complexity is, for Smolensky, the acid test as to whether a model is cognitive. One important task that cognitive models undertake is what Smolensky calls the "prediction-goal", that is, to predict missing features of the environment from the features that are present in the stimuli. Closely related to this goal is the "prediction-from-examples" goal, that is, to use previous examples to continuously improve performance on the prediction problem.

Smolensky answers the argument of Fodor and Pylyshyn (1988) (see the next section) that connectionist models are limited in their usefulness, since mental states have constituent structure, like that represented in a parse tree, and connectionist models don't Clearly, this applies to localist connectionist models, which are subject to combinatorial explosion in the number of nodes, since there must be a node for every combination of concepts (e.g., the-tall-blond-man-with-one-black-shoe node), but Smolensky, who advocates distributed representations, thinks that they are less vulnerable to this kind of criticism. He considers the idea of Pylyshyn (1984) that in a distributed connectionist system the representation of "coffee" is equal to the representation of "cup with coffee" minus the representation of "cup". If the representation for "cup with coffee" consists of units representing features like "solid container", "handle", "brown liquid", "curved liquid", etc., then when we remove all of the features of "cup" from this representation, we are left with a representation of coffee, but in the context of cup, that is, we have a representation of coffee that has the coffee in the shape that is contained by the cup. Other representations of coffee could be made in other contexts; for Smolensky, there is no context-free representation of coffee.

The difference between local symbolic representations of a word and distributed connectionist representations is that, with the former type of representations, the context is established by the connections that it makes with other local symbols (as in a semantic network); with the latter type, the context is contained in the pattern of activation itself. This disturbs people who believe in context-free symbols.

Smolensky argues that connectionist models should be intrinsically continuous, that is, have activations that are real-valued rather than discrete, in order to escape from the brittleness and inflexibility of conventional symbolic models. This allows for the integration of multiple constraints with different weight, which all-or-none rule-based systems cannot give you.

Smolensky believes that even the many connectionist models which use binary data in their computations need not be fundamentally discrete, but can all be mapped onto models that use real-valued variables. He argues, therefore, that little is gained by the use of discrete models, and their common use is based on the fact that digital computers are basically discrete, and so researchers have a tendency to think in discrete terms. But the brain is a highly parallel analog computer, which deals with real values, and analog computers can be built that embody connectionist models: for example, Smolensky cites Anderson (1986b) and Cohen (1986).

Smolensky reformulates the idea that multiple "soft" constraints can simultaneously contribute to a solution to a problem, such as mapping an input to its correct output, in terms of what he calls the "Best Fit Principle". This principle says that the system as a whole arrives at a solution which is statistically the "best fit" to the input, as specified by the various constraints known to the system. This is expressed mathematically in terms of the harmony function H, which is maximized by the machine. Harmony theory (Smolensky 1986) gives the theoretical underpinnings of the harmony function and the dynamic behavior of networks with respect to it.

Smolensky gives an example of how a network can exhibit behavior normally thought of as rule-governed: his system that does qualitative physics. In this system, the knowledge of Ohm's law is embodied in the configuration of parts of the system representing current, voltage, and resistance. Each of these computes its value in parallel, with hundreds of microdecisions (activation changes). Macrodecisions are the result of many microdecisions. If a system changes, as the result of receiving input, to a state in which Ohm's law is satisfied, this is a macrodecision, even though underlying behavior is following Ohm's law as such. The relationship is like that between quantum mechanics and Newtonian mechanics; examined at a gross level a physical system seems Newtonian, but underneath it is really obeying quantum mechanics.

Harmony theory is illustrated by the work on schemata of Rumelhart and his co-workers (1986f) (see section 4.2). This model simulates the look-up of schemata on the basis of some triggering information. Basically, what it does is perform a search in harmony space. Although no schemata are explicitly stored—just correlations between rooms and objects—the schemata are emergent phenomena. When primed on some of a room's contents—say an oven and a cabinet—the system performs a search in harmony space, which leads to a peak which corresponds to the complete set of the room's descriptors. Yet the schemata are not directly present; they are higher-level descriptors of rooms than are explicitly represented.

1.9. Connectionism: A New Form of Associationism?

Fodor and Pylyshyn (1988) advance a detailed critique of connectionism, and a defense of the classical view (as they term it) of cognition as rule-governed manipulation of symbols, as in LISP-based AI or production systems. Basically, they view connectionism as a more sophisticated form of associationism, masquerading in new clothes. Associationism, in one of its forms, behaviorism, reigned as the supreme psychological theory through the 1950s, until it was displaced by classical cognitivism. For a history of cognitivism and its victory over behaviorism, see Gardner (1985). Fodor and Pylyshyn feel that many of the same arguments used against the associationism of the 1950s—one of the most famous of which was Chomsky's review of Skinner's *Verbal Behavior* (Chomsky 1959)—can be used against the associationism of the 1980s, connectionism.

This is not to say that connectionism and behaviorism can be equated; connectionism, for one thing, is representational, believing that structures in the brain and mind represent objects and states of affairs in the world. Behaviorism (at least in the forms advanced by Skinner in his famous arguments against mentalism, which is what he called theories that use mental representations) is not representational, it is what Fodor and Pylyshyn call "eliminativist". This means that behaviorism does not think representations are important, but rather that behavior is, and, in fact, all talk about representations is unscientific. Fodor and Pylyshyn think that all the distinctions made in the connectionist literature between symbolic and sub-symbolic representations miss the main point: that all nodes in a connectionist network are symbolic. (A representation is the same thing as a symbol, in their opinion.) A single node is a symbol; so is a pattern of activation across nodes, much as a bit is a symbol (if it is causally attached to something in the world), and so is a bit vector.

Connectionist representations are typically collections of activated nodes representing microfeatures (or rather, features, since what is typically used in the connectionist literature as a "microfeature" is something like "human", which is hardly an elementary concept). Fodor and Pylyshyn's main objection to this form of representation is that it is unstructured; that is, it exhibits little of the compositionality of representation that classical representations exhibit. For instance, they posit that if the sentence "John loves Mary" is represented by three activated nodes (+john-subject +loves +mary-object), and we receive the additional information that "Bill hates Sally", so that we now have the vector (+john-subject +bill-subject +loves +hates +mary-object +sally-object); we now have crosstalk producing the additional sentences "John loves Sally", and "Bill hates Mary", "John hates Mary", "Bill loves Mary", "John hates Sally" and "Bill loves Sally". One way to avoid this is to have one node representing the entire complex concept of each sentence; the problem is there are so many possible sentences that no physically realizable brain could possibly contain enough nodes. The other way would be to allow the representations to have an internal tree-like structure such as {((John subject) loves (Mary object)) ((Bill subject) hates (Sally object))}. The problem with doing this, according to Fodor and Pylyshyn, is that no one, to their knowledge, has shown how to do this in a connectionist architecture. Touretzky (1989a) discusses issues involved in doing compositional semantics in connectionist networks, with reference to the problem of attaching prepositional phrases to noun phrases in sentences.

The key to this problem is that each link between nodes in a neural network represents a causal relationship between the nodes. Semantic networks, which can be more general than neural networks, allow for labeled links; the links can signify "causes", "is contained in", "precedes", etc. A connectionist network that Fodor and Pylyshyn suggest that draws inferences from a node standing for both A&B to ones standing for A and B is shown in Figure 1.3. Although the nodes are labelled to make it clear what they signify, these labels are not part of the connectionist representation. Fodor and Pylyshyn point out that the difference between this network and the classical implementation of this inference is that, in the classical case, the symbol string "A&B" contains as a part the strings A and B, whereas this is clearly not true of the top node in the diagram.

The causality shown in Figure 1.3 is insufficient to account for the compositionality, at least in this simple form.

Fodor and Pylyshyn point out, additionally, that connectionist models learn that concepts are statistically related. So, for instance, a connectionist model learns that A follows from A&B because the two statements are statistically related in the environment. It does not observe the structure of A&B in order to infer A, which is obviously one of the salient features of A&B.

Figure 1.3. A connectionist network that represents the assertion that A&B implies A and B individually. From Fodor and Pylyshyn (1988). Reprinted by permission.

Two basic properties of language augur well for the classical theory and badly for connectionist theory, according to Fodor and Pylyshyn. These are two well-known properties of language, its productivity and its systematicity. Any natural language consists of, for all practical purposes, an infinite number of well-formed sentences; this is referred to as the language's productivity. They quote a remark of Rumelhart and McClelland (1986e) in which they say that recursive center-embedded sentences—such as "The dog the man walked barked"—are hard to process, and that this is evidence that recursive capabilities are not central to cognitive capability. Fodor and Pylyshyn dispute this point, citing examples in which recursive embeddings are both easily understood and natural. In order to handle recursive embeddings, you need a classical (Von Neumann machine) architecture—one might presume—or a connectionist implementation thereof. So if you think that recursive productive features are critical to language, one might be tempted to choose a classical theory, according to Fodor and Pylyshyn.

Many sentences of the same structure occur in any given language, such as "the tree is in the park" and "the man is in the office"; this is the systematicity of language. This is what has caused linguists to posit the existence of syntactic categories. These categories necessitate the creation of linguistic structures that go beyond the simple lists of features that connectionist structures imply.

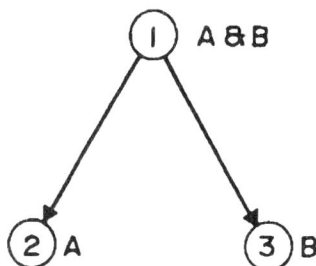

Fodor and Pylyshyn take some time to consider some of the issues that have made connectionism so appealing to so many in cognitive science. First of all, the issue of parallelism: the idea is often advanced that since the brain has many neurons active at once, and no apparent central control, any plausible cognitive architecture would have to be "massively" parallel. Of course, on the lowest level, a standard Von Neumann computer is highly parallel, since electrical signals are active throughout both CPU and memory, but on a higher level of abstraction it is not parallel. Fodor and Pylyshyn point out that not only connectionist models that are parallel; classical symbolic programming languages can be parallel, for instance Hewett's (1977) ACTORS and Hillis's (1985) parallel version of LISP for his Connection Machine.

Designing algorithms for networks of traditional processors and shared-memory multiprocessors has become a fertile area of computer science research. Fodor and Pylyshyn point out that not only connectionist representations can be distributed. A traditional memory register can be distributed; all that is necessary is for it to divide its contents and spread them out across the machine's memory. If it is desired, a transformation like a Fourier transform can be applied to the data so that, if part of the transform is lost (after it is split into chunks and distributed across the memory), the original signal can still be constructed, albeit with a loss of quality (the sort of "uniform degradation" that connectionists often talk about). They point out that an array can be functionally local, but distributed across the entire machine (using a hash table, for instance); representations are damage-resistant unless they are physically localized in memory and non-redundant.

Another point about connectionist models that is often raised is their ability to deal with representations and stimuli that are continuous rather than all-or-none. Fodor and Pylyshyn point out that there are lots of classical models that use continuous variables; for instance the use of Bayesian probabilistic inference techniques in expert systems or systems that use fuzzy logic (Zadeh 1973). Statistical properties of stimuli can emerge from the interaction of many smaller deterministic processes. (For instance, to over-simplify, the classification of a bird can emerge from a set of features, some of which are necessary; the classification process may depend on how many non-necessary features are present, their strengths, or a function thereof.)

It is often maintained that connectionist architectures implicitly model rule-governed behavior whereas classical architectures make the rules explicit (and presumably implicit rules are better). Fodor and Pylyshyn claim that classical architectures can be rule implicit, when functions are wired in to the machine. Connectionist architectures can be rule explicit, as well, but only by implementing a classical recursive machine. They add that if explicit rule learning turns out to be an important part of psychological theory, then connectionist systems are in trouble.

A major argument that is advanced for connectionist architectures is that they are biologically plausible, that is, that they are consistent with known facts about the brain. Fodor and Pylyshyn briefly summarize these facts as follows: connection patterns are important to how the brain processes information; memory is distributed, not localized; neurons work with synaptic thresholds; a neuron is more likely to fire, given a certain amount of input at its synapse, if it has recently fired. Fodor and Pylyshyn claim that none of these facts strongly constrain what type of architecture the mind must have. Low-level structure—and this is a point that Fodor has emphasized in many of his books—does not necessarily reflect high-level structure; the theory of atoms, doesn't look anything like biology, for instance. There is no reason that the brain could not implement a recursive classical architecture. Moreover, Fodor and Pylyshyn lament that the naive implementation of these "brain-like" models has created a revival of associationist psychology.

Fodor and Pylyshyn do not want to dismiss connectionism totally, they just want to reduce it to the level of a theory of how specific psychological algorithms are implemented. Such "properties" of computers such as the idea that their memory is permanent, that they use exhaustive search, that they are logical and don't make mistakes, are not properties of an algorithm but of its underlying implementation in a digital computer; algorithms can be devised that "forget", that perform faulty reasoning, make errors in retrieval, etc.; basically any process that can be theorized about can be embodied in a conventional computer (this is the Church–Turing thesis, the widely accepted statement that Turing machines are universal, that is, that they can compute anything we can conceive of computing).

According to David Marr (1978), every process can be understood on two levels: the level of formal specification (theory), and the level of implementation. The problem that Fodor and

Pylyshyn have with connectionist models is that their authors offer them as theories of cognition, not as implementations of higher-level formal processes. I would add, in defense of connectionists, that studying lower-level neuronal implementations may produce interesting new insights about higher-level processes, much as physics has informed theory formation in chemistry. Of course, there is no reason that neural theories need constrain psychological theories much at all, if the brain turns out to be a general purpose machine, like a Von Neumann computer.

Fodor and Pylyshyn consider four possible routes that connectionism could take from here, which are: (1) to maintain its present course; (2) to admit structured mental representations but retain an associationist account of their processing; (3) to reduce connectionism (and neuroscience) to the status of an implementation theory; or (4) to accept connectionist accounts of a certain subject of cognitive processes—notably the forming of statistical inferences from sets of stimuli—but do not accept connectionist accounts of such phenomena as linguistic productivity and regularity. It is hard to say what route connectionism will take; much depends on the success of the current research program.

2

Neural Network Methods for Learning and Relaxation

2.1. Introduction

Most work in neural networks involves learning. The goal of most neural network models is to learn relationships between stimuli. There are at least three ways that learning models can be classified. The first way concerns the nature of what is learned. A learning model can be a *hetero-associator* or an *auto-associator*. A hetero-associator is a network that computes a function between a set of inputs and a set of outputs. An auto-associator is a network that completes an incomplete input pattern. These two types of models are not different in principle, because a hetero-associator can always be reduced to an auto-associator by concatenating an input pattern and its associated output pattern, to make an input pattern of the auto-associator. Thus the performance of the hetero-associator can be then achieved in the auto-associator, by simply presenting, as the partial input of the auto-associator, the input pattern for the hetero-associator, and having the machine complete the pattern to produce what was the output pattern of the hetero-associator.

Auto-associative memory is extremely useful for the organism, and it is the way that the human memory system seems to work. Everyone has the almost constant experience of having a memory evoked by a particular cue that formed part of the memory: for instance, seeing a hat similar to one one's father used to wear reminds you of him wearing that hat. Content-addressable memories are also useful for database applications, because one typically wants to look up some record in a database based on some part of it (which is called the key.) Traditional approaches have involved building indices on each item of a record that one wants to look for. Organizing your memory in such a way so that content-addressability is an automatic feature would be desirable; it seems that this is what the brain has done.

The second way that learning models can be classified applies only to hetero-associators. These can be classified based on what they compute. Typically they compute either a general function of their input, in which there are about as many outputs as inputs, or a classification, where a large set of input patterns is mapped onto a relatively small set of output patterns, which represent sets into which the input patterns are classified.

Yet another way that learning models can be classified is in terms of the amount of guidance that the learning process receives from an outside agent, typically referred to as the *teacher*. *Unsupervised* learning occurs without a teacher; such a learning algorithm— the various kinds of competitive learning discussed in sections 2.15 through 2.18 are examples—that learns to classify the input into sets without being told anything. It does this clustering solely on the basis of the intrinsic statistical properties of the set of inputs.

Supervised learning adjusts weights on the basis of the difference between the values of output units, given an input pattern, and the desired pattern, given by the teacher. Error back-propagation (see section 2.12) is a supervised learning procedure.

The third type of learning has a long history in psychology: reinforcement learning. This is a type of supervised learning in which very little information is given the algorithm; typically one bit, which signifies if the output that the network provided to the given stimulus is good or bad. Many people feel this type of learning (which must of necessity proceed more slowly than supervised learning, since less information is given) is more psychologically valid, since people are not normally provided with a complete example of the desired behavior, especially in situations in which they are not explicitly taught (such as in child language learning).

While most work in connectionism is limited to learning of weights, many other things can also be learned, such as the topology of the network, the activation functions, even the learning rules themselves. Several authors have explored the possible of learning where in a net to place nodes and connections (see, for example, Ash 1989, Dieterich 1988, Honavar & Uhr 1989b, Honavar & Uhr 1989a).

Relaxation is the process whereby the unit activations (not the weights) change over time until they evolve to a state in which activations are no longer changing, and thus the network can be said to have "relaxed", i.e. fallen into a state of little activity. Relaxation differs from learning in that only activations change; in learning, the weights change. Some network paradigms, notably feed-forward networks, which will be discussed later on in this chapter, require only one update per unit in order to reach their final state. Other types of networks, such as the Boltzmann machine (also discussed later in this chapter), require many updates, and thus undergo relaxation. Relaxation is especially applicable to constraint satisfaction problems such as vertex-labeling in line drawings (Waltz 1975) and line and edge detection and enhancement (Zucker, Hummel & Rosenfeld 1977). Mackworth (1977) supplied a useful discussion of methods for the satisfaction of multiple constraints. For more recent discussions of relaxation, see Hummel & Zucker (1983) and Geman & Geman (1984).

The following sections give an overview of the main neural network designs and learning methods. We start with a review of the different types of model neurons devised by Feldman and Ballard (1982), which can be used to construct connectionist models. We then discuss two of the earliest devices, the Adeline and the Perceptron, which are relatively simple and limited in their computational power. In both of these models the error—difference between the desired and actual output—is used as a corrective to bring the performance of the model closer to that desired. Thus these two models employ supervised learning.

We then proceed to another simple associative network that uses Hebbian learning, that of Anderson. This is a network that uses matrix multiplication to compute associations between input and output vectors, and which uses as correctives to its matrix values correlations (products) of single components of these vectors. Thus, following Hebb (1949) connections between components that are simultaneously active are strengthened. This is a simple form of associative learning.

We then move on to another type of associative learning, that of Kohonen (1988). In the auto-associative version of Kohonen's work, he views an input vector as a corrupted version of its true value. He uses a mathematical technique, the Gram–Schmidt process, to compute the stored vector that is closest to the noisy input.

These first four models are linear associators, since, in each, their output is a linear combination of their input. The remainder of the models discussed are non-linear, i.e. their outputs are non-linear functions of their inputs. A non-linear model can compute a much greater variety of functions than a linear model, although it is surprising how much linear models can handle.

The first non-linear model we discuss is that of Hopfield. In this model, neurons reset themselves randomly and asynchronously if their weighted inputs exceed a threshold. Hopfield's network is auto-associative. By setting the weights in his network in a particular fashion, Hopfield is able to show that the state of his network always converges to a stable state. Any such network, Hopfield shows, has a set of stable limit points, which can be used to store memories. Thus the network functions as an auto-associator, because each input—that is, initial state of the network—leads to a stable state that corresponds to a stored memory. Moreover, unlike a linear associator, the stored patterns need not form a linearly independent set.

We then discuss the more complex neuron model offered by Hopfield and Tank, in which a neuron's behavior is modeled by a differential equation. We discuss the application of this neuron model to problems in optimization, in particular, the traveling salesman problem.

Hopfield used his initial network to store memories that correspond to local minima in a function that, borrowing from thermodynamics, he defines as the energy function of the network. If the goal of the model is not to store a set of memories, but to find a global minimum in the energy function that corresponds to an optimal solution of some constraint-satisfaction problem, then an extension of the Hopfield network, called the Boltzmann machine, is used. The Boltzmann machine is basically a stochastic version of the Hopfield network. The state of a given node in the network is based both on how much input it is receiving as well as a parameter called the temperature. The higher the temperature, the more randomness there is in the system. This type of network lends itself well to finding global minima. We also discuss a learning rule to make a Boltzmann machine reflect the state of the environment.

Next, in our discussion of network paradigms, we turn to the best-known neural network algorithm, the error back-propagation algorithm. This is an extension of the Perceptron to systems with one or more layers of hidden units between the input and the output.

In this algorithm, the difference between the desired output and the actual output is used to adjust the connections first between the output layer and the hidden layer right below it. This error is then propagated backward in the network to layers below the top hidden layer and ultimately used to adjust connections between the input units and units above them. Rumelhart and his co-workers show that this algorithm converges to a local minimum in the error—that is, in the difference between the desired and actual outputs.

We discuss a variety of problems to which Rumelhart and his co-workers applied the back-propagation algorithm. These include computing the exclusive-or function, which the two-layer Perceptron was unable to handle.

We then turn to a variety of unsupervised learning methods. The first three examples we consider are versions of competitive learning, in which various digits or sets of units compete to recognize features in the input. These algorithms resemble Darwinian natural selection. We then consider a class of algorithms that, while not explicitly neural network algorithms, also take their inspiration from evolution: genetic algorithms. These are algorithms that model populations of organisms as populations of bit strings, in which each bit string is itself a solution to a problem. Both competitive learning and genetic algorithms "evolve" solutions to problems.

The final type of algorithms that we consider are reinforcement algorithms. The three main ones that we discuss all were developed at the University of Massachusetts, in Andrew Barto's group. The first of these algorithms is called the associative reward/penalty (A_{R-P}) algorithm, which is used to classify a set of inputs. The system learns the classification of inputs based on a reinforcement signal. We then discuss the work of Sutton on what he calls temporal difference methods, which are useful in predicting events that are in time series.

We then discuss the work of Anderson, one of Barto's students. Anderson applied both back-propagation, and the A_{R-P} algorithm, to a set of problems. He also adapted the work of Sutton to use in the problem of learning heuristics for problem solving for problems normally associated with heuristic search. This type of problem solving has not been attacked by many other researchers using the connectionist paradigm.

Chapter two concludes with discussions of various extensions of the error back-propagation algorithm, of attempts that have been made to model sequential phenomena in neural networks, of a method for compressing information using back-propagation, and of an attempt to embody recursive structures in a neural network.

2.2. Types of Model Neurons

Feldman and Ballard (1982) reviewed a variety of different kinds of model neurons. The simplest kind is the p-unit. The output v of the p-unit is proportional to its potential (activation) p, and p is adjusted based on its weighted total input:

$$p'=p+\beta\sum w_k i_k$$

where p' is p's value after adjustment, the w_k and i_k are the weights and the inputs, respectively, on the input lines entering the unit, and β is the rate of change. If the potential is less than a threshold θ, then the unit's output is zero, otherwise it is simply the potential p, rounded off. Feldman and Ballard limited the number of output values to the integers from 0 to 9; this is an attempt to model the limited information transmission capacity of the individual neuron in a single firing. P-units were used in the Perceptron and the Adeline, which were early learning models, described in section 2.4.

A more complex unit they devised is the max-of-sum unit. For example, if we have a series of inputs $i_1, i_2, ..., i_7$ such that i_1 and i_2 are connected to one input site, i_3 and i_4 are connected to a second site, and i_5, i_6 and i_7 are connected to a third site, then the potential of a max-of-sum unit is

$$p'=p+\beta Max(i_1+i_2-\varphi, i_3+i_4-\varphi, i_5+i_6+i_7-\varphi)$$

where φ is a noise threshold. Of course, units can be connected in whatever combinations are desired. This rule is the continuous analog of a disjunction of conjunctions, which is disjunctive normal form, a standard form for expressing logical expressions. Since disjunctive normal form can express any assertion in propositional logic, a network of max-of-sum units can compute arbitrarily complex logical functions of their input.

Another kind of unit that Feldman and Ballard discuss is the q-unit, which is a discrete unit. Every binary q-unit has two states, firing and null. If a unit has n inputs, then its behavior is described by a table with rows corresponding to states of the input units; the last item in each row is the output, given the input state in that row. These units can be built out of standard digital logic; q-units are at the boundary between digital logic and neural networks. One can also have 3-valued or n-valued q-units.

Feldman and Ballard have also devised a unit that is a hybrid of p and q, called, naturally enough, the p-and-q-unit. One way to construct such a unit is to have it respond like a p-unit—continuously—while it is in one of two states, which they refer to as the normal state. When it is in the other state, the recover state, the unit ignores input. This unit is intended to model the behavior of real neurons, which need some time to recover between firings. The way this is implemented is to negate the potential when it exceeds some threshold, and put the unit into the recover state, for some number of updates, after which it goes back into the normal state and its potential starts to respond to input.

The general definition of p-and-q units augments the p and v of p-units by a set of states $\{q\}$. p, q, and v are updated by three functions f, g, and h:

$$p'=f(i,p,q)$$
$$q'=g(i,p,q)$$
$$v'=h(i,p,q)$$

where i is the vector of inputs to the unit in question, and q is the current state, drawn from the set $\{q\}$. These functions are usually logical, linear, or semi-linear, although they can be arbitrary. Feldman and Ballard also introduced weights into p-and-q units.

Many of the network techniques discussed by Feldman and Ballard are discussed elsewhere in this book, such as winner-take-all networks and coarse coding, but I want to mention one such technique here, that of one unit mediating the connection between two other units in a gated connection One way to do this is to have the activation of a unit multiply the input that would otherwise be sent along the connection between two other units. The concept of a third unit mediating the connection between two other units can be generalized to three units that are connected to each other via a central point and which satisfy equations which predict the activation of any one unit given the activation of the other two.

2.3. Types of Activation Rules

A neural network can be characterized by the type of rule that is used to compute the activation of units in it. Normally, the activation A of a node j is some function f of the total weighted input I coming into j:

$$I = \sum_i w_i x_i$$

where i ranges over the nodes inputting to j, x_i is the activation of the ith node and w_i is the weight on the connection from node i to node j.

The major rules that have been used by connectionist researchers are:

(1) a linear activation rule:
$$A = kI$$
where k is some constant

(2) a binary-threshold activation rule:
$$A = 1 \text{ if } I \geq \mu_0$$
$$A = 0 \text{ if } I < \mu_0$$
where μ_0 is a threshold

(3) a semi-linear, sigmoid activation rule
$$A = \frac{1}{1 + e^{-I}}$$

Linear	Threshold	Semilinear

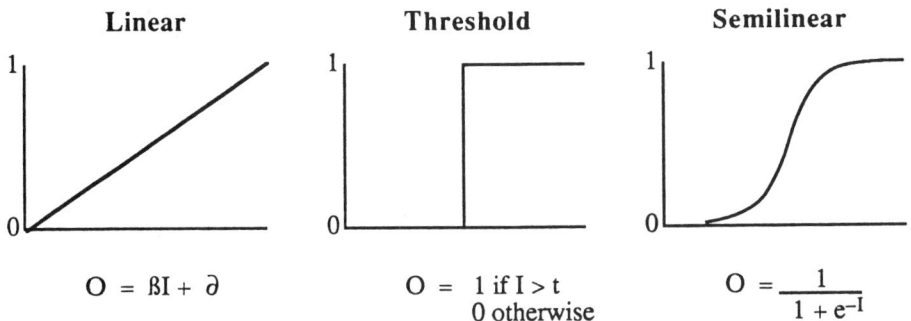

$$O = \beta I + \partial \qquad \begin{aligned} O &= 1 \text{ if } I > t \\ &\quad 0 \text{ otherwise} \end{aligned} \qquad O = \frac{1}{1 + e^{-I}}$$

Figure 2.1 Some neuronal activation rules. From Oden (1988a). Reprinted by permission.

These rules are plotted in Figure 2.1. As we will see, the linear rule is limited in the number of functions that networks that are built using it can compute. The other two rules have been used in systems that do not have this limitation. They both have the interesting property that they transform their input to produce an activation between zero and one.

2.4. Early Learning Models

Two of the first neural network models introduced were the *Adaline* (<u>Ada</u>ptive <u>Lin</u>ear <u>El</u>ement) of Widrow (1962) and the *Perceptron* of Rosenblatt (1961). The adaline is composed of a set of input units x_i and a single output signal y. It was originally specified in terms of an electrical circuit. The output y is related to the input values x by

$$y = \sum_i w_i x_i + \mu_0$$

where w is a weight vector and μ_0 is a bias. (In its original formulation, the adaline also contained a quantizer which output -1 if its output were negative and +1 otherwise. This was irrelevant to the learning process.)

The adaline does supervised learning: the purpose of the machine is to compute a particular function based on the training given it in input/output pairs. If y_k is the output on the kth time step, and the desired output is y, then the adjustment in the weights is given by

$$w_{i,k+1} = w_{i,k} + (y_k - y)\alpha_k$$

where α_k is the learning rate on the kth time step. Thus the weights are adjusted by a term involving the error in the output signal. It can easily be shown that if the set of input vectors presented is linearly independent, the weights will converge; otherwise they will oscillate. This weight change rule is called the adaline convergence rule, although though it might just as well be called the adaline oscillation rule!

In order to remove the oscillations, the learning rate α_k would have to decrease over the course of the learning. Kohonen (1988) shows that the adaline convergence rule minimizes the error

y_k-y when the output of the adaline at time step k, y_k, is viewed as a random variable with expectation y.

The Perceptron (Rosenblatt 1961) is quite similar to the adaline. In one version there is a set of binary input units, each of which is completely connected to a set of binary output units (see Figure 2.2). For each of these output units, zero is output if the weighted sum of the inputs at a given output unit is less

Figure 2.2. The Perceptron. The bottom layer is the input layer; the top layer is the output layer. Activation flows upward.

than zero; one is output if this weighted sum is greater than zero. If w_{ik} is the weight between the ith input unit x_i and a given output unit, and y_k is the actual output and y the desired output (both at time step k) then the learning rule is given by:

$$w_{i,k+1} = w_{i,k} + \lambda(y_k\text{-}y)x_i$$

The main difference between this and the adaline is that, in the perceptron, the x_i and y_k are binary rather than real-valued. If the above formula converges, the machine is capable of computing the function on which it is being trained. Unfortunately, it has been shown that the above equation often does not converge, so the perceptron is severely limited in the number of functions that it is able to compute. For instance, one can prove that it is impossible to compute the exclusive-or function using the perceptron. For details, see Minsky and Papert (1969).

Both the perceptron and the adaline are *feed-forward* networks—that is, activation flows in one direction, from the input units to the output units. In networks that are more complex than these simple two-layer models, additional layers may be placed between the input and output units. If activation always flows in one direction, from input to output, the network is still feed-forward. The error back-propagation algorithm (see section 2.12) normally uses a feed-forward network.

Some of the literature refers to a network with an input layer and an output layer as a one-layer system, not counting the input layer; under this convention, a system with one hidden layer is a

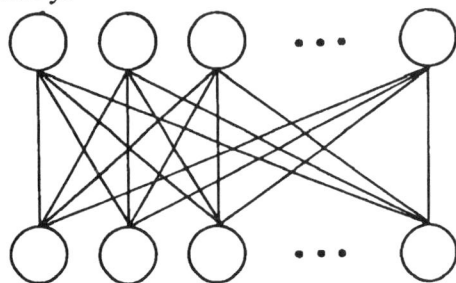

two-layer system, etc. In this book, we will be counting all the layers when we describe a system.

A third early model, the learning matrix (Steinbuch 1963) was developed to explicitly simulate classical stimulus–response (S–R) conditioning. In this system, binary stimuli were presented on one set of lines, and responses were trained and evoked on the second set of lines. The two sets of lines crossed so as to make a matrix, and there were connections made at the crossing points. The machine was trained by placing stimuli and responses on the matrix and then adjusting the weights of the connection points.

If the input lines are denoted by x_i and the output lines are denoted by y_j, then the weight of the connection w_{ij} is increased during training if $x_i = 1$ and $y_j = 1$ (positive reinforcement); it is decreased if $x_i = 1$ and $y_j = 0$ (negative reinforcement). This increase or decrease in weight was a small fixed amount.   The model achieves the same result as that achieved by classical conditioning, which this model was designed to simulate. If all the changes are small and fixed in absolute value, then the weight w_{ij} comes to approximate the expected value of the input line x_i, given that y_j is activated, as Kohonen (1988) points out. In a simple associative network, the possibility of negative reinforcement is removed (Willshaw, Buneman & Longuet-Higgins 1969). In this case, as Kohonen shows, the recall process involves a correlation of the current input pattern with all of the input patterns given during training, to determine which output pattern (or linear combination thereof) of the ones given during training should be produced during recall.

A similar model to the learning matrix was developed by Taylor (1956). This used Hebb's (1949) learning rule(see the next section).

2.5. Hebbian and Associative Learning

Hebb (1949) proposed a simple rule for learning in neurons, which has recently been shown to be biologically plausible (Schwartz 1988). In this rule, the strength of a synapse between two neurons is strengthened when both of them are active.

Anderson (1983), among others (e.g. Cooper, Liberman & Oja 1979, Bienenstock, Cooper & Munro 1982), has studied simple Hebbian associative learning. He takes a set of input neurons, whose activations are considered as a vector f, and a set of output units, whose activations are g. If every unit in f is connected to every unit in g, these connections can be represented by an $n \times n$ connectivity matrix A. This matrix can learn the association between f and g by the modified Hebbian learning rule in which the change in the value of the matrix element A_{ij} is $\Delta A_{ij} = k g_i f_j$ where k is a constant, the learning rate. In vector notation, this is: $\Delta A = k g f^T$, where f^T is the transpose of f (the transpose is used so that the dot product can be written in vector notation).

When $k=1$, in which case the network learns the association between g and f in one learning step, then g can be obtained by inputting f using the formula $g = Af$, since A has come to have the value $g f^T$, assuming it was initially zero.

In general, one wants to store a set of associations g_i-f_i in the connection matrix A, not just a single association. You can use the same learning rule as above, and mix different associative pairs in training the matrix. Each matrix element may participate in the association between several pairs of vectors, so this is a distributed memory model.

This will work well only if the input vectors are orthogonal to one another; that is, if their dot products are zero. Otherwise there will be crosstalk; if f_1 and f_2 are not orthogonal, and g_1 and g_2 are their desired outputs, the output that one obtains when inputting f_1 or f_2 will be some linear combination of g_1 and g_2, rather than either one of them. This is a problem with linear associative networks that Hopfield's work and other work on non-linear methods was designed to fix (see section 2.8). The surprising thing is the wide range of phenomena for which linear methods are adequate.

Since there can be at most N orthogonal patterns in an N-feature input vector, the matrix is limited to N associations. N N-feature vectors chosen at random will tend to be close to being orthogonal to one another, but not absolutely so, thus there will usually be some level of error.

Anderson applied this model to learning a prototype of a category. He borrowed his input patterns for category formation from an experiment done by Posner and Keele (1968a,b). Posner and Keele showed subjects patterns of dots on a two-dimensional screen. The initial patterns of N dots that subjects were shown were called prototypes. Then they were shown examples of the prototype, which were formed by randomly perturbing each dot in the prototype a relatively small distance. This was repeated for several different prototypes, and subjects were then asked to classify a stimulus (which may or may not have been presented as one of the examples) as belonging to one of the prototype classes that have been shown.

Knapp and Anderson (Knapp & Anderson 1984) repeated the Posner–Keele experiment, varying the number of examples that subjects saw of each prototype, and measuring the percentage correct classification rate. They then modeled the subjects' performance. They stored the patterns on a hypothetical two-dimensional visual cortex, where a dot in the input represented a sharp Gaussian peak in the response of the cortex. As trials proceeded, this surface received peaks from all examples of a prototype, and thus came to represent the average of all the examples (see Figure 2.3).

MEMORY FORMATION

From the point of view of the associative model given above, each two-dimensional cortical activity pattern was collapsed to a single row in the matrix A, and the output patterns were 1000... , 0100..., 0010..., etc. representing the N different classification decisions. Each row of A represented an averaged pattern of activity of all the examples of a prototype; since only one node is activated in the output, learning trials result only in the modification of one row.

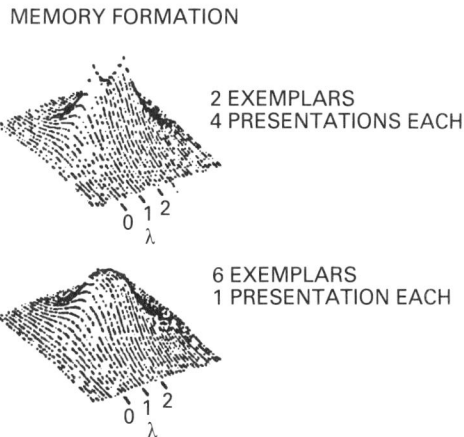

2 EXEMPLARS
4 PRESENTATIONS EACH

6 EXEMPLARS
1 PRESENTATION EACH

Figure 2.3. Response surfaces from Knapp & Anderson (1984). Reprinted by permission.

Given a particular example, more than one row may respond to it, and thus more than one output unit (the output units o_i respond to a dot product of the ith row of A with an example input f_j) may respond. To make the classification of the input into a prototype class, Knapp and Anderson simply chose the output unit that responded the most, thus making their model non-linear. The model exhibited correct classification response curves on new, old (that is, previously seen by the system), and prototype input patterns with respect to the number of learning trials that were qualitatively quite similar to those exhibited by human subjects.

Anderson also employed a simple non-linear associative model, the so-called "brain-state-in-a-box" (BSB). The BSB update rule is given by

$$x(t+1)=x(t)+Ax(t)$$

where $x(t)$ is the the input vector, and $x(t+1)$ is the auto-associative output. Bounds are placed on each of the dimensions of x, typically +1 and -1, so that it is bounded by a hypercube, and the system will naturally drift into one of the corners of the hypercube.

He applied the BSB model to a simple reasoning task designed as a pattern recognition task. In this task, there were triples of words: the first word in a triple was drawn from a set of human or divine names, e.g. Plato, Zeus; the second word was drawn from (man,god), and the third was drawn from (mortal,immortal). Each of these symbols was encoded as a string of -1's and +1's (a value of zero on all the places in the string indicated the absence of a symbol.) The patterns for the various symbols were not orthogonal.

He did Hebbian learning, of the type described above, using each word as a stimulus, with zeros in the positions of the remaining two words. The model was also taught valid pairs of words. After learning was complete, and it was presented with a valid pair of words, it always filled in the missing word correctly. Thus the system learned to do syllagistic reasoning via pattern completion; for instance, it completed the pattern (Socrates man –) as (Socrates man mortal). Nonsense inputs, such as (Zeus man immortal), the model cannot handle; it refuses to converge to a corner of the box in either the name or species location.

In related work on Hebbian learning, Linsker has shown in a recent series of papers (Linsker 1986a,b,c,1987) that many of the receptivity characteristics of neurons in the primate visual cortex can be discovered using this method of learning, extended to a multi-layer network.

2.6. Kohonen's Work on Associative Learning

Kohonen (Kohonen, 1988) has studied auto-associative and hetero-associative mappings. The simplest such mapping is that used by Anderson: a linear associator of the form $y=Ax$, where x is the input vector and y the output vector. There are a set of such pairs x_k and y_k Kohonen studied mappings that are optimal in the sense that if the x_k are corrupted by noise, the y_k are still arrived at. For an auto-associative memory, each x_k can be viewed as a fragment that functions as a key to retrieve the concatenated total vector $z=(x$ followed by $y)$.

Suppose that, in a given associative example, the x_k are viewed as vectors spanning a sub-space of R^N, where N is the dimensionality of the vectors. Then any particular vector x is the sum of a linear combination of the x_k which best approximates x's projection on the sub-space spanned by the x_k, plus a residual. Thus

$$x = r + \sum_k a_k x_k$$

If x is close to one of the x_k, say x_j, the linear combination will be close to $a_j x_j$. There is a mathematical technique to compute this best linear combination, the Gram–Schmidt process (see Kohonen 1988 for details). Of course, the x_k have to be known.

It turns out , and Kohonen demonstrates mathematically, that if the vector in question x is a noisy version of one of the vectors x_k, say x_r, so that $x = x_r + r$, then the linear orthogonal projection

$$\sum_k a_k x_k$$

of x onto the x_k's space, as computed by the Gram-Schmidt process (in conjunction with least squares), is a better approximation to x_r than x itself. This result can be the basis for retrieval of the best-fitting pattern from a noisy input, and has been demonstrated to be quite effective by Kohonen. Here x_r is the pattern to be retrieved, and x is the noisy input. For instance, Kohonen stored 100 photographs of faces, and he used keys missing chunks of the photos, or seriously blurred by noise, to successfully index into this database, using this method.

The complement of this auto-associative mapping, which retrieves the best x_r from x, is what Kohonen calls the "novelty filter". This extracts just what is new, that is the residual r. This can detect "missing" or "new" pieces to a pattern. For instance, if a capital A is one of the stored patterns, and a capital A is presented, but without its horizontal bar, then the horizontal bar is the output of the novelty filter. This can be readily obtained by simply taking the difference between between x and x_r.

Kohonen also did, by the same orthogonal projection technique, an auto-associative experiment. Here images of faces were concatenated with an identifying tag, and then auto-associative recall of faces missing their tags was attempted, with half the image serving as key. The tags were unit basis vectors in which one element was unity and the rest were zero, that is, 1000..., 0100..., etc. In all the recall experiments the tag bit was set significantly higher than the rest of the bits in the tag by the retrieval algorithm, with the quality of recall improving with increases in the proportion of the reference image used as key, and worsening increases in the number of reference faces that are stored.

2.7. Willshaw's Binary Associator

Willshaw (1981) devised an associative network consisting of an array A of mxn units with binary states, which is designed to associate ordered pairs of binary vectors in which the first vector (x) is of length m, and the second (y) is of length n. It does this by setting the state of unit A_{ij} to 1 if $x_i=1$ and $y_i=1$. Each output unit is receives input from all of the array units in its column. The output units have a threshold of q, where q is the number of input units that are active at any given time. This allows the the output unit to accumulate enough "votes" from active input units to set itself to one. The only way that an output unit can come on erroneously is if m outputs exist in the same column from other associations. Willshaw showed that if q is approximately equal to log m, the probability of such crosstalk becomes low. Willshaw's net can also be used as an auto-associator, in which case the array is square, and it can be used to complete noisy or incomplete patterns.

2.8. Hopfield's Non-linear Auto-associator

Hopfield (1982) notes that while people can design computers to perform specific tasks, evolution provides no such designer. Thus configurations of neurons must have computational properties that are emergent from their individual properties and connections to one another. These networks can be "designed" by evolution in the sense that the connection schemes that prove useful to the survival of the organism are preserved.

Hopfield considers a wiring scheme for implementing a content-addressable memory (auto-associator). He begins with a certain class of physical system whose behavior gives you an automatic form of content-addressability. The state of a system like this can be described by giving values to a set of coordinates X_1, X_2, ... , X_n in an N-dimensional space, called a state space, and the way the system evolves in time corresponds to a flow in this state space (in ordinary 3-dimensional space, this would simply be a curve through space.) Given certain types of equations—such as those described below—governing the state of the system over time, there are stable points in the state space towards which all the points in the immediate neighborhood flow towards. These are called locally stable limit points. Thus if the state at the limit point is the memory that is stored, and the states near the limit point represent partial knowledge of this memory, then starting the system at the partial knowledge state will cause it to settle into the complete knowledge state. This is Hopfield's method of achieving content-addressability.

More specifically, he uses neurons with binary states. The activations of the neurons correspond to the individual coordinates in the state space. Each neuron i has two possible values for its firing rate (activation) V_i, 0 and 1. If two neurons i and j are connected, the strength of their interconnection is given by T_{ij}. Each neuron has a fixed firing threshold U_i. Each neuron resets its state at random times, but the average rate of state resetting is W. Thus the system, like the brain, is asynchronous, since neurons in the brain do not all fire at the same time. Each neuron resets itself based on the following rule:

$V_i \leftarrow 1$ if input $> U_i$
$V_i \leftarrow 0$ if input $< U_i$
where input $= \sum_{j \neq i} T_{ij} V_i$

The total input that a neuron i receives is the sum of the activations of all the neurons connected to it, weighted by the strength of its connection to each one of them. This rule is similar to that used by perceptrons, Hopfield points out, but, as he notes, perceptrons are strictly feed-forward, whereas his network is bi-directional.

Each state of the system can be represented by a bit vector of length n. Hopfield has his network store a set of k such states. He does this by using the following "storage prescription" for the weights:

$$T_{ij} = \sum_s (2V_i^s-1)(2V_j^s-1)$$

where i and j are neurons and s is one of the k states. Each of the terms in parentheses can take on the value 1 or -1, since the V_i are binary; thus the value of the product is 1 if the two bits of the state in question are the same, or -1 if they are different. Each state that is being stored is given an equal "vote" in determining the overall weight; hence the summation sign.

There are about n^2 connections; effectively what Hopfield is doing is encoding K n-bit vectors in n^2 weights. By substituting in the formula for the activation of an individual neuron the formula for the weights, he obtains

$$input = \sum_j T_{ij}V_i^{s'} = \sum_s (2V_i^s-1) \left[\sum_j V_j^{s'}(2V_i^s-1) \right]$$

The mean value of the bracketed term in parentheses, Hopfield finds, is 0, since any two neuron states tend to be uncorrelated, and $(2V_i'-1)$ is as often 1 as it is 1, except when $s=s'$, in which case, the average value is $n/2$, since on average half the bits in a state s are 0 and half are 1. Thus the input is approximately equal to

$$\frac{n}{2}(2V_i^{s'}-1)$$

since all the terms in the initial summation go away except for the s' term.

A critical aspect of Hopfield's model is that it is non-linear. The model has a step function response to input. Actual neurons have a response that is similar to a sigmoid function. Hopfield's non-linear constrasts with models that have a linear response, such as Anderson's and Kohonen's models (see sections 2.5 and 2.6).

Borrowing from thermodynamics, Hopfield defines the energy E of his system to be

$$E = \frac{1}{2} \sum_{i,j,i\neq j} T_{ij} V_i V_j$$

in the case where $T_{ij} = T_{ji}$, that is, when you have symmetric connections. The change in E based on a change in a single neuron's state is

$$\Delta E = \frac{1}{2} \Delta V_i \sum_{i,j,i\neq j} T_{ij} V_j$$

This is a monotonically decreasing function for the following reason. ΔV_i can take on the values -1 (when it goes from 1 to 0) and +1 (when it goes from 0 to 1). When V_i becomes 0, the summation is negative, since

$$\frac{n}{2}(2V_i^{s'} - 1)$$

is negative. When it becomes 1, the summation is positive. ΔE is therefore always positive, since it is either the product of two negative or two positive numbers. The model will continue changing state until it reaches a local minimum for E. Thus the model has stable limit points.

Hopfield ran simulations of his model for 30 and 100 neurons, using random initial states. This was done for the case where $T_{ij} \neq T_{ji}$, that is, in the case in which the connections were non-symmetric, to see if the stable limit points still existed. In most of the cases the model would settle to one of two or three stable states; occasionally it would oscillate between two states or roam around in a small area in state space. Hopfield has a mathematical argument for why stable states persist in the case of non-symmetric connections; this is important for the biological validity of the model, because asymmetric mutual connections often exist in the brain. Some neuroscientists question the neural plausiblity of Hopfield's model and of its extension to *simulated annealing*. (For information on simulated annealing, see the next section; for a critique, see section 2.19)

Hopfield discovered experimentally that his n neuron network was capable of storing about 0.15 n states, before a severe degradation in recall occurred. At 0.15 n, about half the states are recalled well, and half are recalled badly. It is necessary to reduce the number of stored states to 0.05 n to get perfect recall.

Each of the stored states, as a limit point, "attracts" flows from those states that are most similar to it, thus providing a content-addressable (auto-associative) memory. If a given starting state is intermediate between two or more of the stored states, a choice must be made. The statistical behavior of this choice is such that the probability of choosing one state or the other is related to the similarity of the intermediate state to one or the other stored state.

2.9. Modeling Neurons with Differential Equations

Hopfield and Tank (1986b) developed a sophisticated model of neuronal firing rates in a network. Each cell i is characterized by a capacitance C_i and a resistance R_i. These, together with the electric current that is input to the cell, determine the input potential v. The strength of a synaptic connection between two neurons, as in the earlier binary model, is given by T_{ij}. Hopfield and Tank derived the following differential equation for the behavior of the cell potential U_i over time:

$$C_i \frac{\partial U_i}{\partial t} = \sum_{j=1}^{N} T_{ij} f_j - \frac{U_i}{R_i} + I_i$$

These three terms are respectively due to input currents from neurons that have synapses with the neuron in question, and input current that is due to neurons that are external to the circuit in question. This equation is still an approximation, but it is a closer approximation to real neuron behavior than the two-state activation model that Hopfield offered earlier (see the last section.)

Hopfield and Tank have applied their model to a variety of optimization problems. An optimization problem is a problem for which an optimal solution must be found, out of a (typically) large set of possible solutions. Many problems can be stated as optimization problems. For example, language understanding can be viewed as the problem of assigning an optimal meaning to a sentence; speech understanding can be thought of as trying to make an optimal interpretation of a sound pattern as a series of words. One of the classic optimization problems is the traveling salesman problem, in which a salesman needs to visit a set of cities; the problem is to find the shortest tour that visits every city once, returning to the starting city at the end. Hopfield and Tank have devised a neuronal circuit to do this.

An n city tour is represented by an n by n matrix; each city has a row in the matrix. Each of the n units that are in a given row represent the n possible positions that the city can have in a tour. Thus a solution corresponds to a single neuron being "on" (highly activated) in each row, and the rest being "off". The requirement that only one city can be in a given position in a tour translates to the rule that only one neuron in each column may be activated. These two constraints are achieved by hooking up all the neurons in each row and in each column as a winner-take-all network with lateral inhibition between each pair of them.

A winner-take-all network is a network in which each node is connected with inhibition to each other node in the network, as well as receiving input or activation from outside. Generally, such a network settles to a state in which only one node in the network is activated and the rest are deactivated. In Hopfield and Tank's network, a unit's activation ranges between 0 and 1.

The distances between cities are put into the system by using them as the weights between neurons along a possible tour path. For instance, if neuron $A2$ represents city A in position 2 in the tour, and $B3$ represents city$B$ in position 3, then there is a connection between these two neurons whose strength is set to the distance between A and B. Since the smaller weights (distances) contribute less to the energy function, and since the updating function tends to minimize the energy function, the system will tend to find a solution containing those units such that the sum of their weights is minimal. Hopfield and Tank found that, in a 30 city problem, the network found one of the best 10^7 solutions out of a total possible of about 10^{30}, thus reducing the problem space by a factor of 10^{23} in a single convergence. They point out that since the values of the units range from 0 to 1, and that a unit's activation represents the certainty that that unit participates in the solution (i.e. that a given city is in a given position in the tour), the network can consider a large number of possibilities simultaneously, instead of having to enumerate them the way a standard serial computer would. Hopfield and Tank point out that this property of having the unit activation be between 0 and 1 is similar to properties of systems built using the certainty factors found in fuzzy logic and fuzzy set theory (Zadeh 1973), which has been applied to artificial intelligence and psychology.

Hopfield and Tank point out that their solution to the traveling salesman problem and other optimization problems is an example of "forward engineering"; that is, specifically devising a neural circuit to handle a specific computational problem. They note that neurobiology is generally a problem of reverse-engineering, understanding circuits whose mode of functioning is unknown. They point out that accumulating experience in designing circuits gives one a set of principles to use when analyzing them. This experience may lead one to discover the principles used by biological evolution.

Hopfield and Tank emphasize the immense time savings involved in neural solutions to problems like the traveling salesman problem. They have implemented their designs in hardware. They note that a 30 city traveling salesman problem could be solved in about 0.1 seconds in a biological network of their design, using actual neurons, if it were possible to build such a network, whereas a conventional serial microcomputer could do it, using a conventional algorithm, in the same time, but would require 10^4 more devices (transistors). An electronic implementation of their algorithm would require only about 1 microsecond.

They have devised neural versions of algorithms for other problems, including graph coloring, the Euclidian match problem, and the transposition code problem (Hopfield & Tank 1985, 1986a).

Their work raises the following interesting question: does the brain make use of special purpose neural structures for vision, language processing, and speech processing, or does it adapt structures that already exist by changing the strength of synaptic connections? It is clear that in the case of the early visual system, specialized connections exist, but the question as to what extent the brain uses hard-wired, specialized circuits for other problems is debatable. Clearly, people are able to learn new solutions to new problems; how problems are represented in the brain, and how the brain adapts solutions to them, are hard questions not directly addressed by Hopfield and Tank's model.

2.10. Simulated Annealing in the Boltzmann Machine

The Boltzmann machine (Ackley, Hinton & Sejnowksi 1985), like Hopfield's network, is a neural network with bi-directional links between units so that two units that are connected have the same weight on a connection in both directions. The units have binary states, and the goal of the system, like that of Hopfield, is to achieve a minimum energy

$$E=\sum_{i<j} w_{ij}s_i s_j+\sum_i \theta_i s_i$$

where θ_i is a threshold. (They use a slightly different notation than Hopfield: his T_{ij} are their w_{ij}, his U_i are their θ_i, and his V_i are their s_i.) This energy function is a little more complex than Hopfield's, since it includes the thresholds θ_i. Each unit k can locally calculate the difference in the energy between what it is if it is activated ($s_k=1$) and if it is not ($s_k=0$); this is easily seen to be

$$\Delta E_k=\sum_i w_{ki}s_i - \theta_k$$

Thus, if the unit turns itself "on" when its input (summation term in the above equation) exceeds its threshold, then the energy is minimized. This is equivalent to what Hopfield does, although he does not include the thresholds in the energy function.

This deterministic algorithm was used by Hopfield, and it was fine for his purpose, which was to recall an exemplar pattern from an input pattern similar to it (or to recall a whole pattern from part). The above network will converge to a local minimum, and Hopfield uses the local minimum network states to store his exemplars. This is no good, however, when you are using the network to solve constraint-satisfying optimization problems; then you want the network to find *the* global minimum state. Ackley and his co-workers, following (Metropolis, Rosenbluth, Rosenbluth, Teller & Teller, 1953) and (Kirkpatrick, Gelatt & Vecchi 1983) get the network out of local minima by introducing noise. Instead of having each unit turn itself on asynchronously if its input exceeds a threshold, it turns itself on with a probability p_k that is a function of the energy gap ΔE_k on the iteration k

$$p_k=\frac{1}{(1+e^{-\Delta E_k/T})}$$

where T is a parameter that plays the same role in this system that temperature plays in a thermodynamic system. This decision rule is the same as that for a thermodynamic system in which each particle has two energy states. The reason why this system is of interest is that it will find an equilibrium state (corresponding to a global minimum) no matter what state it is started in.   At high temperatures it converges rapidly to a solution, but it does not discriminate finely between different energy states; at low temperatures convergence is slower, but it is able to make this fine discrimination.   One way to approach equilibrium quickly and accurately is to start with the system at a high temperature, then lower the temperature slowly. This is called *simulated annealing*, because it is the computational analog of the physical process known as annealing.

A VLSI chip that implements the Boltzmann machine is being built by Alspector and Allen (1987). This will run simulations about one million times faster than could be done by a VAX (Hinton 1987).

2.11.Learning Weights in the Boltzmann Machine

The Boltzmann machine, like Rumelhart and his co-workers' back-propagation algorithm (see section 2.12), solves the *credit assignment problem* of assigning optimal weights to connections to hidden units in a neural network. This problem is a classical one in learning; it dates back to such work as that of Samuel (1963) on checkers, in which a complex function was used to evaluate moves in a game of checkers. If the move was successful, it was difficult to determine which of the terms in the function should be given credit. In terms of a neural network divided into hidden units, input units, and output units, the credit assignment problem is simply that of setting these weights so that the correct associations between input and output are embodied in the network—that is, assigning credit (or responsibility) to the hidden units.

Ackley and his co-workers' technique, which is a learning algorithm, goes beyond simulated annealing alone. Simulated annealing is not a learning algorithm, since it does not change the weights. The following algorithm may be used to discover the optimal weights.

In this scheme, a Boltzmann machine is divided into v visible units and h hidden units. During training, the visible units are clamped—their states are fixed—and the machine is allowed to settle into equilibrium. Then another input is clamped. There are 2^v possible inputs, each with a certain probability of being chosen as the input. A Boltzmann machine is said to model its environment (that is, this probability distribution of the set of inputs) if, when it is left running freely (with no input—no units clamped), it achieves the same probability distribution as its environment.

Information theory (and common sense) tells us that our Boltzmann machine needs to have $0(2^v)$ units to store the 2^v probabilities needed to specify the behavior of the environment. Thus in general, the system will not model the environment correctly if it contains less than $0(2^v)$ units. If the environment contains regularities (such as patterns with odd parity being presented more frequently), the system can do better with less units. In order to get the two probability distributions to match, it is necessary to minimize a measure of the discrepancy between the two. Such a measure is

$$G = \sum_\alpha P(V_\alpha) ln(P(V_\alpha)/P'(V_\alpha))$$

where $P(V\alpha)$ is the probability of state $V\alpha$ in the environment, and $P'(V\alpha)$ is the probability of that state when the network is running freely. G is zero when $P'(V\alpha) = P(V\alpha)$ for all x, and is positive otherwise. Ackley and his co-workers show that a rule that minimizes G is

$$\Delta w_{ij} = \varepsilon(p_{ij} - p'_{ij})$$

The term Δw_{ij} specifies the change in the weight between units i and j; in order to change the probability distribution the weights must be changed; the relaxation process only changes the states of the neurons. p_{ij} is the probability that units i and j will both be on in the clamped state, and p'_{ij} is the probability that they will both be on in the unclamped state. ε is a constant, the learning rate. Both of these probabilities can be estimated by observing the network run. Note that though this formula minimizes G, each connection can adjust its weight by observing locally available information (the states of the units it connects). The parameters of the learning process are ε and the length of time over which p_{ij} and p'_{ij} are estimated. Errors in the estimation of the probabilities, which are necessitated by the requirement of observing them over finite lengths of time, can lead to short climbs in G.

Instead of using the above formula for Δw_{ij}, Ackley and his co-workers often implemented the variation whereby w_{ij} was incremented by a fixed amount y if $p_{ij} > p'_{ij}$, and decremented by y otherwise. This gives the advantage of allowing the network to take larger steps when the gradient surface is relatively flat, so that it can proceed more quickly to the center of a wide trough in the surface.

One problem that Ackley and his co-workers applied this learning algorithm to is the encoder problem. In this problem, there are two sets of visible units, V_1 and V_2., each composed of v units. In each group there is a single unit turned on, so that the visible units have a total of v^2 states. There also is a set of hidden units H. Each group of visible units is completely connected to itself and to H, but the two visible groups are not connected to one another. The goal of the system is to have the two groups of visible units agree on a code in the hidden units whereby they can communicate their state to one another. There must be at least $log_2 v$ hidden units in order for this to work totally; for instance, a 2-bit binary number in the hidden units is sufficient to encode a 4-bit unary number, which is what is being stored in the visible units. There were v inputs to the system, in each of which one unit was turned on in each of the two sets of visible units.

They ran instances of the encoder network with low values of v. The first instance they ran was the case where $v = 4$, the 4-2-4 network. Each of four input vectors was presented to the system, which was then brought to equilibrium using simulated annealing. The co-occurence probabilities p_{ij} and p'_{ij} were measured by repeating this process with each input, and was repeated for many cycles. As the network learned, it first built up winner-take-all networks that reflected the fact that the only one unit in each set of visible units was activated at a time.

The network then chose encodings of each 8-bit input as a 2-bit hidden unit vector; often it first chose redundant encodings (that is, two or more inputs had the same encoding), but it later learned unique encodings. If three hidden units are provided, it quickly finds 4 unique encodings of the input, and then runs for some time longer as it spreads the inputs out optimally (in terms of their encodings). In their simulation of an 8-3-8 machine, it found 8 encodings in 16 out of 20 trials and 7 encodings in the other four trials. It took over ten times as long as the 4-2-4 case to find the unique encodings, apparently because the weight space is much larger. They also ran a 40-10-40 encoder, which achieved 98.6% correct performance in retrieving encodings, after learning. The ten hidden units were more than the $log_240 \cong 6$ units required.

Ackley and his co-workers note that their learning algorithm represents a way in which the distributed representations of concepts may be learned; the encoder problem illustrates this. They also note that the encoder problem illustrates a way in which concepts can be communicated between different parts of a connectionist system.

2.12.Error Back-Propagation

Rumelhart, Hinton, and Williams (1986d), developed a method, *error back-propagation*, or more simply, *back-propagation*, for learning associations between input and output patterns using more than than the two layers of Rosenblatt's original perceptron. Similar methods were developed independently by Parker (1985), Le Cun (1987), and Werbos (1974). Error back-propagation is a procedure, like Ackley and his co-workers' learning algorithm (see the last section) for learning optimal weights and thus solving the credit assignment problem. They note that Minsky and Papert, in their book *Perceptrons* (1969), pointed out the limitations of the two-layer perceptron, in that there were some functions from input to output that such devices could not compute. The solution to this problem is the insertion of hidden units intermediate between the input and output units, as in Figure 2.4. These are the "internal representations" that the authors speak of in their paper.

A classic example of a function that cannot be computed by a perceptron without hidden units is the exclusive-or (xor) logical operation. This cannot be computed with only two binary-valued input units and one output unit: rather, an additional (hidden) unit must be placed between the input and output that detects the conjunction of the two input units. The resultant network is shown in Figure 2.5.

Back-propagation is a supervised learning technique that compares the responses of the output units to the desired response, and readjust the weights in the network so that the next time that the same input is presented to the network, the network's response will be closer to the desired response.

Back-propagation is also called the *generalized delta rule* because it is a generalization of the original two-layer perceptron convergence procedure introduced by Rosenblatt (see section 2.4), specifically, the version developed by Widrow and Hoff (1960), which Rumelhart and his co-workers call the delta rule. (See also section 2.12).

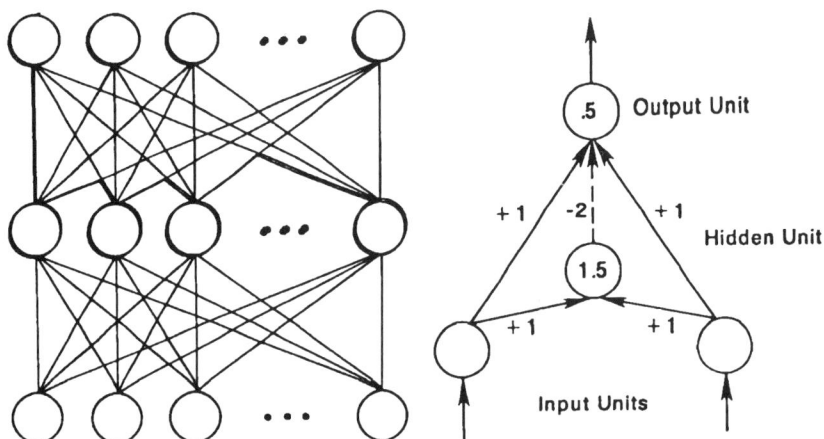

Figures 2.4 (left) and 2.5(right). Fig. 2.4: A three layer perceptron. The bottom layer is the input layer, the middle layer is the hidden layer, and the top layer is the output layer. There may be different amounts of units in each layer. Activation flows upward. Fig. 2.5: A network for computing the exclusive-or function from Rumelhart et al. (1986d). Reprinted by permission

The delta rule is as follows: If the network is presented with input pattern p, let the response of the network on output unit j be o_{pj}. If the desired target output is t_{pj}, then the difference is given by $\partial_{pj}=t_{pj}-o_{pj}$. If the ith unit of the input pattern has input I_{pi}, then the change in the weight connecting units i in the input with j in the output is given by

$$D_pW_{ji}=z\partial_{pj}I_{pi}$$

where z is some constant. This formula is applied iteratively, and may cause a convergence of the actual and target output.

The generalized delta rule was developed in the context of a layered, feed-forward network that has units with a semi-linear activation function. To review, a layered feed-forward network is one in which there are distinct layers of units; the input is the lowest layer, and the output is the highest, and all activation flows from lower to higher units. A semi-linear activation function is defined for their purposes as one that is a non-decreasing function of input that is differentiable everywhere. Thus a sigmoid activation function such as that typically used to model neuron response qualifies as semi-linear; a binary threshold does not, because it is not differentiable at the threshold point.

The form of the generalized delta rule is the same as that of the regular delta rule. For unit i whose output is o_i, the change in the weight connecting it to a unit j to which it outputs is $\Delta_p w_{ji} = k \partial_{pj} o_{pi}$. The generalized delta rule's error signal ∂_{pj} differs from the standard error signal. If unit j is an output unit, then

$$\partial_{pj} = (t_{pj} - o_{pj}) f'_j(net_{pj})$$

This formula is the same as before, except for the addition of the term $f'_j(net_{pj})$. This is the derivative of the activation function, evaluated at net_{pj}, which is the net input that unit j is receiving. (see the next section for a description of $f(net_{pj})$). Thus this term represents the rate of increase in the input that unit j is receiving.

In the case where j is not an output unit, the error signal is a function of the error signals of units that it is connected to, higher up in the network. This is the origin of the term back-propagation. The errors on the connections from the top level of hidden units to the output units are computed directly with the above formula. Then the errors in the connections from units in layers below the top two layers (the top hidden layer and the output layer) that are connected to the top two layers are computed in terms of the errors on the connections between the top two layers, and so on. Thus, while activation in the network propagates forward (upward), when computing the output, errors propagate backward, in order to adjust the weights. The error in a connection that is below the top is given by:

$$\partial_{pi} = f'_j(net_{pj}) \sum_k \partial_{pk} w_k.$$

where k ranges over all the units that unit j outputs to. Thus the error for a hidden unit is the weighted sum of the errors in the units that that hidden unit outputs to, multiplied by the rate at which the input to that hidden unit is changing.

Rumelhart and his co-workers have shown that the delta rule minimizes the total sum squared error (between the target and actual output) in the case of units with a linear activation rule. If you have *n* output units, the weights connecting them with the input units form a *n*-dimensional space. If the error is assigned an additional dimension, making a *n+1* dimensional space in this conceptualization, then it is a "hyper-surface" in the space. Rumelhart et al. have shown that the delta rule finds a minimum value for the error in this surface, and thus always sends the error plummeting most steeply, which they call steepest gradient descent.

The error surface can be visualized as a hilly landscape. Each point on its surface corresponds to a particular set of values for the weights in the network; the height at that point corresponds to the error. Steepest gradient descent means that, wherever you are on the surface, you always go in the steepest direction toward the valley. Of course, this only guarantees that the algorithm will find the nearest valley (local minimum) from where you happen to be on the error surface; it will not necessarily find a global minimum in the error.

The generalized delta rule was derived based on the desire that it have this behavior, steepest gradient descent. Taking this as an assumption, Rumelhart and his co-workers were able to derive the above formulas for back-propagation.

Hinton (1987) has observed that back-propagation typically learns in what appears to be $O(N^3)$ steps on a conventional serial machine, where N is the number of connections in the network. This would be reduced to $O(N^2)$ on a parallel machine with one processor per connection.

2.13. Applications of Back-propagation

Having developed the rule, they proceeded to apply it to a variety of problems. For their simulations, they used the sigmoid semi-linear activation rule

$$o_{pj} = \frac{1}{(1+e^{-(\sum_j w_{ij}o_{pi}+q_j)})} = f(\sum_i w_{ij}o_{pi}+\theta_j) = f(net_{pj})$$

They used a constant ζ in their weight change rule that was small enough to avoid sharp changes in the error surface that would throw off the gradient descent.

They used the network shown in Figure 2.5 for solving the exclusive-or (xor) problem. They solved it hundreds of times using different random initial weights, and the network settled into a solution state except in two cases, in which it found a local minimum in error space. They also solved it using different network topologies; for example, with a network with two hidden units instead of one.

They also used back-propagation to solve the parity problem, that is, determining whether an even or odd number of input units are activated. Like the exclusive-or problem (which is a special case of the parity problem), this is a problem that Minsky and Papert (1969) showed that a two-layer perceptron could not handle. Rumelhart and his co-workers handle it by using a three-layer

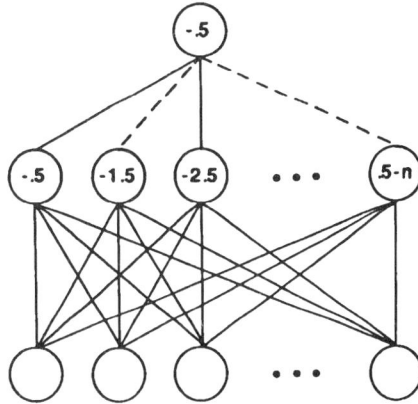

Figure 2.6. A network for computing the parity problem from Rumelhart et al. (1986d). Reprinted by permission.

perceptron with an equal number of input and hidden units and a single output unit (see Figure 2.6). They trained this network to respond correctly.

2.14. Learning Family Relationships

Hinton (1986) gave an interesting example of how concepts can come to be embodied in distributed representations using back-propagation, and how this leads to automatic generalization when inputs are given that are novel, that is, not included in the training set. The knowledge domain used by Hinton is that of family trees; the relationship between any two people in a family tree can be represented by a triple: (person1 relationship person2).

The five-layer feed-forward network that Hinton devised had two sets of input units, for the first two items in the above triple respectively. There are 24 input units for (person1), locally encoding the 24 possible people. There are 12 input units representing the 12 possible relationships. These 36 units comprise the first layer Each of these input units is connected to its own set of 6 units in the second layer, which learn distributed representations of the input. Each unit in both sets of 6 is connected to all of the 12 units in layer 3, which are in turn completely connected to 6 units in layer 4. Finally, all the units in layer 4 are connected to a layer of 24 output units in layer 5 representing the third item in the triple (person2). The only place that this feed-forward network is not completely connected is in the connections between layers 1 and 2.

Thus the network functions as a triple completion machine. Hinton used the two family trees shown in Figure 2.7; these contain 104 relationships, of which 100 were used for training with back-propagation. After 1500 sweeps through the 100 training instances, the network performed correctly on all of them, with correct performance defined as the correct output unit having an activation of greater than 0.8 (out of 1.0) and all of the rest of the output units having an activation of less than 0.2.

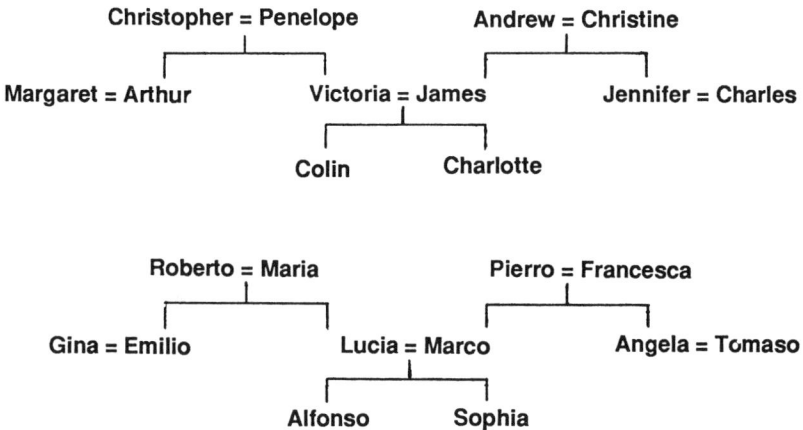

Christopher = Penelope   Andrew = Christine

Margaret = Arthur   Victoria = James   Jennifer = Charles

Colin   Charlotte

Roberto = Maria   Pierro = Francesca

Gina = Emilio   Lucia = Marco   Angela = Tomaso

Alfonso   Sophia

Figure 2.7. Family trees used by Hinton (1986). Reprinted by permission.

Some aspects of the distributed representations learned in the hidden units are particularly interesting. Unit 1 in the hidden units in layer 2 representing person1 encodes nationality. Unit 2 encodes what generation in the family tree person1 belongs. Unit 4 encodes the branch of the family tree the person belongs to. Unit 1 in the six hidden units in layer 2 encoding the relationship encodes the sex of person2; it is encoded here because the relationship (e.g., brother, mother) also describes the sex of person2. There was no need to encode the sex of person1 because this placed no constraints on the identity of person2, given the set of relationships used.

The isomorphism between the two family trees led to an economy of representation. The two items occupying the same slot in their respective family trees had a similar representation, except for the one unit encoding the English/Italian distinction.

Generalization was tested using the four relationships that were not used in the training. The training was repeated twice, using different initial random weights. In one of these cases, it got all four novel stimuli correct; in the other it got three out of four correct. Here, out of necessity, the criterion for what is correct was relaxed somewhat; a correct response entailed activation of over 0.5 on the correct output unit and less than 0.5 on the remaining units.

2.15.   Competitive Learning

Competitive Learning is a mechanism in which units in higher layers in a connectionist network compete to recognize features in an input layer. It is a type of unsupervised learning, since no information is presented other than the input data to help a competitive learning algorithm to form features. Many versions of competitive learning exist: we discuss a few: the version of Rumelhart and Zipser, that of Carpenter and Grossberg, and that of Kohonen. Others include the work of Von der Malsburg (1973), Fukushima (1975), and Amari (1983). We then turn to the Neuronal Group Selection theory of Reeke and Edelman, which is an competitive learning theory of the brain.

2.16.   Competitive Learning Using
Feed-forward Networks

Rumelhart and Zipser (1985) studied one form of competitive learning. The type of competitive learning networks studied by Rumelhart and Zipser are feed-forward, with an input layer and one of more feature-recognition layers.

Nodes in each of the feature-recognition layers are grouped into clusters, and each unit in a cluster inhibits all the others, resulting in a winner-take-all situation within the cluster, whereby one unit becomes activated at the expense of all the rest. Each unit in the cluster receives input from the same set of units in the layer(s) below, but has different weights on these connections, resulting in different activation. The weights of only the winning unit are adjusted. In the version they studied, the weights coming into a unit summed to one.

For simplicity's sake, let us consider a two-layer system of input units and inhibitory clusters. The connection to a unit j in one of the clusters from a unit i in the input layer are weighted by w_{ij} The activation received by a unit equals

$$\sum_i w_{ij} c_i$$

where c_i is the activation of input unit i. In Rumelhart and Zipser's model, all the c_i's are binary. The activation of the units in a cluster range between zero and one; after winner-takes-all competition within each cluster has taken place, the activations in the clusters are also binary—one unit in each cluster has value one and the rest are zero. The w_{ij}'s for the unit that wins are then adjusted according to the following rule:

$$\Delta w_{ij} = g\left(\frac{c_{ik}}{n_k} - w_{ij}\right)$$

where g is a constant (the learning rate), c_{ik} is the *ith* component of the stimulus k, and n_k is the total number of input units that are activated in the stimulus k. Thus, on each iteration of the learning process, the vector of weights moves closer to a normalized version of the input presented in that learning cycle. If all the inputs were the same, say the constant vector c, the vector of weights of the winning unit would come to be equal to c/n_0, where n_0 is the number of ones in c. If all the inputs are not the same, individual units would come to be responsive to clusters of similar inputs, with the weights representing an input in the center of each cluster, in a similar manner to the self-organizing maps of Kohonen (see section 2.18)

Rumelhart and Zipser trained such a network to respond to adjacent dipole stimuli on a 4x4 grid; that is, each dipole stimulus was composed of two active nodes on the input grid, which were vertically or horizontally adjacent. They first connected each of the 16 input units to an inhibitory cluster of size two. Learning caused one of these units to become more responsive to activation on half the grid, and the other to be more responsive to the other half. The grid was divided in such a way horizontally, vertically, or (occasionally) diagonally, depending on the initial configuration of the weights, which was random. Thus the network detected the locality in the input.

The inhibitory cluster's size was then increased to four units. After one convergence, the input grid was partitioned into four regions, each of which had a maximally responsive unit, three of which were 2x2 squares and one of which was divided into two pieces (see Figure 2.8). When a stimulus bordered two regions, it was classified into one or the other region. More units would classify the stimuli even more locally, up to a limit of 24 units, each of which would respond to one of the 24 possible dipole stimuli on this grid.

The next experiments in competitive learning that Rumelhart and Zipser conducted involved letter and word recognition. They used a 7x14 grid to present two letters to the system; each letter was contained in a 7x5 section of the grid, with two blank columns to the right of each letter. They used the letters A, B, C, D, E, and S as stimuli. The specific experiments, stimuli, and output cluster descriptions are given below.

Since these letters only sparsely occupied the grid, as they are hollow, so some units are rarely or never activated, there is the possibility that some of the units in the output classification cluster will never win. They suggest two solutions for this problem. The first changes the learning rule so that it is "leaky", so that both the winning unit and all the losing units have their weight vectors moved toward the input vector, but the winner is moved faster—Rumelhart and Zipser moved it an order of magnitude faster. This moves all units into regions into which they can eventually win. The other idea, due to Bienenstock, Cooper, and Munro (1982), is to associate with each unit an additional number,

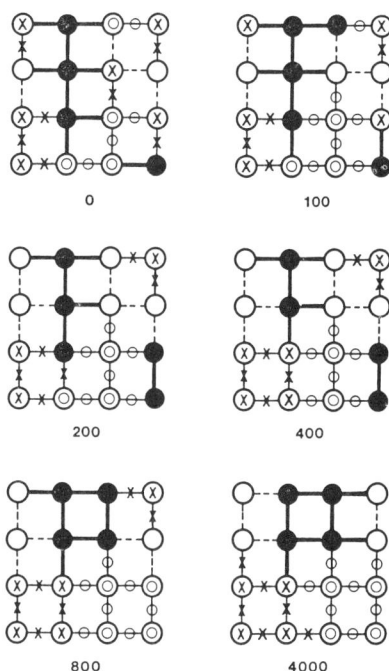

Figure 2.8. The 4 by 4 grid of input units used by Rumelhart and Zipser (1986) marked by four symbols (O,X,black square, white square) according to which of 4 units in an inhibitory cluster responded most to that each input unit. The numbers measure how long the system has learned. Reprinted by permission.

called its sensitivity, which becomes a multiplicative factor in the formula for its activation. The sensitivity is based on the number of inputs that a unit wins on; it increases its sensitivity when it fails to win, and decreases it when it wins. By this mechanism, every unit can come to win and thereby move closer to some cluster of inputs. Rumelhart and Zipser used both techniques; which one was used mattered little, they found.

Rumelhart and Zipser's first experiment presented four pairs of letters, AA, AB, BA, and BB; their output was composed of an inhibitory cluster of two units. In some cases, one unit responded to AA and AB, and the other to BA and BB; in the others, one unit responded to AA and BA, and the other to AB and BB. By examination of the weights, it was clear that in the former case, one unit responded to A in position 1, and the other unit responded to B in position 1; in the latter case, the same responses were found with respect to position 2. Each unit had similar connections to the position to which the two units were not responding. When the number of units in the inhibitory cluster was raised to four, one unit responded to each of the four patterns. Thus the same competitive learning mechanism can be used for both position-specific letter detectors and word detectors.

Next, Rumelhart and Zipser changed the stimulus patterns to AA, AB, AC, AD, BA, BB, BC, and BD. With two units in a cluster, they always became sensitive to the letter in the first position, because there were two possibilities there; with 4 units, each unit responded to one of the four possible values in the second position.

They demonstrated the ability of their network to classify stimuli by presenting the letters A, B, S, E to an inhibitory cluster of two units. The cluster correctly classified B with S and E with A; each element in each of these pairs is quite similar to the other, in terms of the patterns that they used. They then presented the patterns AA, BA, SB, EB to an inhibitory cluster of size two. As before, the cluster became a detector of which letter was found in position two, but the units also responded to the E or S in position one. One unit responded to a B in the second position and an E or S in the first; the other unit responded to an A in the second position and an A or B in the first. Thus the units come to respond to all the clustering information available in the input, even though it was redundant.

Rumelhart and Zipser's final experiment attempted to get the units in a cluster to respond to vertical and horizontal lines. They used a 6x6 grid, and presented as input the 12 possible vertical and horizontal lines of length 6. The trouble with recognizing horizontal vs. vertical in a single perceptron output layer is that every output unit participates in both a horizontal and a vertical line. They had hoped that each of the two units in an output cluster would respond to parallel bands of vertical or horizontal activation. Unfortunately, the system failed to classify the inputs in this way. Instead, each of two units responded to half of the vertical and horizontal lines. One unit responded to the vertical and horizontal lines that intersected the lower right quadrant of the input grid, and the other unit responded to those that intersected the upper left quadrant. The units clustered inputs in this fashion because clustering in this form of competitive learning is based on overlap in input patterns, and none of the vertical stripes overlap with one another, and neither do the horizontal stripes.

Rumelhart and Zipser forced the system to recognize the horizontal/vertical distinction by adding additional input units. In the case of the horizontal stripes, a static horizontal stripe in the additional units was added to each input. The same was done with the vertical stripes; in this case, a static vertical stripe was added. This fixed the problem, but there was nothing about the original classes of stimuli themselves that caused the system to distinguish them, other than the fact that two distinct static teaching patterns had been added, one of which was associated with each class. The fact that the static teaching patterns happened to be stripes and matched the rest of the input was irrelevant.

To approach the learning of the horizontal/vertical distinction in another way, they also built a three-layer system which had a middle layer of two clusters of four units each right above the input layer, and a top layer of a cluster of two units, each of which was connected to the eight units below it. Each of the four units in a cluster in the middle layer came to respond to either half the horizontal stripes, or half the vertical ones. The units in each cluster usually came to recognize different sets though, which gave the units in the top cluster enough information to perform the vertical/horizontal classification.

The vertical/horizontal distinction is an example of a classification that is not linearly separable. This means that there is no weight vector that, when the dot product between it and an input vector is taken, can determine by the value of the dot product what the classification of the input should be. A competitive learning system involving three or more layers often solves this problem.

2.17.   Competitive Learning using
Adaptive Resonance Theory

Carpenter and Grossberg (1987) propose a network that does competitive learning (self-organization) based on Grossberg's Adaptive Resonance Theory (ART) (1976). This network is sensitive to novel stimuli, as people are. Their system is divided into two subsystems; an attentional subsystem, which processes familiar stimuli, and an orienting subsystem that detects unfamiliar input patterns, and resets the attentional subsystem when it detects such a pattern. The network as a whole forms its own clusters of patterns, and thus acts as an unsupervised classifier.

Their system uses "self-scaling" units. This is needed because a feature that is "necessary" in one pattern may be superfluous or noise in another. The self-scaling property of units is the ability for them to recognize that in different types of patterns there may be a different number of critical features. This is quantified by a parameter called the vigilance level.

When familiar patterns are encountered, little settling of the network occurs and the system functions like a look-up table, quickly finding the (network-created) category for that familiar pattern. The environment can also act as a teacher; the network learns to respond to the differing precision of a category's definition by automatically detecting statistical properties of categories. Thus, if the examples are all very similar, any new example would have to be just as similar in order to be classed in the same category. If the category is looser, so is classification. This is designed to reflect human performance (Posner 1973); people pay attention to detail if it is necessary. If the system receives negative reinforcement from the environment, it will become more discriminating in its judgment, for the category in which a misclassification has occurred.

Their system, shown in Figure 2.9, is layered. The input I, which may be preprocessed in some way, becomes an activation pattern X across a set of nodes in layer 1, F1. Nodes in F1 are linked to nodes in the next layer up, F2, by connections that have corresponding nodes in long-term memory (LTM). The signal received at a node in F2 is the product of the node value in F1 and the value in LTM; the LTM value is said to *gate* the F1 value (functioning in a manner similar to a weight). Each node in F2 adds up all the information that it receives along all the gated connections that it has with nodes in F1 to create a pattern Y in F2. F1 and F2 together are the system's short-term memory (STM). The nodes in F2 interact with each other to get further contrast enhancement, that is, to separate the input patterns from each other in terms of the response in F2. The other parts of Figure 2.9 will be explained below.

One method of doing this contrast enhancement is by a process whereby the nodes in F2 become a winner-take-all clique (as in the competitive learning scheme of Rumelhart and Zipser), but in general, more than one node in F2 can be active at once. A winner-take-all clique in F2 can function as a classifier. The gated connections between F1 and F2 are called the "adaptive filter" by Carpenter and Grossberg.

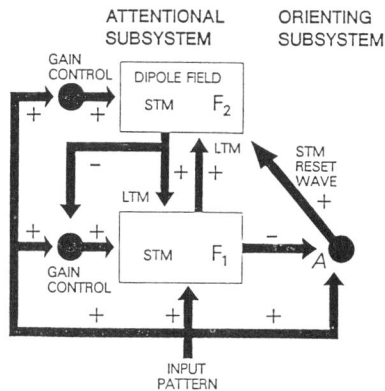

Figure 2.9. The network of Carpenter and Grossberg (1987). Reprinted by permission.

After F1 activates F2 to create Y, F2 gives feedback to F1 via another adaptive filter, also gated by LTM. This creates a new (modified) activation pattern across F1, X^*. If X^* differs significantly from X, this attenuates the initial activity in F1, and a subsystem, called the orienting subsystem detects this attenuation, and sends a burst of inhibition to all the active nodes in F2, which lasts for some time. The purpose of the orienting subsystem is to create novel responses to novel stimuli.

X^* thereby disappears and X is reinstated by I, thereby precluding further (immediate) bursts of inhibition from the orienting subsystem. The system then attempts to create a new pattern Y' in F2, which cannot be the same as Y, because the active nodes in Y continue to be inhibited for some time. The system continues to search for the right pattern in F2 until it finds a pattern whose top-down activation to F1 does not produce a significant attenuation in F1, which would reactivate the orienting subsystem.

The orienting subsystem responds to novel stimuli because only novel stimuli will produce attenuations in F1.

Two additional concepts apply to the attentional mechanism of the system; attentional priming and attentional gain control. Attentional priming occurs when top-down feedback to F2 creates a pattern in F1 before the input has a chance to affect the F1 nodes. An expectation is thereby created in the F1 nodes. The attentional gain control controls the degree to which F1 responds to top-down versus bottom-up input, thus allowing the system to respond differently to the two situations.

Carpenter and Grossberg use what they call the 2/3 rule to determine whether or not the F1 units produce output. In order for them to produce output, 2 out of the 3 sources for input to F1 must be active: these are the input pattern, feedback from above, and the attentional gain control. Since only the presence of an input pattern can trigger the attentional gain control, the 2/3 rule guarantees that only input from stimuli allows the F1 neurons to fire. The 2/3 rule is necessary to maintain consistent pattern classification over time; without the rule a pattern A may become classified by the responsiveness of F2 node q and later by a different F2 node r.

Carpenter and Grossberg note that, at a fixed vigilance level, their system may classify two stimuli A and B differently and C & D the same, even if A differs from B on exactly the same features on which C differs from D. If the system has been initially trained with a vigilance level that allows it to distinguish A from B, it will not distinguish C from D in its classification if C and D have more features than A and B. This behavior, Carpenter and Grossberg point out, is akin to "attentional focusing" in people; that is, discrepancies are less noticed if they are a smaller proportion of the total pattern being paid attention to; when you "zoom in" on part of a pattern, discrepancies become more apparent.

They note that the vigilance level is directly related to the number of categories that the input patterns are classified into. For instance, they classified bit patterns representing letters using their algorithm. With a vigilance threshold of 0.5, the system classified the 20 letter patterns presented into four groups; with a threshold of 0.8, it classified them into nine groups. The critical patterns that were stored as top-down weights in the system were significantly different in the two cases, being more specific in the latter case. If the vigilance level is set high enough, each letter would be classified into its own (singleton) set. Thus the total resource requirements of the system is a function of the vigilance level and the total number of input patterns.

The response of units in Carpenter and Grossberg's system is described by non-linear differential equations; Lippmann (1987) has shown them to be equivalent to the following simpler mathematical formalism; I borrow his notation.

There are n input units (F1) and n output units (F2). There are top-down and bottom-up connections between each input unit i and each output unit j, the weights of which are denoted by t_{ij} and b_{ij} respectively. These connections comprise what Carpenter and Grossberg call the adaptive filters. All the t_i are set to 1 initially, and all the b_{ij} to $1/n$. Binary input is applied to F1 and each unit in F2 computes its activation m_j as follows:

$$m_j = \sum_i b_{ij}(t)x_i$$

where x_i is the input applied to the input units. In this example, a winner-take-all network is used, so that only the largest unit is selected to be activated. The sum of the activation in F1:

$$|X| = \sum_i x_i$$

is compared to the sum weighted by the top-down connections

$$|T \cdot X| = \sum_i t_{ij}x_i$$

If $|T \cdot X|/|X|$ is greater than a vigilance threshold ρ, this signals a misclassification. The output unit that formerly responded to the F pattern is disabled, and a new output unit wins the competition. This is repeated when the vigilance threshold is not exceeded, and another output unit that corresponds to the current classification has been chosen. The system then integrates this information by changing its weights in the following manner, if j^* is the correct output node

$$t_{ij*}' = x_i t_{ij*} \text{ for all } i$$

$$b_{ij*}' = \frac{x_i t_{ij*}}{\sum_i x_i t_{ij*} + \frac{1}{2}} \quad \text{for all } i$$

where the bottom-up connections are normalized so that the average activation received by an output node will not exceed one in magnitude. Over time, the top-down and the bottom-up connections to an output node come to represent an average of all the examples that have been successfully classified using that output node. The vigilance threshold controls the dispersion of the examples in a category. Carpenter and Grossberg allow negative reinforcement to change the value of the vigilance threshold to allow the system to respond differently to categories of differing "fuzziness".

2.18.   Kohonen's Self-organizing Topological Maps

Kohonen's (1988) model of self-organization is based on the idea that the brain tends to compress and organize sensory data spontaneously. Self-organization is Kohonen's term for unsupervised learning. He starts with the observation that neural networks in the brain tend to consist of layers of neurons, which obey the "Mexican Hat" function; that is, units strongly excite those units nearby them, and inhibit those not so near (see Figure 2.10). He uses networks with large numbers of lateral connections to implement this, and a sigmoid activation function for his units. These types of networks tend to contain "clusters of activation". If there is more lateral inhibition, clusters tend to be smaller; if there is more excitation, they tend to be bigger

The purpose of Kohonen's self-organizing mappings is that patterns of high dimension (i.e., long vectors) are transformed into one or two-dimensional patterns, such as the two-dimensional clusters just described. For example, in a situation where input units are mapped onto

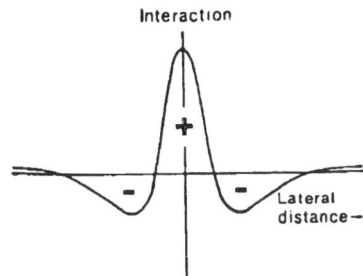

Figure 2.10. The "Mexican Hat" function of Kohonen (1988). Reprinted by permission.

corresponding output units, a self-organizing system would give a localized response—that is, a single output unit responding most, with activation falling off in the units around it, for each input pattern provided.

He defines a topology-preserving mapping onto a one-dimensional set of output units as one that reproduces some ordering that is placed on the input patterns. For instance, if the input patterns are ordered as $(x_1, x_2, ...,x_n)$ a topology-preserving mapping (e.g., state of the internal weights of the system) is one in which unit o_1 is most active when pattern x_1 is presented, unit o_2 is most active when x_2 is presented, etc., where the o's are the output units. Thus the spatial relations of the output units reflect the ordering of the input patterns. Kohonen notes that this can be thought of as a projection of the original high dimensional vector onto a linear scale.

If this is extended to two or more dimensions, the mathematics that describes what is topology preserving becomes more complex, but the intuition of a projection still holds. For instance, if the various input points are, as vectors, distributed on a curving, twisted surface, they will be mapped onto units on a flat plane. Distances between points will not be preserved but their topology will—that is, input vectors that were adjacent to each other will still be adjacent to each other: more strictly, if B is between A and C, this will be the case after the mapping as well.

Kohonen gives the example of a two-dimensional self-organizing system, that is a two-dimensional rectangular or hexagonal lattice, in which each unit in the grid receives input from each input unit, and forms a function of the weighted sum of these inputs, in which the weights are adaptive. The purpose of Kohonen's system is to evolve localized response patterns to input vectors. If two input vectors are similar, they evoke similar localized response patterns.

The way this is accomplished is as follows: each output unit has a vector of weights which connects it with the input units. These weight vectors are initially random. At each time step, the dot product of the weight vector of each unit with the current input vector is formed:

$$o_j = \sum_i w_{ik} x_k$$

where x_k is the kth component of the input vector, o_j is the activation of the jth output unit, and the w_{ik} are the weights connecting them.

After the activation of each output unit is computed, the output unit with the maximum activation level is selected. This is the unit whose weight vector is most similar to the input vector. This weight vector is then adjusted to be even more similar to the input vector by the rule

$$\Delta o(t_{k+1}) = \alpha(t_k)(x(t_k) - o(t_k))$$

in which x and o are the input and output vectors respectively, α is the learning rate, Δo is the change in o, and t_k and t_{k+1} are the kth and $(k+1)$st time step respectively. This is a version of the perceptron convergence rule (see section 2.4), and is similar to the competitive learning scheme of Rumelhart and Zipser (see the last section.)

At each time step this rule is applied to the maximally responding unit and to all the units within a certain distance d of this unit. The fact that that the rule is applied to nearby units is what leads to the topology-preserving properties of the mapping, and distinguishes it from the competitive learning schemes discussed in the previous two sections. As the learning proceeds, d is decreased, as is the learning parameter α. Relatively high values of these two parameters allow areas of units to quickly respond to different types of input patterns, whereas "fine structure" aspects of the topology of a set of input vectors are worked out in the later stages of the learning, as d and α decrease.

An example of a self-organizing system that Kohonen gives is one in which the output units come to recognize ranges of signal frequency; adjacent output units recognize adjacent ranges. The input units are resonators that each respond to an initially random (but then fixed, for each resonator) range of frequency. Each of these input units is randomly connected to a set of output units. When the system is trained on an input set of randomly chosen frequencies, using the protocol for a self-organizing system given above, the first output unit comes to recognize the highest frequencies in the input range, the next a slightly lower value.

Kohonen gives two examples of systems that capture a hierarchical set relationship between input elements in a topological map. In his first example there are 32 symbols each represented by a sequence of five octal digits, which code hierarchical relationships For example, if symbol C is represented by 30000, F by 31000 and G by 32000, F and G are viewed as more specific versions of C. The complete code is shown in Figure 2.11, and the result of a hierarchical clustering analysis is shown in Figure 2.12.   When   the   self-organizing algorithm using the codes as training data was run using a two-dimensional hexagonal array of output units, the result shown in Figure 2.13 was obtained. Here, for each symbol, the unit responding maximally to it is shown.   One can see that the topological map duplicates the information given by the hierarchical clustering process, although the straight lines in Figure 2.12 are deformed in Figure 2.13.   Nevertheless, all the topological clustering information is present.

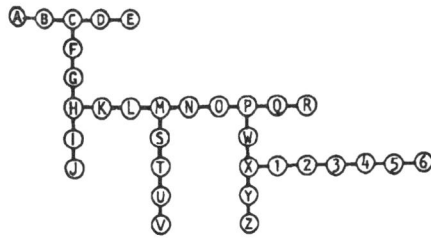

Figure 2.12. The result of a hierarchical clustering analysis of the code given in Fig. 2.11. From Kohonen (1988). Reprinted by Permission.

   The second example of classification in a two-dimensional array is given by a system that came to recognize and cluster natural phonemic data. After training on this data—sampled at 15 different frequency values—the system arrived at the map given in Figure 2.14. This map shows similarity relations between phonemes, based on the metric used by the system, which was the scalar product, taken between two phoneme input patterns. In Figure 2.15, the phoneme to which each unit responded maximally is shown. As expected, clusters are apparent.

Item

Char.	A	B	C	D	E	F	G	H	I	J	K	L	M	N	O	P	Q	R	S	T	U	V	W	X	Y	Z	1	2	3	4	5	6
ζ_1	1	2	3	4	5	3	3	3	3	3	3	3	3	3	3	3	3	3	3	3	3	3	3	3	3	3	3	3	3	3	3	3
ζ_2	0	0	0	0	0	1	2	3	4	5	3	3	3	3	3	3	3	3	3	3	3	3	3	3	3	3	3	3	3	3	3	3
ζ_3	0	0	0	0	0	0	0	0	0	1	2	3	4	5	6	7	8	3	3	3	3	6	6	6	6	6	6	6	6	6	6	6
ζ_4	0	0	0	0	0	0	0	0	0	0	0	0	0	0	0	0	0	1	2	3	4	1	2	3	4	2	2	2	2	2	2	2
ζ_5	0	0	0	0	0	0	0	0	0	0	0	0	0	0	0	0	0	0	0	0	0	0	0	0	0	0	1	2	3	4	5	6

Figure 2.11. An Encoding of 32 sysmbols by 5 octal digits. From Kohonen (1988). Reprinted by Permission.

o	*	*	a	æ	*	*	*	*	*
*	*	*	*	*	*	ø	e	*	i
*	u	*	h	*	*	*	*	j	*
v	*	*	*	r	y	*	*	*	*
*	*	*	*	*	*	*	ℓ	*	*
*	*	*	*	ŋ	*	*	*	*	*
d	*	n	*	*	*	m	*	*	s

o	o	a	a	æ	æ	æ	e	e	e
u	o	a	a	æ	ø	ø	e	i	i
u	u	h	h	r	ø	ø	e	i	i
v	v	v	r	r	ø	y	j	i	i
v	v	d	r	r	y	y	ℓ	j	i
n	v	n	d	n	ŋ	m	n	s	s
n	n	n	n	n	m	m	m	s	

B	C	D	E	*	Q	R	*	Y	Z
A	*	*	*	*	P	*	*	X	*
*	F	*	N	O	*	W	*	*	1
*	G	*	M	*	*	*	*	2	*
H	K	L	*	T	U	*	3	*	*
*	I	*	*	*	*	*	*	4	*
*	J	*	S	*	*	V	*	5	6

Figures 2.13-2.15. Topological maps formed by a self-organizing algorithm. From Kohonen (1988). Reprinted by Permission.

2.19.   A Population Biology Approach to Connectionism

Reeke and Edelman (1988) criticize approaches to connectionism that are inspired by physical systems, such as those given by Hopfield, and by Ackley and his co-workers (see sections 2.8 and 2.10). Although these approaches take their inspiration from biology insofar as they attempt to use realistic model neurons and use brain-like terminology, they are not modeling anything that is really present in the brain, according to Reeke and Edelman. To quote, "in the attempt to find regularity in biological systems, many features have been introduced into their simulation in connectionist system that are quite unbiological."

Reeke and Edelman take issue with the idea that the organism is simply a vessel for information already structured in its environment instead of a creator of information, which it synthesizes by applying criteria to its environment. They note that each individual must construct his or her own categories. In other words, they are advocating a model of the mind as an unsupervised learner in which much of the clustering of stimuli into classes is not readily inherent in the stimuli.

They note that the nervous system is composed of distinct areas, and each area has a distinct pattern of connectivity and is specialized for a different task. Different sub-networks interact and exchange information, building up more complex functions, which none of them could compute on their own. They note that regions seem to have been gradually added to the brain over the course of evolution, adding additional functions while coordinating their work with older sections. The brain is asynchronous; that is, events in different parts of the brain are not synchronized with one another. No one neuron is essential for the operation of a given network, and there are typically many paths connecting any two neurons that are connected at all. Apparently patterns of activation are what is important in the brain, not local activations of individual neurons. Thus representations are distributed.

One factor that Reeke and Edelman emphasize that seems to have been left out of most discussions of connectionism is the diversity of neuronal populations. This diversity takes two main forms. First of all, because of stochastic variation in development, genetically identical animals—twins—have different numbers of neurons and they are arranged differently. Even corresponding individual neurons differ from one another. They note that it is easily calculated that the human DNA does not contain enough information to totally specify the location and connectivity of the approximately 10^{11} neurons in the brain. Thus much of actual brain structure must be due to random and epigenetic events that occur during development. The local physical and chemical environment of a neuron influences that cell's development. Thus, Reeke and Edelman point out, the brain is not an optimally devised computer, but a variable structure. This variability is likely to be functional, since it can be used by natural selection.

Reeke and Edelman suggest that selection plays an important role in deciding what structures are used in development, and how their functioning develops during the brain's maturity. They think that these active structures are selected from a set of "repertoires", each of which is a set of interconnected neurons, and these selected repertoires come to play a major role in the functioning of the brain. This selection takes place over the lifetime of the organism (as opposed to Darwinian natural selection, which takes place over the lifetime of a species and its precursors). They have called their theory neuronal group selection (NGS). In terms of the models we have seen so far, it is a form of competitive, unsupervised learning, but it differs from the others in that it is explicitly a theory of brain function.

NGS theory provides for two forms of selection. The first occurs during the prenatal period of the brain's development. Selection between competing neurons during this period leads to the development of connections. After birth, the connectivity patterns are fixed, and the second form of selection occurs, whereby neurons compete to participate in active pathways and networks. This form of selection adjusts the weights of synaptic connections, but does not change the connectivity of the brain.

Reeke and Edelman list three required attributes of a selective system: there must be a variety of entities able to respond to the environment, these entities must receive input from their environment, and they must be able to receive differential reinforcement, so that one or the other entity wins out. They estimate that the selective groups (repertoires) contain 50 to 10000 neurons each. They note that individual groups of neurons can neither be too specific in their responses to stimuli nor can they be too general; in the former case, it is impossible to have, in the brain, enough groups to handle all the possible stimuli, and in the latter case, the groups cannot discriminate between stimuli.

Reeke and Edelman's system differs from simple competitive learning in that the competitors are not individual neurons, but rather groups of neurons. Each group has internal and external connectivity that is determined during development; the strengths of synaptic connections can be adjusted afterwards.

Another concept used in the NGS theory is re-entry. This is simply the ability for the different neuronic groups to receive inputs from one another. This concept encompasses lateral, feed-forward, and internal connections, and provides a mechanism whereby classifying groups can combine their outputs to form more complex classifications.

Re-entry is a very general concept describing any situation of combining outputs or of feedback, that is, the fact that the motor activity of the organism affects what the organism is seeing as a form of re-entry.

Reeke and Edelman cite evidence supporting the NGS theory. Growth patterns of neurons do not seem to have their connections specified by genetics, and different individuals have different patterns of connectivity.

They have built three automata, named Darwin I,II and III. They have built each system from repertoires, each of which is a set of cells, consisting of (up to) several layers. Each repertoire has its own fixed connectivity, but synaptic strength that can vary over time. Reeke and Edelman's third automaton, Darwin III, which we discuss here, differs from most connectionist systems in that it actually has a simulated motor component, consisting of a multi-jointed arm and a moveable head.

The automata receive their input in the form of a retinal array. The arm can actually move objects that are in the visual field; the head movements perform translations of the field. There is no a priori information given about the classifications of the stimuli. Reeke and Edelman claim that this distinguishes their system from other AI and connectionist systems, but this claim is false: all unsupervised learning methods operate without any external information.

They designed into their system feature-detecting elements. The features that are useful are the ones that long processes of selection have shown to be useful. The systems are set up so that the networks can adjust their synaptic strength based on the adaptive value of a particular response or behavior. Darwin III is divided into two parallel repertoires, Darwin and Wallace. For each stimulus, Wallace matches it to the closest prototype, based on the correlation of various features in the stimulus. Darwin provides a unique response for each stimulus; Wallace provides the same response for all the objects in a given class, and thus performs categorization. Darwin and Wallace are intended to be two sample modules; many other parallel channels would be needed in a real brain simulation. Each of these channels has its own sampling of the input. Each of their two networks is organized in a hierarchy, in which cells higher up in the hierarchy respond to increasingly more complex features, as in a multi-layer perception.

The specific response of the Wallace subsystem in Darwin III is used to guide the systems along the edges of connected areas in the stimulus. It uses sensory neurons in the arm to detect continuities in objects so that it can trace them.

The two repertoires are connected to one another only at the higher levels. It is necessary that they not be connected on the lower levels in order for each repertoire to serve as an independent perceptual agent. Each repertoire has its own connectivity, determined by its functionality. They use a Hebbian scheme to modify connection strengths. A connection is strengthened when both its inputting and outputting neurons are firing above a given threshold. They also have a mechanism for weakening connections when their input or output neurons are not responding so that all connections do not eventually saturate.

They note that their system is capable of four basic processes: categorization, recognition, generalization, and association. The Wallace subsystem does categorization by means of a unique output for each class of stimuli, but they state that it does not do naming, in that it does not use a conventional symbol for the category. Of course, the output itself could be considered a symbol.

Recognition, as they describe it, is a process of gradually strengthening responses to stimuli which the system has seen before. Their system becomes habituated to stimuli in this fashion.

The Wallace subsystem is capable of generalization, which is the ability to classify heretofore unseen stimuli. It gets this ability by the way it classifies stimuli, which is by correlating features. Wallace can give input to Darwin so as to make Darwin's responses to similar stimuli more similar over time. Association occurs in their system when a stimulus evokes a response associated with another stimulus in the same category; Wallace's categorization abilities coupled with Darwin's recognition capabilities produce this associative behavior.

Reeke and Edelman claim that these four basic processes of recognition, classification, generalization and association must precede "more conventional learning" in any learning process; in other words, they are prerequisites for more complex learning (such as, perhaps, language learning, or learning of complex skills).

They feel that their theory indicates that object motion is particularly important in learning how to discriminate objects; if objects did not move then it would be difficult, in the absence of prior knowledge, to tell where one object began and the other one ended. Of course, Reeke are Edelman were not the first to recognize the importance of object motion in region segmentation and object recognition; researchers in computer vision have attempted to make use of this information for quite a while (Cohen & Feigenbaum, 1982).

The performance of Darwin III is as follows: visual layers of cells are connected to motor layers of cells controlling the "eye". Initially all the connections can be amplified by selection. This amplification is related to the extent to which a stimulus is centered on the retina. Thus the system rapidly learns to center any object that is presented to it, and then learns to recognize and categorize the object. The eye tracks the stimulus by always keeping itself in the center of the moving stimulus. Since the eye always directs itself to the center of the stimulus, and keeps itself there, the system is able to perform position-independent classification and recognition. The system then becomes habituated to the stimulus, and this allows the eye to wander off and become fixated on another stimulus.

The question of what proportion of the neuronal groups would actually prove functionally useful in real problems remains open.

Reeke and Edelman admit this, but they cannot say what this proportion would actually be. One might think that if the neuronal groups were relatively unstructured prior to learning a large proportion of them might learn no function at all. This is an issue which would have to be addressed in experiments. Reeke and Edelman point out that if some of these neuronal groups turn out to have the same functionality, then this could benefit the organism in the case that some of them failed to function. They point out that although their system may require a large number of units, the time latencies are less than a system performs relaxation. They urge researchers in AI to adopt more biologically-motivated models, as opposed to models drawn from physics, such as Hopfield's, or those drawn from more formal ideas of what intelligence is, such as those found in traditional symbol-processing AI. Of course, many people would agree with Reeke & Edelman that more attention needs to be paid to biology. Unfortunately, little is known about brain architecture, on the level of cellular connectivity, outside the sensory and motor systems.

2.20.   Genetic Algorithms

Many problems that have been studied using neural networks can be viewed as optimization problems. For instance, many networks, such as those wired with back-propagation, that compute input to output mappings have the goal of finding the optimal set of weights to best compute this function. They search a space of solutions to find the optimal one, in this case a weight space.

Another class of algorithms that do a stochastic search on a solution space are the genetic algorithms, invented by Holland (1975). Like the NGS theory of Reeke and Edelman, these algorithms are directly inspired by biological evolution. In a genetic algorithm, there is a population of bit strings, called chromosomes. The population changes over time. Each bit string encodes a solution to the particular problem being attacked. One problem-specific method is used to compute the fitness (or "goodness", or quality) of each bit string, that is, how good a solution it is to the problem at hand. Those bit strings with higher fitnesses will be allowed to have proportionally more "children" than those with lower fitnesses.

Children are formed by crossover between the two parents, so that a child would be formed by taking some bits from one parent then some from the other, then some from the first, e.g., bits 1-10 of the child are bits 1-10 of one parent, bits 11-20 of the child are bits 11-20 of the other parent, etc. There is also a mutation rate; some bits in each child are randomly set. Because more fit individuals reproduce more, the population will see an increase over time of the average fitness of its individuals.

To illustrate this class of algorithms, we consider work done by Axelrod (1987) on the Prisoner's Dilemma, a classic problem in game theory, using a genetic algorithm. In the Prisoner's Dilemma, there are two prisoners who are suspected of working together on a crime. Both are independently offered the opportunity to turn stool-pigeon. If neither one turns State's Evidence, they both get a light sentence. If only one of them becomes a stool-pigeon (defects) he or she goes free, and the other gets a stiff sentence. If they both try to become stool-pigeons, they both go to jail, and serve a moderate sentence. This poses a dilemma because it always pays to defect, no matter what the other person does. But if both people defect, they do worse than they would if they cooperated.

Axelrod held a tournament in which the game was the iterated Prisoner's Dilemma, in which different strategies competed in a round-robin tournament to see which one was most successful. The iterated Prisoner's Dilemma is simply the Prisoner's Dilemma repeated over and over again, which allows each player to base his or her behavior on the history of his or her interaction with an opponent.

Many people submitted strategies to the tournament, some of them very complex, yet a simple strategy won, dubbed TIT-for-TAT. TIT-for-TAT cooperates on the first turn, and does whatever the opponent did on the previous turn in all subsequent turns. After the first tournament's results were announced, a second tournament was held. The contestants in the second tournament were aware of what the TIT-for-TAT strategy was, and that it had won the first tournament. Despite this, TIT-for-TAT won the second tournament as well; people were unable to construct a strategy to beat it.

Axelrod constructed the following genetic algorithm for this problem. At each move, each prisoner can cooperate with the other prisoner (C) or defect to the state (D). If the previous three moves are taken into account, the algorithm must deal with 64 possibilities, since there are four possibilities at each move (2x2), and therefore, in three moves there are $4^3 = 64$ possible combinations. Thus a strategy can be specified by giving a string of 64 Cs or Ds (bits; 0=C, 1=D) indicating which action should be taken in each of the 64 possibilities. Also 6 bits are devoted to the strategy's hypothesis of what the three moves that might have preceded the start of the game were, for a total of 70 bits.

The space of possible strategies is therefore huge; there are about $2^{70} \cong 10^{21}$ strategies. The genetic algorithm searches this space very rapidly.

Axelrod implemented a genetic algorithm with a population size of 20 individuals. Games consisted of 151 moves. In each generation, each individual met eight representative strategies in games. These representative strategies were chosen by the fact that play against them accounted for 98% of the variance in the performance of the other strategies.

The populations were initially random, but they evolved—in 50 generations—into populations whose median individual, that is, the individual that was median in performance, achieved performance that was comparable to TIT-for-TAT. 40 runs were made of 50 generations each. In 11 of these runs, the median individual actually did better than TIT-for-TAT by taking advantage of the weakness of one of the eight representatives, and by breaking—under particular conditions—the motto of the TIT-for-TAT strategy, which is: never be the first to defect.

He tried the same simulation without sexual reproduction, so that only one parent contributed to the genes of the offspring. The genetic algorithm still worked, but not as quickly—or as effectively—within a given span of generations.

He also tried having the individuals in the population compete against one another. Initially this leads to a decrease in cooperation, but eventually this trend reverses itself, and the population becomes more and more cooperative; over time, there are fewer and fewer defections.

In related work, a learning procedure called "iterated genetic hill-climbing" has been developed, which combines features of genetic algorithms and hill-climbing algorithms (Ackley 1987, Brady 1985). This algorithm improves on the performance of both techniques alone. Mjolsness, Sharp and Alpert (1988; see also Mjolsness & Sharp 1986) have introduced a class of "genetic nets" with recursively-structured connectivity, in which learning is applied to rules rather than weights, and which are based partly on genetic algorithms. They claim that these nets scale better to large problems than do nets based on weight learning, because they are hierarchically structured.

2.21.   Reinforcement Algorithms

Reinforcement algorithms are a class of algorithms for learning automata. The automaton takes one of a set of actions based on a set of corresponding probabilities, and the environment ("teacher") responds to the automaton's action by indicating "success" (+1) or "failure" (-1). The automaton then adjusts its behavior based on this feedback by altering the set of probabilities. This is repeated, until, all being well, the automaton's behavior converges to good performance.

One specific instance of this class of algorithms is the Linear Reward–Penalty (L_{R-P}) algorithm (Narendra & Thathachar 1974). In this algorithm, the set of actions is denoted by $(a^1,...,a^r)$ and the respective probabilities for these actions on the kth iteration are $(p_k^1,...,p_k^r)$.

On the kth iteration, a reinforcement signal b_k, which is either -1 or +1 is supplied (but no other input). If the action taken on iteration k is $a_k = a^i$, and $b_k = 1$, then:

$$p_{k+1}^{(i)} = p_k^{(i)} + a(1 - p_k^{(i)})$$
$$p_{k+1}^{(j)} = (1-a)p_k^{(j)} \qquad \text{for } j \neq i$$

If $b_k = -1$, then

$$p_{k+1}^{(i)} = (1-b)p_k^{(i)}$$
$$p_{k+1}^{(j)} = \frac{b}{r-1} + (1-b)p_k^{(j)} \qquad \text{for } j \neq i$$

This notation is taken from Barto and Anandan (1985). Thus this algorithm increases the probability of an action that is successful by increasing it by some fraction of the difference between it and one, and decreases the probability of all the other actions. In the case of the action's failure, its probability is decreased and every other probability is increased. a and b are the learning rates of the algorithm.

This can readily be translated to a connectionist network. There are r units. If unit r fires, this corresponds to action a^r being taken. The probability density in time that any unit will fire is given by the probabilities above. After the one unit fires, the environment immediately feeds the reinforcement to all the units, and they reset their own firing probabilities accordingly. See Figure 2.16.

This algorithm gets only one bit of information at a time from its outside environment. It can learn to adjust its behavior so that its responses are constrained in an interesting manner, but it can not perform association and classification, two processes of primary interest to cognitive science. Barto and Anandan (1985) therefore extended it to perform these tasks.

In their first extension, which they call associative reinforcement learning , the environment provides not only the reinforcement, but an input vector x_k on the kth iteration as well. The r possible responses of 1 or -1 the network can be viewed as a classification of the set of input vectors into r groups; the network will learn to make the right classification, provided the teacher gives consistent reinforcements. The teacher has an array $d(x_k, a_k)$ which determines what the reinforcement to action a_k should be, given input vector x_k. See environment. Figure 2.17 for a diagram of the network.

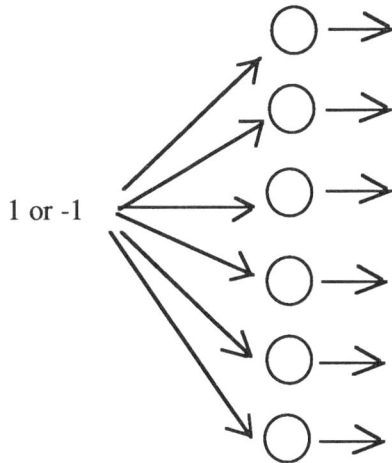

Figure 2.16. An array of units recieving reinforcement from the environment.

In the case of two possible outputs a_1 and a_2, corresponding to a partition of the input into two sets, it is known that the number of classification errors of input x is minimized if output a_1 is chosen for x when $P(a_1/x) > P(a_2/x)$, and a_2 is chosen when the inequality is reversed. The only trouble is that the system has no way of knowing these conditional probabilities (in the case of disjoint sets, one of them will always be one and the other zero; in the case of overlapping sets, they will both be non-zero for vectors that are in the intersection of the two sets).

Instead of these probabilities, they use a vector θ to approximate them, such that $\theta \cdot x \cong P(a_1/x) - P(a_2/x)$. If $\theta \cdot x$ is positive, a_1 is chosen; if $\theta \cdot x$ is negative, a_2 is chosen. θ changes over the course of the learning.

Z is defined to be the class label of an input x; if x is in the set corresponding to a_1, then $z = 1$, if a_2, then $z = -1$. It can be shown

(Duda and Hart 1973) that if $E((\theta \cdot x - z])^2)$ is minimized (where E denotes the expected value), then the error in classification is minimized. This makes intuitive sense, since you want $\theta \cdot x$ to be positive when $z=1$ and negative when $z=-1$, and the above formula is small under both of these circumstances.

Barto and Anandan use a gradient descent procedure, the Robbins-Monro algorithm (Kasyap, Blaydon & Fu 1970). The partial derivative with respect to θ of the above expected error formula on the kth iteration of the algorithm is given by:

$$2[\theta_k \cdot x_k - z_k]x_k$$

This is used to adjust θ in the course of the learning:

$$\theta_{k+1} = \theta_k - \rho_k[\theta_k \cdot x_k - z_k]x_k$$

The ρ_k are constants which vary over the course of the learning; they, at some point in the learning, get progressively smaller, and are subject to some formal requirements for convergence (see Barto & Anandan 1985 for details).

The components of θ can be interpreted as weights on connections connecting each component of the input to a single perceptron output unit, which outputs 1 if its input is positive and zero otherwise. (If one unit for each of the classes a_1 and a_2 is desired, the connections can be duplicated for a second unit, whose polarity is reversed). See Figure 2.18 for a diagram. This interpretation of these equations as a neural network applies to the rest of our discussion.

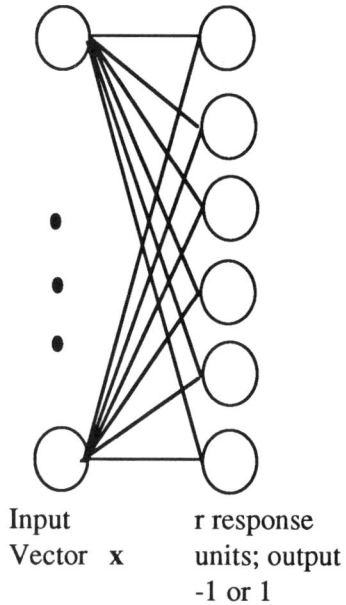

Input Vector x r response units; output -1 or 1

Figure 2.17. An associative reinforcement learning network.

They add an element of randomness to this associative reinforcement learning algorithm to create the Associative Reward-Penalty (A_{R-P}) algorithm. Again there are two actions $a_k=1$ and $a_k=-1$, and two reinforcements $b_k=1$ and $b_k=-1$. The rule for choosing the action is changed to:

$a_k= +1$ if $\theta_k \cdot x_k + \zeta_k > 0$
$a_k= -1$ otherwise.

ζ_k is a random variable whose distribution is known in advance. Thus $E(a_k/\theta_k,x_k)$, the expected value of a_k given values of θ_k and x_k, is known. The formulas for updating θ are essentially the same as in the Robbins–Monro algorithm given above, with the expected value of a_k replacing a_k itself. A factor λ is added to allow for differential reinforcement between reward ($b=1$) and penalty ($b=-1$). In the case of reward we have

$$\theta_{k+1}=\theta_k-\rho_k[E\{a_k/\theta_k,x_k\}-b_ka_k]x_k$$

In the case of penalty

$$\theta_{k+1}=\theta_k-\lambda\rho_k[E\{a_k/\theta_k,x_k\}-b_ka_k]x_k$$

If $\lambda=0$, Barto and Anandan call this the associative reward-inaction (A_{R-I}) algorithm.

They show that the A_{R-P} algorithm reduces to other algorithms under certain conditions. If the input vector x is a constant, and the random variable has a uniform distribution over the interval $(-1, 1)$, the A_{R-P} algorithm reduces to the L_{R-P} algorithm. If the random variable is always zero and $\lambda=1$, the A_{R-P} algorithm reduces to their two-category supervised learning classification algorithm given above.

The A_{R-P} algorithm reduces to the perceptron convergence procedure if the expected value $E(a_k/\theta_k,x_k)$ is replaced by a_k, and the distribution of ζ_k is given by a step function, although it will not necessarily converge to a solution. In the case in which the input vectors are

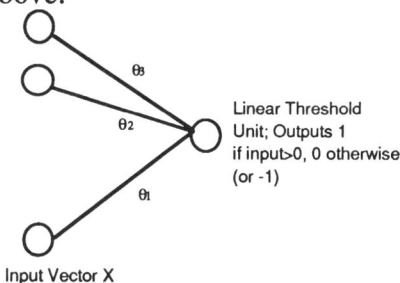

Linear Threshold
Unit; Outputs 1
if input>0, 0 otherwise
(or -1)

Input Vector X

Figure 2.18. Interpretation of θ as a perceptron.

all unit basis vectors, the A_{R-P} algorithm functions as a look-up table.

They show that under the conditions that (1) the input vectors are linearly independent (2) they each occur with finite probability (3) the random variable's distribution is continuous and monotonic (4) the sequence ρ_k satisfies certain conditions which amount to it eventually decreasing to zero, then the weight vector converges, which implies a certain formal type of optimality.

They implemented the A_{R-P} algorithm for use in two tasks, comparing it to the non-associative L_{R-P} algorithm and the selective bootstrap algorithm (Widrow et al. 1973), which is another algorithm that does associative reinforcement learning. As l decreased, the learning rate of the A_{R-P} algorithm decreased, but it approached an asympotote that was more nearly optimal than the selective bootstrap algorithm. The L_{R-P} algorithm, being non-associative, did not detect the input vectors, thus its expected success probability remained at a steady 0.5, rendering it (and all other non-associative algorithms) useless for associative learning. In fact, they could have predicted this behavior without bothering to implement it.

Both tasks involved just two input patterns ($x^{(1)}$ and $x^{(2)}$)and two actions (-1 and +1). For task 1, the success probability matrix d for task 1 was given by $d(x^{(1)}, -1) = 0.8$, $d(x^{(1)}, +1) = 0.1$, $d(x^{(2)}, -1) = 0.2$, $d(x^{(2)}, +1) = 0.9$. In this task, the selective bootstrap algorithm outperformed the A_{R-P} algorithm (in terms of percent success), because the success probabilities, with respect to each action, are far apart and, for each input, one is on each side of 0.5. In the (more difficult) task 2, where $d(x^{(1)}, -1) = 0.2$, $d(x^{(1)}, +1) = 0.4$, $d(x^{(2)}, -1) = 0.9$, $d(x^{(2)}, +1) = 0.6$, the A_{R-P} algorithm outperformed the selective bootstrap algorithm, whose performance oscillated. They provide a mathematical account of why the selective bootstrap algorithm will not converge, along with other algorithms in its class, for "unclear" tasks like task 2.

2.22.   Temporal Difference Methods

Sutton (1988) discusses a type of learning mechanism, which he calls a temporal difference method, in which credit assignment—which, with neural networks, corresponds to the adjustment of weights—is based on the difference between temporally successive predictions of the correct output instead of, as in back-propagation and other error-based methods, the difference between the predicted and desired outputs.

This method is applicable to the problem of learning to predict, that is, using past experience to predict the future behavior of a system like the weather, a game, or the economy. Sutton claims that temporal difference methods require less computation time than ordinary methods and converge faster to an optimum, for a class of learning problems that Sutton refers to as multi-step problems, in which the correctness of a particular prediction is not revealed until several steps after the prediction. He gives the problem of predicting Saturday's weather on Tuesday as an example of such a multi-step problem. Although temporal difference methods are only applicable to multi-step problems, Sutton argues that most real-world problems are of this type. For instance, he points out that the last year's predictions about this year's economy are validated or invalidated gradually as this year passes.

Sutton formalizes a learning problem as follows: $x_1, x_2, x_3 ,..., x_t$ is a sequence of observations (for a connectionist network, inputs), w is a vector of weights, and $P_1, P_2, P_3 ,..., P_t$ is a sequence of predictions (for a network, outputs). Sutton proves that the weight update rule

$$\Delta w_t = \alpha (P_{t+1} - P_t) \sum_{k=1}^{t} \nabla_w P_k$$

where α is the learning rate and ∇_w is the gradient operator with respect to the weight vector, so that $\nabla_w P_k$ is the vector of partial derivatives of P_k with respect to each component of w, is precisely equivalent to the Widrow–Hoff delta rule, the perceptron convergence procedure (see section 2.4). Sutton refers to this algorithm as $TD(1)$, the first-order temporal difference procedure. By extension, he defines the family of learning procedures $TD(\lambda)$ by

$$\Delta w_t = \alpha (P_{t+1} - P_t) \sum_{k=1}^{t} \lambda^{t-k} \nabla_w P_k$$

where gradients into the past are weighted by decreasing factors of λ. Thus recent gradients are favored over older ones. Typically λ ranges between zero and one.

Sutton gives an example of how the temporal difference methods can lead to better performance than ordinary methods. Suppose we have a state A which leads to state B which in turn lead to states C and D. C, which is a losing state, is reached from B 90% of the time; D, a winning state is reached from B 10% of the time. A supervised learning method would associate state A with either state C or state D, so would either associate it with fully winning or fully losing, each time state A and either states C or D shows up. The temporal difference method always will associate A with state B, and will more quickly converge to the 90% goodness value associated with B. This is, as Sutton points out, not a proof that temporal difference methods are better; one can construct scenarios in which supervised learning works better, but Sutton believes these are the exceptions.

In order to more rigorously illustrate the superiority of temporal difference methods over standard supervised learning, Sutton chose a simple problem involving a random walk through a linear sequence of states A-G as shown in Figure 2.19. In this problem, A and G are final states; from each of states B-F there is an equal probability (1/2) of a move to the state immediately preceding and a move to the one immediately following it in the alphabet. All walks start with state D; one example of a walk is $DEDCDCBCBA$.

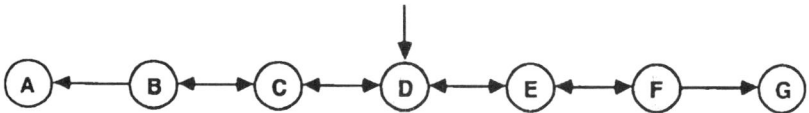

Figure 2.19. A network of states used for random walks by Sutton (1988). D is the starting state. Reprinted by permission.

The problem that Sutton chose to have his systems learn was the probabilities, for each of the states B-F, that the system will end up in state A or G. Each walk is memory-less; thus these probabilities are constant during each walk. This was formalized as follows: $z = 1$ denotes a final state of G, and $z = 0$ denotes A. x_i in the formalization discussed above is the ith state of the walk; the predictions P_i are the expected values of z at each x_i. The learning algorithms $TD(\lambda)$ were trained on 100 training sets of ten sequences (walks) each. Each training sequence was presented repeatedly until convergence. Values of $\lambda=1$ (Widrow-Hoff), and $\lambda = 0, 0.1, 0.3,$

0.5, and *0.7* were used. The learning rate α was also varied, with α taking on values of 0, 0.1, 0.2 ,..., 0.6.

Based on the root-mean-square error computed between the ideal predictions, which can easily be shown to be 1/6, 1/3, 1/2, 2/3, 5/6 for states *B-F*, and the asymptotic prediction in a training sequence, averaged over the 100 training sequences presented to each algorithm, he found that the error (for the best value of α for each λ) declined rapidly as λ was lowered below 1, and was optimum at $\lambda=0$. $\lambda=0$ corresponds to the case where the current prediction is compared only to the previous prediction. This is due to the fact, which Sutton proves, that *TD(0)* minimizes the error on trials presenting *after* training, whereas Widrow-Hoff (*TD(1)*) minimizes error *during* training.

He also did a second experiment in which each training sequence of 10 walks was presented to each algorithm just once. Here, he found that the best value of λ was close to 0.3, again comparing values of λ on the basis of their respective error-minimizing values of α. The reason that the optimum λ exceeded 0 is as follows: because *TD(0)* takes quite a bit of training to adjust the prediction values of states occurring earlier in a sequence (walk), whereas *TD(λ)* with $\lambda>0$ propagates the adjustments backwards faster, within a single learning trial.

Sutton extended the *TD(λ)* class of algorithms to several related problems. His first extension was to the case in which the algorithm, instead of predicting the eventual outcome of a sequence, predicts the remaining cost of the sequence, if a cost function is associated with each step. His second extension was to modify *TD(λ)* so that the weight vector is modified during each sequence, instead of just at the end. Finally, he extended the class of algorithms to handle the problem of, at each point in the x_t, making a prediction for some fixed amount of time later. In this case, for instance, one can use the fact that the prediction you make of Monday's weather on the preceding Monday should be as similar as possible as the one made on the preceding Tuesday. For details, see Sutton (1988).

Sutton's (1984) adaptive heuristic critic (AHC) learning method is closely related to the *TD(1)* class of algorithms. The AHC algorithm is used for predicting cumulative outcomes, such as the total future return on an initial investment. The trouble is that this sum is often infinite, so that is often discounted as follows: if the income generated at time t is c_t, the discounted sum is

$$z_t = \sum_{k=0}^{\infty} \gamma^k c_{t+k+1}$$

where γ ranges from 0 to 1, and is called the discount rate. If P_t is used to predict z_t, then it is readily shown that $P_t = c_{t+1} + \gamma P_{t+1}$. The mismatch between successive predictions is therefore $(c_{t+1} + \gamma P_{t+1}) - P_t$. The AHC method uses this error to adjust the weights in a similar manner to $TD(\lambda)$, as follows:

$$\Delta w_t = \alpha(c_{t+1} + \gamma P_{t+1} - P_t) \sum_{k=1}^{t} \lambda^{t-k} \nabla_w P_k$$

Here the error term from $TD(\lambda)$, $(P_{t+1} - P_t)$, is replaced by the discounted error $(c_{t+1} + \gamma P_{t+1}) - P_t$. Anderson (1986) used a variant of this AHC algorithm in his work on problem-solving in the connectionist paradigm (see the next section).

2.23.   Problem Solving Using Reinforcement and Back-propagation

Anderson (1986a) tackled, in his Ph.D. dissertation, the topic of "Learning and Problem Solving with Multilayer Connectionist Systems". He uses feed-forward networks with no recurrent connections and uses Rumelhart and co-workers' back-propagation algorithm and Barto and co-workers' reinforcement-learning algorithms, and variants of these that he developed, to a variety of tasks that involve the learning of new features. He also developed an algorithm that combines aspects of back-propagation with Sutton's AHC algorithm for learning evaluation functions (see the previous section) and a reinforcement-learning algorithm to learn search heuristics for problem solving. He applied this algorithm to the problem of balancing a pole on a cart, and to the Towers of Hanoi puzzle.

In a connectionist system a concept can be viewed as a region in an n-dimensional feature space, defined by the values of the inputs to the system. This is a definition that Anderson borrows from Utgoff (1986); if the stimuli, in more traditional AI, are strings of symbols, then a concept is a set of strings, which is a region (not necessarily connected) in the space of possible strings. Following this, the exclusive-or task is the task of learning to separate the bit vectors (1 0) and (0 1), which are assigned the value 1, from the bit vectors (1 1) and (0 0), which are assigned the value 0. As Minsky and Papert (1969) have shown, this classification task cannot be accomplished with a two layer perception. As we have seen, it requires at least three layers.

Anderson did not choose the exclusive-or function for his exploration of learning discriminant features, because he wanted a classification task that required more than one hidden unit for its solution. He suspected that algorithms that performed well learning a single feature would not necessarily perform well when required to learn the behavior of more than one hidden unit. The function that he chose for a more complex classification task was a multiplexer function which had two address bits and four data bits in the input vector. The two address bits serve as a binary number indicating which of the four data bits to route to the output. The system must learn to route the correct bit. In terms of concept learning, as outlined above, the problem is of dividing the set of possible input vectors into two sets, one for which one is output, and the other for which zero is output.

Anderson used the perception convergence algorithm (Rosenblatt 1961) to learn the multiplexer function. He defines the error on iteration k, $e_k(t)$ as:

$$\sum_{j \in O} (d_j(t) - y_j(t))$$

where O is the set of output units, t is the time, $d_j(t)$ is the desired output of unit j and $y_j(t)$ is its actual output. He sums this $e_k(t)$ over all the s time steps of an individual convergence procedure, and then averages this sum over a series of runs to arrive at a performance measure

$$\mu = \frac{1}{r} \sum_{k=1}^{r} \sum_{t=1}^{s} e_k(t)$$

Since μ treats all the time steps of a run equally, Anderson developed a second performance measure v which accounts for improvement toward the end of a run. The way this is measured is by freezing the weight values at the end of the run and then presenting the system with all possible inputs (in the case of the multiplexer there are $2^6 = 64$ of these) and summing the errors for all 64 of these to obtain the total error h_k for run k:

$$h_k = \frac{1}{n} \sum_{x \in X} \sum_{j \in O} |d_{xj} - y_{xj}|$$

where X is the set of 64 possible inputs, J is the set of output units, d_{xj} is the desired output of unit j on input x, and y is the actual output. This is averaged over a set of r runs to obtain

$$v = \frac{1}{r} \sum_{k=1}^{r} h_k$$

v is a measure of the quality of a solution, and μ is a measure of how fast the system found a solution.

The multiplexer function is not linearly separable using a single linear threshold perception unit, as Anderson readily shows. He considers the four vectors shown in Table 2.1, with their desired outputs,

input vector	desired output
(0,0,0,1,0,0,0.5)	0
(0,0,1,0,0,0,0.5)	1
(0,1,0,1,0,0,0.5)	1
(0,1,1,0,0,0,0.5)	0

Table 2.1. Multiplexer function used by Anderson (1986a). Reprinted by permission

and notes that, for example, the relationship between components two and three is an exclusive-or. The exclusive-or cannot be handled by a two-layer perceptron, which therefore cannot handle the multiplexer function either.

In order for a single unit to handle the classification task, additional inputs must be added. If the input is $a_1a_2d_1d_2d_3d_4$ (two address bits and four data bits), then the function that is to be computed is

$$\bar{a}_1\bar{a}_2d_1 \vee \bar{a}_1a_2d_2 \vee a_1\bar{a}_2d_3 \vee a_1a_2d_4$$

The four inputs that are added (new features) are therefore the four components of this "or" equation; each of them corresponds to a particular configuration of the address bits and the data bit that that configuration selects.

In addition to the original input pattern $a_1a_2d_1d_2d_3d_4$ and this pattern augmented by the four additional features mentioned above, Anderson considered a third representation in which the input vector had 64 components and each stimulus was represented by a vector with exactly one bit set to one and the rest set to zero. These are called, in vector algebra, the 64-bit unit basis vectors, and there are 64 of them.

Thus 64 6-bit numbers in base two are effectively replaced by 64 numbers essentially in base one. The perception convergence algorithm has no problem classifying these inputs as zero or one, since it has a separate weight associated with the connection to each of the 64 inputs.

As one might expect, the 64-input model converges faster than the six-bit/four additional features model. The original model, without the four additional features, does not converge at all, as expected. The convergence graphs are given in Figure 2.20. The new feature representation gradually comes to learn the proper categories, whereas the 64-component model exhibits perfect performance as soon as it has been presented with all 64 possible inputs, since it is functioning as a look-up table. This is interesting only as an extreme example of presenting the system with the most readily interpretable information.

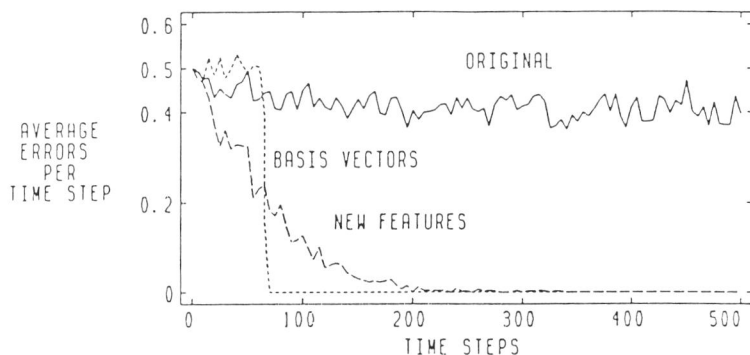

Figure 2.20. Convergence graphs of three models on the multiplexer task of Anderson (1986a). Reprinted by Permission.

Anderson points out that learning new features is most useful if it helps the system to group together those inputs that require the same output; in other words, a new feature should make input vectors that belong in the same cluster seem more similar. Anderson did a series of experiments in which a perceptron was made to learn the association between the 16 unit basis vectors composed of a 16-bit input each, $x_1, x_2, ..., x_{16}$. There was a 4-bit output; $x_1, ..., x_5$ got output (1010), $x_6, ..., x_{10}$ got output (1111)

and $x12$,..., $x16$ got output (0101). His system learned these
outputs with the unit basis vectors alone as input, and augmented by
two- or three-bit class labels added to the input; the three-bit class
labels were (001), (010) and (100), and the two-bit ones were (01)
(11) and (10).

He handled the learning process somewhat differently in this
example. The input units were completely connected to the four
output units, but he trained the system in two phases. In the first
phase the first two output units were trained; in the second phase the
second two units were trained, starting with the weights as they were
at the end of the first phase. The purpose of this is to show how the
learning of features that can aid in input classification (i.e. the first
two bits of the output) can facilitate further learning. The new
features mentioned above were not added until the start of phase 2.

In the absence of the new features, learning proceeds at the
same pace in phases 1 and 2, $\mu1 = \mu2 = 22$ (μ is the measure of the
speed of convergence mentioned above). With the three bits added
in phase 2, $\mu2$ was equal to 4, and with the two bits added, $\mu2$ was
equal to 3. The reason the two bits performed better than the three
bits is because they were the same as the first two bits of the desired
output.

Anderson compared
the performance of a variety
of algorithms on the
multiplexer task, using a
three-layer network (see
Figure 2.21) containing input
units, four hidden units and
an output unit. Error back-
propagation and Barto and
Anandan's (1985) A_{R-P}
algorithm were best and

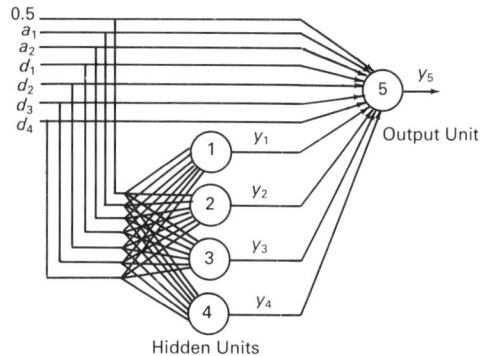

Figure 2.21. Three-layer network used by
Anderson (1986a) for his multiplexer task.
Reprinted by permission.

second-best respectively in terms of speed of convergence. Various
modifications of the A_{R-P} algorithm were designed in order to get
more accurate assignment of credit or blame to the hidden units
beyond the global reinforcement signal, but, even with these
variations, its performance still did not surpass the error back-
propagation algorithm.   This is not surprising, since back-
propagation is given more information than the A_{R-P} algorithm.
Other algorithms that searched the space of weights for minima

were tried, but their results were even worse. The perceptron convergence procedure did not converge to a solution at all, as expected.

2.24.   Problem-Solving Networks

For problem-solving, Anderson uses networks that combined the error back-propagation algorithm with the AHC algorithm of Sutton (1984). His first network, the evaluation network, is used to learn an evaluation function for a general strategy learning task. The second network is used to learn search heuristics formalized as the selection of an action from a set. Both of these networks are three-layer.

The evaluation network is contains of m_h hidden units and one output unit; the action network has m_h hidden units and m_o output units. Each unit in both layers of units receives all of the n inputs from the environment; each unit in the output layer (in the case of the evaluation network, just the single output unit) receives all of the n inputs plus the m_h outputs of the hidden units.

The hidden units produce output which is a logistic function of the sum of their weighted inputs. In the evaluation network, the output of the output unit is simply the weighted sum of its inputs. The action network hidden units behave the same as those of the evaluation network; again, their activation is a logistic function of the weighted sum of their inputs. In the output units of the action network, noise is added to the weighted sum of their inputs. The noise is distributed according to the distribution function

$$\psi(q) = \frac{1}{(1+e^{-q})}$$

The output units are organized in winner-take-all networks; the output unit receiving the most input (including noise) wins the competition, and output one; the rest of the units output zero.

To train the evaluation network, Anderson used the heuristic reinforcement function $\hat{r}(t)$ defined by Sutton (1984). This is given by $\hat{r}(t) = 0$ if the system at time t is in a start state,

$$r(t) = r(t)-p(t-1,t-1)$$

if the system at time t is in a goal or failure state, and

$$\hat{r}(t) = r(t) - \gamma p(t,t-1) - p(t-1,t-1)$$

otherwise. The p's are the outputs of the output unit of the evaluation network at time t and $t-1$; $p(t,t-1)$ is computed using the weights at $t-1$ to avoid having a change in weights affect the heuristic value, beyond the environment itself. γ is a constant called the discount rate, between 0 and 1; $r(t)$ is an (externally supplied) reinforcement value.

The second two terms in $\hat{r}(t)$ measure the change in the heuristic value of p. Thus if p has increased, the effect of the weight change formula is to decrease the weights from those units with negative potential and to increase those with positive potential. The opposite occurs if p has decreased. Therefore credit is assigned to different units based on the strength and magnitude of their potential. The discount rate allows the algorithm to "ignore" a certain rate of increase in the evaluation function, that is, a rate equal to $1/\gamma$. This is appropriate since one hopes that the evaluation function will be increasing over time.

Thus $\hat{r}(t)$ measures both the external reinforcement and the change in heuristic output value; it is used to update the weight values of the network. The equation used to update the weights or connections from unit i in the input or the hidden units to the output unit is:

$$v_i(t) = v_i(t-1) + \beta \hat{r}(t) y_i(t-1,t-1)$$

where v_i is the weight, y_i is the potential of the hidden or input unit i, and β is a constant, the learning rate.

Output unit j of the action network updates its weights according to a similar rule:

$$w_{ij}(t) = w_{ij}(t-1) + \rho r(t)(a_j(t-1) - E(a_j(t-1)/w;z)) z_i(t-1)$$

where w_{ij} is the weight connecting unit j with each of the hidden units and the input, a_j is the potential of the jth action unit, and $E(a_j(t-1)/w;z)$ is the expected potential of the jth action unit, given the particular values of w and z. Thus the weights are adjusted by an amount proportional to the discrepancy between the actual and expected values of $a_j(t-1)$. The expected value is simply equal to the probability that a_j will be equal to 1. Unusual actions therefore create relatively more change in the weights. The $\hat{r}(t)$ term allows increase in the weights if there is an increase in p.

For the hidden layer of the evaluation network, a variant of the error back-propagation network is used, but since we do not know the correct output in each case (which is necessary in order to use ordinary back-propagation), $\hat{r}$ is used as the back-propagated error. Since the weights in the output layer of the action network are adjusted by a term in which the expression playing the role of the error is $\hat{r}(t)(a_j(t-1) - E(a_j(t-1)/w;z))$, this expression is what is used as the error for the purposes of back-propagation. Anderson uses a variant of back-propagation developed by Sutton (1985), in which the sign of the weight instead of the weight itself is used, to decrease the algorithm's sensitivity to its learning rate.

Anderson applied his evaluation and action networks to two strategy learning tasks. The first of these was the pole-balancing task, in which a pole is attached by a hinge to the top of a cart and the system must move the cart so as to keep the pole balanced. The second of these was the Towers of Hanoi puzzle. In this puzzle, you have three pins and n disks. The disks increase linearly in size from 1 to n, and initially they are stacked in order on the first pin, with the largest on the bottom. The goal is to move all the pins so that they are again stacked in order on the third pin. The disks may be moved one at a time, and a larger disk may never be placed on top of a smaller one.

The problem is readily solved with the following 3 step recursive algorithm: (1) move $n-1$ disks recursively from pin 1 to pin 2 (2) move the largest disk from pin 1 to pin 2 (3) move $n-1$ disks recursively from pin 2 to pin 3. Steps 1 and 3 are recursive calls to the algorithm. The Towers of Hanoi puzzle has been studied from the point of view of state space exploration in AI using search heuristics (e.g. Langley 1985) and human strategies have been modeled (Anzai & Simon 1979).

The state of the Towers of Hanoi puzzle may be completely specified by a vector of length n which describes for each disk which peg it is on. (The order on each peg must always be from smallest to largest as one goes from top to bottom on the peg.)

In Anderson's system there are three reinforcements $r(t)$ provided to the action and evaluation networks. If the goal state (in which all disks are on pin 3) is reached, $r(t)$ is set to 1. A reinforcement $r(t)$ of -1 is given if a two-step loop is selected; that is, if the system chooses an action which reverses the previous action. This is to prevent the system from making such loops. This $rloop(t)$ is given only to the action network, not the evaluation network, since we do not want the evaluation of a state to go down simply because it was visited in a loop. Finally, a constant reinforcement $r(t)$ of -0.1 is given on every time step that does not lead to a goal state. This is to encourage the system to select short paths to a goal state.

For his experiments, he used a three-disk system. The input to the evaluation network is the state of the puzzle encoded as nine bits; for instance, the state (123) is encoded as (100 010 001). (This is the state in which disk 1 is on pin 1, disk 2 is on pin 2, and disk 3 is on pin 3.) Actions are encoded by six bits; one for each of the six possible actions (disk movements, which can each be expressed as ordered pair of pins). The action network receives as input the current state and the previous two actions, for a total of $9 + 6 + 6 = 21$ bits.

He first ran simulations of his system with no hidden units; the equations given above for adjusting weights were used, with the single change that $r(t)+rloop(t)$ was substituted wherever $r(t)$ was found. The system with no hidden units usually learned to solve the puzzle with paths that were far from optimal; on average it found a path to a solution of length 30, whereas the optimum number of steps is seven. In the best example, which learned a path of length nine, the evaluation function learned to evaluate more highly states in the search space that were closer to the final state.

The three-layer system performed much better: Only the evaluation network was three-layer; the action network remained two-layer. In nine out of the ten runs in which Anderson trained the network, it learned the optimal path of length 7. He used parameter values that were arrived at by testing 20 sets of parameters to determine which arrived at the best performance. It learns an evaluation function such that if there are two states A and B such that a move from A to B moves toward the goal state, then B is evaluated higher than A. He analyzed how the function is constructed in terms of the contributions of the hidden units, many of which are specialized to evaluate various portions of the state space.

One of the main features of the action network is the development of strong negative connections between actions and their inverses. There are also connections that cause the selection of a particular action on one step to make the selection of another particular action on the next step more probable.

One problem with this technique of learning good behavior on heuristic search tasks is the learning time. It took 100,000 learning steps to learn an optimal solution to the three disk Towers of Hanoi problem, which is a toy problem with a small search space. Since search spaces for more complex problems, such as adversary games like chess or reversi, tend to be large, training times and numbers of hidden units required might be unworkable. More work needs to be done along these lines.

2.25.   Extensions to Learning Algorithms

A number of researchers have developed extensions to the basic back-propagation algorithm given in section 2.12. For instance, Sandon and Uhr (1988) have developed a technique for dealing with the fact that back-propagation sometimes gets stuck in local minima in weight space. Ballard (1988) has also developed a technique for dealing with local minima. Kruschke (1988) discusses techniques for minimizing the number of hidden units required to solve a given problem. McCloskey and Cohen (1987) demonstrated the tendency of back-propagation and other connectionist algorithms to "forget" old memories, and Hinton and Plaut (1987b) have devised a scheme to cope with this tendency, substituting new knowledge for it. I discuss some of these techniques in more detail in the following sections.

Back-propagation and related procedures are prone to the problem of poor convergence in some cases. Hinton (1987) gives the example of the case in which the error surface has steep walls surrounding a relatively flat ravine. Various methods have been devised to deal with such problems. (Widrow & Stearns 1985, Amari 1967, Parker 1987, Plaut & Hinton 1987)

One big problem with back-propagation is that it is biologically implausible. No mechanism has been found whereby neurons transmit error signals backward. One response to this is that back-propagation simply finds interesting networks that biological evolution may have found by other means. Some authors have suggested methods to make back-propagation more plausible, e.g. Parker (1985), Hinton & McClelland (1987a).

2.26.   Escaping From Local Minima

Sandon and Uhr (1988) introduced a new technique for escaping from the local minima that gradient search methods such as back-propagation often lead to. Typical methods for escaping from local minima are: to add noise (such as in the Boltzmann machine), or to jolt the weights from their position in weight space, to escape. Sandon and Uhr suggest the use of what they call a "local interaction heuristic", adapted from ideas in computer vision. Hierarchical methods of visual processing (Uhr 1972, Tanimoto 1978, Dyer 1982) make use of the fact that much of the information that you want to integrate can, at any given level of resolution, be found in a local neighborhood of an image point.

Sandon and Uhr point out that this locality principle can be applied to the general problem of finding global minima in layered feed-forward neural networks. It is based on the idea of clustering. The nodes are grouped into local clusters, and the error function that is propagated back is modified so as to avoid having two nodes in the same cluster respond to the same patterns of activation. Sandon and Uhr point out that such redundancy in the functions computed by nodes means that a needed feature may not be represented.

They applied this to the familiar exclusive-or (xor) problem, with the smallest feed-forward network (in which only adjacent layers are connected) that could solve this problem (see Figure 2.22). In one test-case, back-propagation converged to the correct solution, a global minimum, but in another, with a different initial setting of weights, the network gets stuck in a deadlock with the two hidden units computing exactly the same function. In this second case, they modified the error back-propagated so that the two hidden units formed a cluster. Only the unit that would receive the largest error from normal back-propagation received the same error as under normal back-propagation; the other unit received -1/4 that

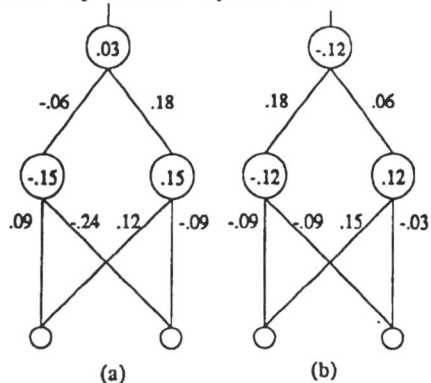

Figure 2.22 Networks used to solve the exclusive-or problem by Sandon and Uhr (1988). Reprinted by Permission.

value, so that the two units receive signals of opposite polarity, and the deadlock is defeated. Using this algorithm "fixed" the second test-case, while the correct results were maintained on the first test-case. They mention other rules for distributing the errors among the cluster; one rule, which set the other unit (that one not receiving maximal error) to +1/4 the value of the maximal unit, still converged to a correct response.

They applied their method to several other problems, such as a network that rotated three bits one bit to the left, in a circular fashion, e.g. 101 to 011, and a two-dimensional shift network (for translating an input pattern). It worked better than standard back-propagation for both cases, although the two-dimensional shift network, being a more complex network, did not achieve very high performance; the best was 59% correct convergence using Sandon's first modified error rule.

2.27.   Creating Bottlenecks

Kruschke (1988) has studied the issue of exactly how many hidden units are needed to accomplish a given mapping, using back-propagation. He gives several reasons why the number of units should be reduced; the first is parsimony: both the amount of computer space and the amount of complexity are reduced with a reduction in the number of units. In addition, with fewer units, each unit is forced to compute efficiently; no units are wasted, and it is often easier to interpret what each unit is competing. Another reason for keeping the number of hidden units to a minimum is that generalization performance tends to be better when fewer hidden units are present.

The disadvantage of using fewer units is, according to Kruschke, that local minima are harder to avoid, and the amount of training time is increased. Kruschke refers to the minimum number of units that compute a particular function as a *bottleneck* (since if there were any less units, the information would not get through). He has devised two methods which result, respectively, in two different types of bottlenecks, *local bottlenecks* and *distributed bottlenecks*. Local bottlenecks are created by starting with many units and gradually attenuating away those units that are redundant in terms of the representation in the hidden units.

He considers the variant of back-propagation that includes, for each unit, a parameter called the *gain* in the activation rule. The activation rule is thus

$$a_i = f(g_i net_i)$$

where a_i is the activation, g_i is the gain and net_i is the input received by unit i. Kruschke notes that a unit with zero gain has constant activation, independent of the input received. Also, as Kruschke shows mathematically, since the gain acts as a multiplicative factor in the back-propagated error, a unit with zero gain also propagates back no error.

The gains are the attenuating factors that Kruschke uses to create his local bottlenecks. The gains compete with one another. Kruschke considers two units redundant if their weight vectors are (nearly) parallel or anti-parallel. Thus, with each adjustment of the weights, the gains are also adjusted by

$$\Delta g_i = -\gamma \sum_j \cos^2 \angle(w_i^s, w_j^s) \cdot g_j^s$$

Thus all the gains are decreasing by an amount that is a measure of their similarity of their weight vector to all the others based on the square of the cosine of the angle between the weight vectors, which is large when the vectors are close to being parallel. The most similar nodes diminish each other's gains by the largest amount.

After each epoch of back-propagation, the gain was reversed if the length of the weight vector for that particular node has increased, and is decreased if it has decreased. Then the weight vector is normalized. This way the gain comes to represent the length of the weight vector and the weight vector itself is a unit vector indicating its direction. This leads to an interaction between Kruschke's gain competition algorithm and back-propagation.

He used these algorithms to minimize the number of hidden units in the 4-4-4 encoder problem (see also section 2.11), in which the 4 unit basis vectors in the set of 4-dimensional binary vectors are each mapped onto another member of the set specifically, he used the identity mapping, 1000→1000, 0100→0100, etc. 4-4-4 denotes 4 input units, 4 hidden units, and 4 output units. His algorithm reduced the number of hidden units required to two by reducing the gain of two of the hidden units, thereby creating a 4-2-4 network in which the two hidden units that remained after the imposition of the bottleneck contained a binary encoding of the input.

The second approach that Kruschke took to reducing the information flow through the hidden layer was the creation of what he called a distributed bottleneck. This is based on Shepard's (1962) concept of multi-dimensional scaling. What Kruschke did was to compute the mean distance between all pairs of weight vectors. Then each pair of vectors that were closer to each other than this mean were moved closer together, and those that were further apart were moved even further apart. This was done in the direction of their difference vector. The effect of this algorithm over time is to make all the vectors either parallel or anti-parallel to one another.

With moderate amounts of this dimensional compression, the network still learned the 4-4-4 encoder, but the learning time was increased. It did this, however, by exploring a smaller area in weight space, in the sense that pairs of weight vectors tended to be closer to being parallel or anti-parallel. Distributed bottlenecks reduce the dimensionality of the back-propagation mapping without reducing the number of units; thus they retain damage resistance associated with redundancy. Kruschke notes that both types of bottlenecks are not limited to back-propagation networks, but can be created in a similar fashion with other learning paradigms, such as that invented by Ackley and his co-workers for the Boltzmann machine (see section 2.10).

2.28.   Sequential Learning

McCloskey and Cohen (1987) considered the problem of sequential learning in connectionist networks. Sequential learning is common in people: for instance, as they point out, children learn simpler addition facts (i.e., the ones involving smaller numbers) before they learn more complex facts. It is possible to train a connectionist network to do addition; some representation can be made of the two operands in a feed-forward back-propagation network with a layer of hidden units, and the network can be trained to add them if random input-output pairs are employed in sequence.

They explored the ability of such networks to learn if the inputs were not all presented at once, but sequentially. They trained networks using both the Boltzmann machine and back-propagation to respond correctly to addition problems involving one (e.g., 7 + 1 = 8). They then took this same network and trained it on problems involving two. Almost immediately after commencing training, even before the network learned to handle the problems involving two, it "forgot" the correct answers to the problems involving one.

This is not the behavior exhibited by human subjects. For instance, in a well-known experiment by Barnes and Underwood, described by McCloskey and Cohen, subjects were trained on an associative pair task of form A-B until they could recall the entire list of A-B pairs, and then were taught A-C associations. Subjects were given context information as to whether they were being asked to provide a response of form B or C. Even after subjects achieved good performance on the A-C list, they still retained better than 30% accuracy on the A-B list. This is in marked contrast to McCloskey and Cohen's model's performance; it forgot all the A-B associations quickly.

McCloskey and Cohen adjusted the representation of the input and outputs (local vs. distributed; more units vs. less) and the number of hidden units to attempt to deal with this forgetting, and changed the learning rate. None of these efforts met with any success. They explain this behavior by reference to regions in the space defined by the set of weights. The solution to the "add-1" problem is represented by a region in this weight space. The solution to the "add-2" problem is represented by a different region. The solution to the combined problem is represented by the intersection of these regions. When trained on stimuli from the combined problem, the system's vector of weights moves quite directly to the intersection region, using gradient descent. If trained on either sub-problem, it moves to that sub-problem's region, but not normally to the intersection region. If then trained on the second sub-problem, it then moves directly toward the second sub-problem's region, but is not constrained to remain in the region of the first sub-problem, so it does not proceed to the intersection region. Only training on examples from both problems will move the weight vector toward the intersection region.

They and others (Hinton & Sejnowski 1986b, Hinton & Plaut 1987b) suggest that rehearsing previously learned information during learning might mitigate forgetting. This may be what people do. Another suggestion is to modify the learning algorithm so that it learns without this forgetting; in terms of the example given above, our modified learning algorithm would remain in the region of the first sub-problem while moving toward the second sub-problem's region, thus ending up in the intersection region. The algorithm would therefore be somehow "keeping in mind" the association from the first set of stimuli. Unfortunately, these associations are not learned explicitly, but in terms of the functional relationship between their parts, so it is difficult for a connectionist machine to rehearse associations.

2.29.   Remembering Old Knowledge

McCloskey and Cohen's work, and that of others, demonstates the problem that it is hard for a network to learn something new without erasing what it has previously learned. Hinton and Plaut (1987b) deal with this problem by proposing that, for each connection in a network, two connections be substituted, with a weight on each of them. One of these would have a relatively rapid learning rate—the "fast weight"—while the other would have a relatively slow one. The slow weights would store the long-term knowledge of the network, while the fast weights would function as a short-term memory.

They propose a novel use of the fast weights in which the fast weights are used not simply to hold new associations, but to "deblur" the system. If the slow weights have come to reflect a set of associations—the "old" set—and are then trained on a new set, they will have a tendency—as McCloskey and Cohen have shown—to forget the old set. Hinton and Plant have devised a scheme in which the fast weights compensate for the changes in the slow weights so that the old associations are still recalled. This is analogous to deblurring in image processing: an algorithm is used to deblur an out-of-focus picture, based on information on how far out of focus it is. For Hinton and Plaut, he fast weights store this information.

They used a feed-forward network and back-propagation to carry out their experiments. This network contained both fast and slow weights with different learning rates. The overall weight of a connection is simply the sum of the fast and slow weights. The fast weights have a built-in tendency to decay to zero, so when the network reaches near zero error they will decay to zero. In the retraining, the fast weights retained information about the earlier slow weights—i.e., how far they had been perturbed from their earlier values.

Their task was to associate one 100-member set of 10-bit vectors with counterparts in another set; the 200 vectors, and the matches between them, were chosen at random, but were then fixed for purposes of learning the associations. The network's slow

weights were trained by multiple sweeps through the data. They
then trained the network on five new associations, until this new
knowledge was stored in the slow weights. They then retrained the
network on a portion of the original 100 associations. At the
beginning of this retraining, the rest of the old associations were
remembered almost as well as the portion used for retraining, even
if this portion was as low as 10%. Eventually, of course, the portion
used in retraining came to be recalled better. Hinton and Plant
account for this by noting that the information about the initial 100
associations is distributed across the entire pattern of the slow
weights, so that, as the network relearns, it is pushed back in weight
space toward the weight pattern representing the complete set of old
associations, which it has visited before. This is what Hinton and
Plaut call the *transfer effect*.

In order to understand the transfer effect, they choose a simple
problem of a three unit network with two input units and a single
output unit (see Figure 2.23). This network's weights are then
trained to learn two simple linear associations: $w_1x_1 + w_2x_2 = y$
and $w_1x_1' + w_2x_2' = y'$. This is represented by the point (w_1, w_2)
in the two-dimensional weight space which is at the intersection of
the two lines in weight space corresponding to the two associations.
For either association, any point on the line corresponding to it in
weight space will do to represent the association; both associations
can be represented only by the intersection.

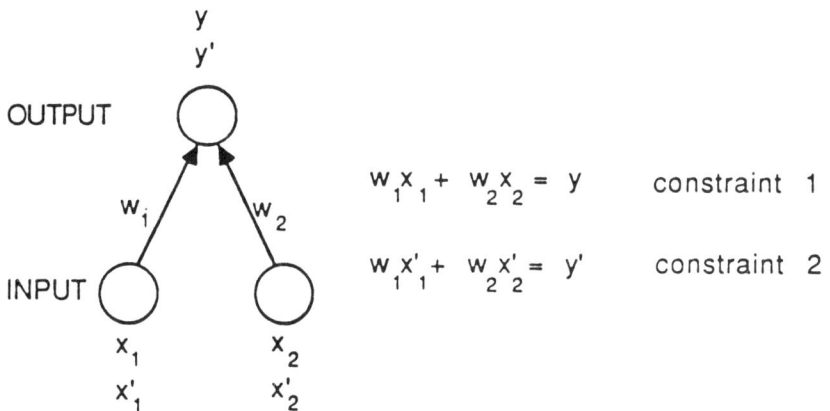

$$w_1x_1 + w_2x_2 = y \qquad \text{constraint 1}$$

$$w_1x_1' + w_2x_2' = y' \qquad \text{constraint 2}$$

Figure 2.23. A network representing two linear constaints used by Hinton and
Plaut (1987b). Reprinted by permission.

They consider what will happen if the solution is perturbed some random distance from the solution point. This is analogous to what occurs during the learning of the new associations. If, after this perturbation, the network is retrained on only one of the two associations, it will tend to make a "bee-line" for the line that corresponds to that association. In Figure 2.24, the random displacement is somewhere in the circle around the intersection point. The two association lines divide this circle into four regions.

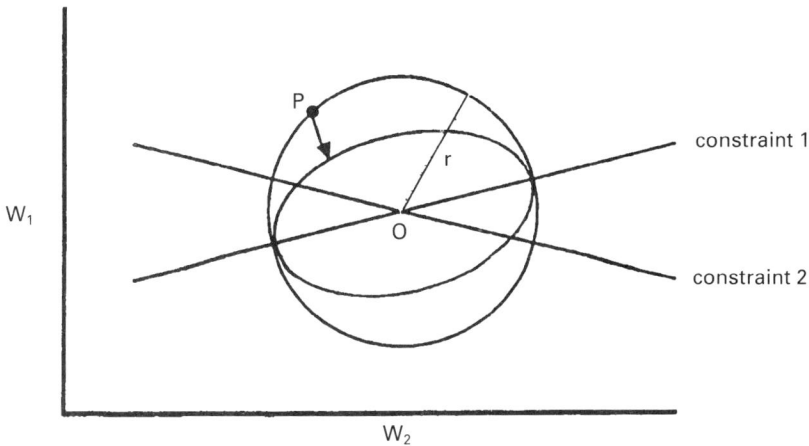

Figure 2.24. Regions in the weight search space surrounding two linear constraints. From Hinton and Plaut (1987b). Reprinted by permission.

Hinton and Plaut point out that if the displaced point lies in one of the two larger regions of the circle, a movement in weight space from the displaced point toward the line associated with one of the associations will also bring the weights closer to the line representing the other association. If the displaced point is in one of the smaller two regions, such a movement will be toward one of the two association lines and away from the other. But the displaced point is more likely to be in one of the larger two areas. They extend this point mathematically to show that in circumstances like those in their simulation, the transfer effect occurs.

They note that as the point moves from one of the larger regions towards the intersection point, the circle becomes an ellipse, and the fraction of area corresponding to what was the larger area in the circle is smaller in this ellipse. Therefore the transfer effect gets smaller as re-learning proceeds.

2.30.   Sequential Processing

Jordan (1986a) has applied connectionist models to sequential tasks in cognition. While much of cognition seems intrinsically parallel, such as the recognition of objects in a visual scene, many tasks, such as speech production and understanding, are intrinsically sequential. Nevertheless, even such a sequential task as speech production, Jordan points out, exhibits a certain degree of parallelism. This is evinced in phenomena such as co-articulation. In co-articulation, the shape of the mouth and tongue during the utterance of a particular phoneme will be influenced by a phoneme that is to follow; Jordan gives the example of the word "freon", the opening of the mouth that is required to pronounce the "n" can start as early as the "e".

The formalism used by Jordan for expressing sequential performance employs a sequence $x_1, x_2, ..., x_n$ of actions taken by the system. The x's, each of which is a vector, are stored, one after the other, over time. That is, x_2 replaces x_1 in the output units, then x_3 replaces x_2, and so on. There is also a static vector p, called the plan. There is another vector sequence $s_1, s_2, ..., s_n$, which is the sequence of states of the system. At any given time step in the operation of the system, the state vector is the "memory" of the system, that is, the system's recollection of all the previous outputs it had.

Jordan's network is shown in Figure 2.25. In order to compute a non-linear function of the plan and state units to arrive at the next output (action), a layer of hidden units are present. The layer of input and plan units is completely connected to the layer of hidden units, which in its turn is completely connected to the layer of output units. As far as we have described it, the network is completely feed-forward.

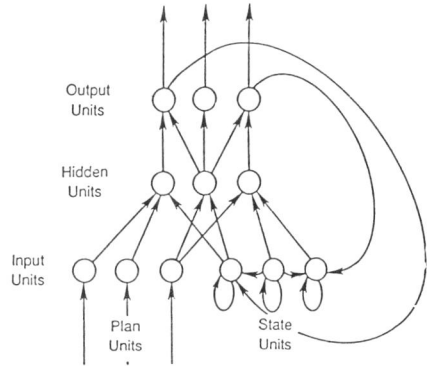

Figure.2.25. Recurrent network of Jordan (1986a). Reprinted by permission.

It also has some recurrent connections. Each of the state units is connected to itself, and each of the output units is connected to the state units. Thus both the previous state and the current output determine the next state, as defined by the state units. A learning algorithm such as error back-propagation is used to train the weights in the system so as to produce the desired sequence of actions.

Generally, it is desirable that the state vector changes continuously in time, that is, a pair of successive state vectors should be similar to one another. For one thing, this makes the associations between them easier to learn, since the state vector can simply flow along a trajectory in state space. But the main reason for this continuity requirement is to provide the kind of parallelism that is illustrated by co-articulation. This parallelism means that there must be aspects of the state vector that are "getting ready for" the next action, and these are similar to what they will be on the next time step.

As an example, Jordan considers the case where the learning system must learn the sequence (1.0 * *) (* 1.0 *) (* * 1.0), in which the state vector has 3 components and * indicates "don't care". In this case, the system will likely learn a sequence such as (1.0 0.8 0.6) (0.8 1.0 0.8) (0.6 0.8 1.0), since each state generalizes from nearby states. This is similar to co-articulation. As more and more components of the state vector are specified on each time step, this parallelism becomes less possible, and learning takes longer.

Jordan observed that in the case of a system that learned a sequence of states under this continuity requirement have a particular property: that their learned states serve as *attractors*. That is, if one of the states in a learned sequence is perturbed somewhat, to a nearby point in state space, and this state is input to the system, the system will correct the perturbation and get back to the correct sequence, although this may take some time, and the correct sequence may only be approached asymptotically. In the case where a system has learned a number of independent cyclical sequences, each of these sequences serves as an attractor for those states similar to states in the sequence in question. This, Jordan notes, is a generalization of Hopfield's network, in which partial representations of states flow into complete representations, called limit points, thus serving as a content-addressable or auto-associative memory (see section 2.8) In Jordan's system, the attractors are not points, but trajectories through state space. Jordan uses the term *attractor dynamics* to characterize the study of his class of systems.

Jordan applied this network formalism to the simulation of the co-articulation data. He notes that his system can be viewed as a discrete version of a continuous process; this has promise in the simulation of continuous sequential processes such as speech articulation.

In related work, Rumelhart, Hinton, and Williams (1986c) have extended the back-propagation algorithm to sequential data. They use networks that have one layer for each time slice.

2.31. Image Compression Using a
Back-propagation Auto-associator

Cottrell, Munro, and Zipzer (1987) devised a method of image compression that is based on back-propagation. Their method is based on the fact that most real images contain large amounts of redundant information. Their compression technique can be applied to any redundant data file, not just images.

In their experiments, they used 8x8 pixel images, with 8-bit pixel values ranging from 0 to 255. The system contained three layers, with the input and output layers both being 8x8 images, and a layer of 16 hidden units in between. The goal was to completely represent the 64 bytes of information in the image in the 16 hidden units. The network is feed-forward, with each layer being completely connected to neighboring ones. For the purpose of back-propagation, the desired output was the same as the input; thus the network was an auto-associator.

The network was trained for 100,000 images, which were patches drawn from a single, much larger image, with a learning rate of 0.25, and then on an additional 50,000 patches, with a learning rate of 0.01. This resulted in a "compression machine", which yielded reasonable results on visual inspection (comparing an image reconstruction from the compressed version with the original).

In order to compare their results to more conventional methods for image compression, they had to limit the hidden units to having a fixed number of output values, so that they could measure the relative number of bits in the compressed vs. the uncompressed versions. There is a trade-off between image quality and compression. There are two ways that the amount of compression can be varied; by changing the number of hidden units and by changing the number of possible output levels that the hidden units might have (which the authors refer to as the quantization).

They compared their algorithm with a standard compression algorithm, the principal components transform (PCT). This transform is based on multiplying the vector of elements representing the uncompressed image by a matrix so as to transform the coordinates in which the vector is represented to ones that display the maximum variance along their axes, thus removing correlations between pairs of coordinates. To decompress, the inverse matrix is used.

In both the PCT method and their method, they note, the resultant image can be viewed as a linear combination of basis images (since the hidden units tend to have inputs that stay in the linear ranges of their sigmoid activation functions). In the two cases, though, the set of basis images are different.

Cottrell and his co-workers argue that their system is an example of a new programming style, called extensional programming. This term simply indicates that the network was not explicitly programmed to solve the problem (of compression), but rather it learned by example. They note that, because a linear solution was found, it was not necessary to use a non-linear system, although they found that the non-linear system generalizes better to novel images. They feel that their technique may be better than the PCT method in certain circumstances, such as in the case in which there is a noisy channel for the transmission of the compressed image, because the variance in the image is better distributed among the various components of the compressed image than it is in the PCT compressed image, so loss of one or two important components of the PCT can cause substantial degradation in the image.

2.32. Representing Recursive Structures
in Connectionist Networks

Many of connectionism's critics (e.g., Fodor and Pylyshyn, see section 1.9) have argued that recursive symbol structures, such as trees, lists, and stacks, are essential to any theory of cognition, including a connectionist one. For instance, many linguistic rules are recursive, such as

NP ←NP PP

which says that a noun phrase may be generated by taking another noun phrase and appending a prepositional phrase to it. This leads to an infinite variety of linguistic constructions such as "the woman", "the woman with the binoculars", "the woman with the binoculars at the zoo", etc.

Touretzky (1986) shows how such recursive structures may be implemented in a connectionist network. He takes the title of his system from the Boltzmann machine (Ackley et al. 1985; see section 2.10), which is the particular neural network type that he used to implement his system, and the LISP operation CONS, which is used to recursively CONStruct a list out of two lists or atoms, and is the basic list-constructing operation in LISP. Each CONS operation creates a CONS cell, which is a record containing two pointers, one to the CAR, and one to the CDR (the names CAR and CDR come from old IBM mnemonics, which no longer have any significance). These CONS cells, as any introductory computer science student knows, can be used to construct many dynamic data structures, such as binary trees, stacks, and linked lists. For an introduction to LISP, see (Wilensky 1986).

Touretzky takes off from his and Hinton's design for their connectionist production system interpreter, DUCS (see section 3.2), in his design of BoltzCONS. As in the production system network, there are 25 distinct symbols, and each unit in the system is sensitive to six symbols in each position of a triple of symbols; thus each unit is receptive to 6^3 triples out of the 25^3 possible.

The BoltzCONS System is divided into 5 modules, as shown in Figure 2.26. The CONS memory is used to store all of the CONS cells. Each CONS is represented by a triple (tag car cdr), where each of tag, car, cdr is one of the twenty-five symbols supported by the system. Each CONS cell has a unique symbol associated with it; thus the system can represent only 25 CONS cells

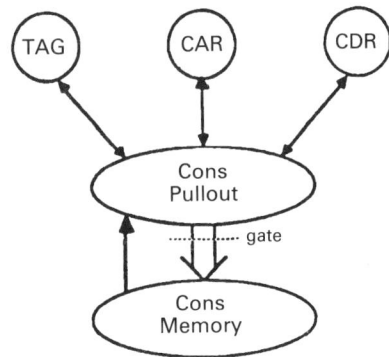

Figure 2.26. The BoltzCONS system (Touretzky 1986). Reprinted by permission.

at once, or less if some of the symbols are considered to be atoms, which are stand-alone symbols that do not denote any CONS cell.

Many triples are stored in CONS memory; the CONS pullout network is used to select one triple from the memory. Three winner-take-all networks are used to store the symbol from each of the three symbol positions; these are called (naturally enough) the tag, car, and cdr networks. Each of these is identical to a bind space in the production system network. The representation of symbols in these bind spaces is itself distributed; each symbol is represented by a unique pattern of activation across the bind space. Each unit that participates in the pattern for a particular symbol, say x, is positively connected to a random subset of the units in car pullout space that participate in the representation of x in the particular position in the triple corresponding to which bind space we are talking about: in the case of the tag space, the first position; in the case of the car space, the second position; and in the case of the cdr space, the third position.

Touretzky gives the example of a stack represented by the triples (p a g) (g B r) (r C s) (s D nil). Note that the first symbol of each triple is the same as the last symbol of the previous one; this provides the links between stack elements. To pop the top element off the stack, the symbols p, A, and g are loaded into the tag, car and cdr spaces respectively, and the triple (p A g) is represented in the CONS pullout space. The triple (p A g) is removed from the CONS memory by activating gated inhibitory connections between corresponding units in the CONS pullout space and the CONS memory. The CONS pullout space and the CONS memory have the same structure, except that, because of inhibitory connections, the CONS pullout space can represent only one triple at a time. In order to move the triple (g B r) to the top of the stack, that is, into the CONS pullout space, the activation pattern corresponding to the symbol g is clamped into the tag space, and then simulated annealing (see section 2.10) is run on the CONS pullout space and the three bind spaces to find a minimum energy state. There are excitatory connections from units in the CONS memory to corresponding units in the CONS pullout space. This annealing causes the triple (g B r) to move into the CONS pullout space, since it is the only triple that has g as its first symbol.

In order to push a new symbol on the stack, say E, Touretzky chooses a new "pointer" symbol, say t, copies the tag space to the cdr space, and puts t into the tag space and E into the car space. The combined influence of these three spaces—if, for example, (g B r) was formerly on top of the stack—causes the triple (t E g) to move into the CONS pullout space, and then via gated excitatory connections, to move into the CONS memory.

Having shown how to implement stack operations, Touretzky moves on to trees. The main difference between BoltzCONS and ordinary LISP is that BoltzCONS has the ability to follow pointers backwards. For instance, Touretzky gives an example of a tree in which the root is (v w y) and its two children are (w A x) and (y D E). If you are at either of the children of the root as you traverse this tree, it is possible to get back to the root. For instance, if you are at (w A x), you know that w must be the car or the cdr of the parent; it may take two attempts to find the parent node, in which w is loaded into the cdr and cdr spaces, one at a time, to find the appropriate triple, but BoltzCONS can find it. Touretzky shows that is possible to implement a tree traversal in terms of BoltzCONS operations alone, without using an auxiliary stack, which a conventional implementation of a tree traversal would require, since a tree traversal is a naturally recursive operation, and recursive operations require a stack.

In the initial implementation of BoltzCONS, a program in LISP controlled BoltzCONS's operations, such as clamping a space (holding its activations constant, at fully activated), starting annealing, etc. in the spirit of making the system completely connectionist. Touretzky implemented the control module as a connectionist network as well, using his and Hinton's (1985) production system interpreter, DUCS, suitably modified. The sequential nature of the control module is implemented using a set of production rules that execute in sequence.

Touretzky argues that systems like BoltzCONS and the connectionist production system interpreter, DUCS, are interesting not because they can compute solutions to problems that Turing machines can't, but because they can compute them in a way that is biologically plausible in that they use distributed memory and massive parallelism to solve constraint satisfaction problems.

Touretzky also notes that the modules employed in BoltzCONS and in DUCS, that is, bind spaces, pullout networks, and distributed representations of symbols, are generally applicable to symbol processing in the connectionist paradigm. For Touretzky's more recent connectionist work, much of it in the same vein, see (Touretzky 1989a,b,c).

3

Production Systems and Expert Systems

3.1. Introduction

Work in the development of connectionist rule-based systems, which can be used to simulate expert performance, can be divided into two areas. The first type of work, exemplified by the work of Touretzky and Hinton (1985) , simulates the firing of rules, as in a production system. The second type of system, such as that developed by Gallant (1988), or that of Saito and Nakano (1988), uses a neural network learning algorithm, such as error back-propagation, to learn relationships between inputs and outputs; these relationships are normally considered expert knowledge. For instance, the inputs might be configurations of symptoms and the outputs might be diseases. As has been done with many symbolic expert systems, both Gallant, and Saito and Nakano, use a medical domain to demonstrate the expert capacities of a neural network. The network, once trained to exhibit expert knowledge, can be examined and rules can be extracted from it, based on correlations between particular inputs and outputs.

The work of Gallant, and that of Saito and Nakano, illustrates the applicability of connectionist systems to expert systems. Since no rules need be explicitly programmed into a connectionist expert system, the development time of such a system is substantially reduced from that required for a traditional symbolic rule-based system, in which the process of discovering rules is slow and painstaking.

The work of Touretzky and Hinton is interesting not because of its practicality for use as a tool to implement an expert system, but because it illustrates how a rule-based system can be implemented in a distributed connectionist system. In this it is similar to Touretzky's BoltzCONS (see section 3.2), which shows how a LISP-like system may be implemented in a connectionist network.

In the following sections we discuss the systems of Touretzky and Hinton, of Gallant, and of Saito and Nakano in detail.

3.2. A Connectionist Production System

Touretzky and Hinton (1985) consider the problems of pattern matching and variable binding within the connectionist paradigm. These operations are critical to implementing a standard AI production system. They devised their system partly to respond to criticisms that connectionist systems were unable to deal with standard symbolic stimuli as encountered in AI. These criticisms have been effectively been taken care of by their system and others; the debate has shifted to whether or not connectionist systems are an efficient mechanism for implementing such standard AI symbol processing systems such as production systems.

They use a distributed connectionist system, which they call DUCS, consisting of binary threshold units. They use rules of the form

$$(F\ A\ A)\ (F\ B\ B) \rightarrow +(G\ A\ B)\ -(F\ A\ A)\ -(F\ B\ B)$$

This rule can be interpreted as follows: replace the triples *(F A A)* and *(F B B)*, if they are present in the working memory, with the triple *(G A B)*. In the second version of their system, they added variables to the first position of a triple in a rule if the triple appeared on the left side of the rule.

Their system is comprised of five groups of cells. The main one of these is the working memory. There are two "clause spaces" called *C1* and *C2*, and each holds a single triple. There is a space representing the production rules, and another space representing the variable bindings.

The system behaves like a standard production system, which repeats a recognize–act cycle over and over; recognizing the left side of a rule, and taking the action specified on the right side of that rule. In the recognize phase, cells in working memory influence cells in the *C1* and *C2* clause spaces, and the rule and binding spaces.

Relaxation takes place until a state that corresponds to a match is achieved.

The working memory represents triples of symbols. They have chosen to represent 25 different symbols. They preferred a distributed representation using coarse coding to a local one. The latter would have required $25^3 = 15,625$ distinct neurons. Their representation requires 2000 cells, each of which responds to $6^3 = 216$ triples, because each cell responds to six randomly chosen symbols in each position of a triple. Because the cells recognize $2,000 \times 216 = 432,000$ triples, each triple is recognized by approximately $432,000/15,625 \approx 28$ cells. Thus each triple is represented by a pattern of activity over about 28 cells. A triple is stored by activating all of the cells that are receptive to it. Conversely, a triple is present if all but a few of the cells that are receptive to it are activated. The system is relatively insensitive to noise, in that a few cells can be missing from the representation of a triple and the triple would still be considered to be present in working memory. This is necessary, since it is essential that one be allowed to remove triples from working memory as well as add them. The problem with removing triples is that a given node can serve in the representation of more than one triple. This is why it is not required that all the nodes associated with a given triple be activated in order for that triple to be considered present, because some of its nodes could have been deactivated as the result of the removal of other triples from working memory.

Note that, since coarse coding is used, when many similar triples are stored, the system is unable to tell which of them is in fact present.

The two clause spaces $C1$ and $C2$ each has exactly the same number of cells as the working memory, 2,000. Each cell in the spaces is connected to a corresponding cell in working memory. Thus $C1$ and $C2$ are structurally identical to working memory, except that the cells in clause space inhibit one another in such a way so as to limit the total number of cells in the space that can be activated at the same time to 28. This is because each space is designed to hold only one triple at a time. Since the rules have two antecedents each, the idea is that the two triples on the left side of the rule come from the two clause spaces, one from each space.

Rules are represented in a distributed manner; each rule is represented by a collection of 40 rule cells. Each rule cell is positively connected to the clause spaces. If triples *T1* and *T2* are the two triples on the left side of the rule *X*, then each of the 40 rule cells of rule X are connected to a random subset of the cells representing *T1* in the *C1* clause space, and to an equal number of randomly selected cells that represent *T2* in *C2*. The 40 cells comprising the rules form a clique. Cells inhibit cells outside their clique. Thus the rule space is a winner-take-all network; after the network settles all the cells representing a single rule will be activated, and no others. They chose a distributed representation for rules partly so that if two rules match, the one that matches more strongly would be activated.

The rule cells perform the rule by being connected to cells in working memory that represent the triples that the rule takes action on. If the rule inserts a triple into working memory, each node representing the rule is positively connected to a random subset of the cells representing the triple in working memory. If it deletes them, then the connections are negative. The system is set up so that the rule firing connections are gated; that is, the rules are not allowed to take any action until a single rule has settled into place. Touretzky and Hinton can show that each phase, rule recognition and firing, corresponds to Hopfield energy minimization (see section 2.8).

In order to handle variable binding, they use another set of cells called bind cells. There are 25 possible values that a variable can take on, since there are 25 distinct symbols that the system recognizes. As in the rule space, each symbol is represented by a clique of 40 cells. Each of these cells is connected to a random subset of all the nodes in *C1* and *C2* that have that particular symbol in their first position. If the clause spaces settle into the representation of two triples, each of which begins with the same symbol, then the bind space will settle into a state in which the nodes representing that symbol are activated. In order for the system to work properly when variables are allowed, the rule cells must be given larger receptive fields, because a rule antecedent that contains a variable has a larger number of possible triples that it can match.

One problem with their system is that it doesn't allow for conflict resolution; that is, it cannot deal with the situation in which more than one rule is ready to fire at a given time. All standard production system interpreters provide some form of conflict resolution. If such a conflict occurs, DUCS will not function properly. This is a serious limitation. However, the system, like many other connectionist systems, is subject to crosstalk, whereby many weakly activated rules may cause a triple to incorrectly enter the clause space, and cause the wrong rule to be activated.

In a simulation, their system is much, much slower than an standard symbolic production system interpreter such as OPS5 (Forgy 1981). If it were built in hardware, it would be much faster, probably comparable in speed to OPS5 running on a conventional computer. The point of their work, however, was to show that connectionist systems can handle very general form of symbol processing, not that they can do it more efficiently than conventional systems. Their system has properties that are more human-like than a conventional system, such as graceful degradation of performance if the working memory gets overloaded.

Another disadvantage of this system, as opposed to standard systems, is that the rules have to be wired into the system, as opposed to being fed in as data. An interesting extension of this work would be a system that learns production rules, which is effectively what is done in the work described in the next two sections, although rules are not represented explicitly.

3.3. Saito and Nakano's Connectionist Expert System

Saito and Nakano (1988) applied a connectionist network to a problem in medical diagnosis that has been traditionally within the area of application of rule-based systems. They use a three-layer feed-forward network to represent the diagnostic information. It has 216 input units, which are divided into small sets, each set corresponding to a question given to the patient; for each possible response to a question one of the input units in a set corresponding to that question is active. The middle layer consists of 72 hidden units; the output layer uses 23 units corresponding to the 23 diseases that the system knows about. Each of the layers is completely connected to each unit in the layer above it.

For the purposes of training the network, 394 patient records were utilized, in which the output disease was given, as well as all the diagnostic data. Back-propagation was used to train the system. After the training period, the network responded "perfectly" to an additional 300 cases. They defined a perfect response as one of the output units responding with an activation greater than or equal to 0.75, and all the others responding with activation less than 0.25. Note that a perfect response, as they define it, is not necessarily a correct one; it is just one in which a single unit is responding. It would be surprising if the network achieved a percentage of correct diagnostic responses that is significantly better than that given by expert physicians.

Saito and Nakano define two measures of the system, precision and recall. Precision is the ratio of the number of diseases that the system diagnoses correctly to the total number of diseases that it diagnoses, and recall is the ratio of correctly diagnosed diseases to the actual number of diseases present in the patient. Their system gave a recall result of 0.54 and a precision result of 0.21; this is based on the (low) threshold for a disease being present of 0.25. This low value biases the system in favor of recall, with a loss of precision (many inaccurate diseases are diagnosed). Accuracy was defined as the fraction of diagnoses in which one of the diseases diagnosed was actually found to be present in the patient. Their system had an accuracy of 67%. A symbolic expert system programmed to handle the same task achieved accuracy of about 70%. Of course, these numbers are not really useful for comparing symbolic vs. connectionist expert systems, since they are implementation-dependent.

The expert neural network can be viewed as a source of information for knowledge acquisition. Knowledge acquisition has been long recognized as a "bottleneck" in the construction of expert systems; although expert behavior may be rule-governed, it is notoriously difficult and time-consuming to determine what the rules are, and what the relation factor (RF) relating antecedent and consequent of each rule may be. (The RF is a number that quantifies the strength of the association.) If it is possible to extract RFs both from a connectionist network and from interviewing experts, then the best of both worlds could be built into a system, resulting in a system with maximal performance.

Saito and Nakano define two methods for determining the RFs. In the first method, the output of a node representing a disease D is given by $B(D)$, when no symptoms are input (zero input vector), and $A(S,D)$ if only the input node corresponding to symptom S alone is activated, and no others. In this case, $RF_1(S,D) = k_1(A(S,D) - B(D))$, where k_1 is a constant. This formula measures the effect of a single symptom on the presence of a given disease, ignoring the effects of other symptoms. The second estimate is given for an actual set of patients. Here $C(S,D,P)$ gives the change in the output value of D when patient P 's symptom S is switched from 1 to 0 and defines the sum of the C's over the patients as

$$sum(S,D) = \sum_P C(S,D,P)$$

Saito and Nakano let $N(S)$ be the number of patients for which this has been done. They define $RF_2(S, D) = k_2(sum(S, D)/N(S))$, where k_2 is a constant. Thus this measures the average effect that S has on D in an actual patient set.

RFs relate only single symptoms with single diseases, and cannot represent non-linear or conjunctive relationships between symptoms of diseases. To cope with this problem, Saito and Nakano invented a method for extraction of rules from their neural network. They did this by considering sets of symptoms, setting all the symptoms in such a set "on" in the neural network, and then seeing if a given disease D is activated. If it is, then a rule of the form: if D then (set of symptoms) is generated. If, at this point, activation of a second set of symptoms causes D to be de-activated, then the rule is modified to : if D then (set of affirmative symptoms)(set of negative symptoms).

Since for n symptoms there are 2^n sets of symptoms, one must find a way of considering only a small subset of this power set, to avoid combinatorial explosion. They restrict their sets of affirmative symptoms to symptoms that are found in conjunction in actual patients, and sets of negative symptoms to symptoms that are all absent together in actual patients. Secondly, Saito and Nakano restrict the size of the symptom sets that can occur; in their example of role extinction they limited the size of the affirmative symptom set to three and that of the negative symptom set to a single symptom. Using the 216 input nodes representing symptoms of the network described above, they extracted 443 rules about the single disease muscle contraction headache, of which 303 were affirmative rules and 140 were negative rules, such as "if (muscle-contraction headache) then (the headache continues all day long)" and "if (not muscle contraction headache) then (previous headache has happened more than 3 years before) and (when the headache is serious it is too severe to hear)". Physicians to whom they showed the rules thought that they made sense and were reasonable. An enormous number of rules can be extracted by this method.

These rules, once they are extracted, can be used to confirm patients' symptoms, to extract symptoms that patients are only partially conscious of, and to reject symptoms that are the result of errors made by patients in the course of answering a questionnaire. Saito and Nakano have automated this confirmation procedure as a feedback loop between diagnosis and confirmation, which iteratively improves the quality of a diagnosis.

3.4. Gallant's Connectionist Expert System

Like Saito and Nakano, Gallant (1988) developed a connectionist system which deals with a specialized domain in medical diagnosis, acute theoretical diseases of the sarcophagus. There are nodes in three layers corresponding to each symptom (layer 1), disease (layer 2), and treatment (layer 3) that is relevant to this domain; the nodes are 3-valued, with 1 denoting the activation of a disease, symptom, or treatment, -1, the de-activation and 0, the absence of knowledge. Connections between nodes reflect dependencies between pairs of three types of nodes. There are no cycles in the network. Additional cells were added between the input cells (symptoms) and layers 2 and 3 to increase the computational power of the network. The cells are threshold cells that take value 1 if their total weighted input is positive, -1 if it is negative, and 0 if it is zero. There are cells intermediate between each adjacent pair of layers. Gallant uses a learning algorithm that he calls the pocket algorithm

The pocket algorithm is a variation on the perceptron learning procedure. The basic idea behind the pocket algorithm is that for each vector of weights impinging on an internal or output node, there is another vector in your "pocket" as it were. Over the course of training, if the vector of weights results in a longer string of correct classifications than the vector of weights in your pocket, then you replace the pocket weights with this vector. Each internal or output node u is trained independently, and it is presumed that a set of pairs E^k, C^k is used for training, where E^k is a vector of the activations of the nodes that are inputting to u and C^k is the activation of u, all on the kth iteration. After each iteration, the weight vector P is modified by the formula $P' = P + E^k C^k$, to move it closer to the current pattern of activation. In the case of two output values and a weight vector P, a correct classification is when $P \cdot E^k > 0$ and $C^k = 1$, or when $P \cdot E^k < 0$ and $C^k = -1$.

The pocket algorithm is not guaranteed to converge to good performance, but it does monotonically improve performance by always successively selecting better sets of weights.

The connectionist inference system that Gallant has developed is called MACIE (for <u>Ma</u>trix <u>C</u>ontrolled <u>I</u>nference <u>E</u>ngine), because Gallant uses a matrix to represent his weights. It reasons on the basis of incomplete information. Any node a_k in the system representing a disease or treatment is dependent on, and therefore receives input from, a set of nodes lower down. Some of these nodes—let us refer to them as u_i—have known values, and some of them—v_j—have unknown values. It is often possible to reach a conclusion about the value of a node in the system in a given situation. If the maximum amount of output that the unknown nodes could be giving,

$$MAXUNKNOWN = \sum_j w_{jk}$$

is less in magnitude than the amount of input that the known nodes are given, which is

$$KNOWN = \sum_i w_{ik} u_i$$

then the unknown nodes cannot change the sign of *KNOWN*, and therefore the value can be set to 1 if *KNOWN* is positive, and -1 otherwise.

He also computes, for each node, the confidence that it will be eventually activated. For known cells, the confidence is defined as simply the cell's activation. For unknown input cells, the confidence is zero (nothing is giving us any information about their status). For other unknown cells, the confidence is defined as the weighted sum of the confidences of all the cells impinging upon a given unknown cell (computed one level at a time, from the bottom up), normalized by the total weight attached to unknown cells:

$$\frac{\sum_j w_{ij} conf(u_j)}{\sum_{j, \, u_j \, unknown} w_{ij}}$$

This is just one of many possible heuristics.

As in all expert systems, it is useful to know what additional data to gather in order to clarify the value of an unknown variable. For instance, if there is a collection of output variables, none of which has been verified or falsified (possibly representing diseases or treatments), the system selects the variable u among these with the highest associated confidence. It then repeatedly searches backward in the system through the layers, starting with u, at each layer choosing the unknown variable with the largest weight connection to the variable in the layer above. Eventually, in this fashion, an input variable is reached, and data can be gathered on the value of this input variable. This information is then fed forward through the layers of the system, and it may resolve the value of the output variable in question. If not, the whole process is repeated. This technique may be used to prove or disprove hypotheses, or both. It is a connectionist implementation of the back-chaining technique normally used in expert systems. The system also allows the user to enter "unobtainable" to a request for information, and then that node's value is marked as permanently unknown.

Like Saito and Nakano's system, Gallant's system also explains its behavior by extracting rules from the network as follows. For a given node u_i, all the nodes with known values u_j directly affecting it are considered in order of the absolute value of the weight w_{ij} on the connection between i and j. For instance, node u_5 (state 1) might receive input from nodes $u_1, u_2, u_3,$ and $u_4,$ with states 1, -1, 1, -1 and weights -3, 6, -5, 4 respectively. Nodes u_2 and u_3 would be chosen to participate in the rule because their absolute weights are largest and the sum of their absolute weights (11) exceeds the sum of all the remaining weights (7). The following rule is therefore formed: if ((not u_2) and u_3) then u_5. This, of course, is just one of the many rules that might be formed, but it has the advantage of selecting a set of decisive variables. The rules so generated were judged to be reasonable by physicians.

The system, like that of Saito and Nakano, achieved performance of about 70% in making the correct diagnosis in an application that detected causes of infantile diarrhea. Experts achieve roughly the same performance. Gallant has applied his system to a variety of domains.

Gallant states that his system is not a model of human reasoning: rather it is designed for practical use. He views his work as providing a framework for knowledge engineers to use in building expert systems: he believes that the engineers need good knowledge of connectionist principles in order to use such tools effectively, and that connectionist approaches to knowledge engineering can not "automate away" the knowledge acquisition process.

One interesting extension of such attempts at connectionist expert systems would be to integrate them with connectionist attempts at knowledge representation that embody such properties as inheritance (see the next chapter). This would be in keeping with the general trend in research on expert systems toward modelling the domain-specific knowledge of an expert in a way that reflects the structure of the system that the expert is dealing with. For instance, an expert system for kidney disease would incorporate a model of the kidney's structure and function. For a discussion of these issues, see Patil (1987).

4

Knowledge Representation

4.1. Introduction

Work in knowledge-representation in connectionist systems is closely related to that in natural language understanding, the topic of chapter 7. Connectionist attempts at knowledge representation must succeed at embodying some sort of structured data object or set of objects in a system. For early discussions of how this might be done, see Minsky (1977) and Hinton (1981a).

There are many approaches to this. Some of them are distributed, like Touretzky's DUCS (1985), in which each concept is represented by a pattern of microfeatures. Others are localist, such as Shastri's (1988), in which single nodes are associated with concepts, and the casual relationship between concepts is represented by the strength of connections between them.

One way of thinking about the difference between distributed and local methods of knowledge representation is that distributed representations handle the set containment relation by having the subsets (microfeatures) form parts of a superset's representation, whereas local representations handle the same subset-superset relation by connections between local nodes. The former approach is taken in the work of Touretzky on representing schemata in a neural network. The latter approach is taken in the work of Shastri on knowledge representation.

Inheritance of features of classes by class members is implemented in connectionist networks by Shastri and by Dolan and Dyer. Minsky (1977) and Hinton (1981a) have also done work in this area.

4.2. Storing Schemata in Neural Networks

One of the first efforts to embody structured knowledge representations—often known as schemata—in neural networks was made by Rumelhart, Smolensky, McClelland, and Hinton (1986f). They represented in the network information about five different types of rooms—a kitchen, office, bedroom, bathroom, and living room. There were forty room descriptors, which were items one could find in one or more of these rooms. They interviewed subjects on each of the rooms and asked for each of the descriptors, asked whether that descriptor was likely to be found in that room. For each room, 13 subjects judged each descriptor. This allowed the estimation of probabilities that room descriptors co-occur. Note that certain descriptors were characteristic of all rooms—for example, ceiling, walls, and floor—while others were highly specific to particular room—for example, stove, toilet, and bed. Once the co-occurrence probabilities were estimated, they were used to set the weights in a completely connected neural network of 40 units representing the room descriptors in the following manner:

$$w_{ij} = -ln \frac{P(x_i = 0 \ \& \ x_j = 1) \ P(x_i = 1 \ \& \ x_j = 0)}{P(x_i = 1 \ \& \ x_j = 1) \ P(x_i = 0 \ \& \ x_j = 0)}$$

where x_i and x_j are the binary activations of descriptor units i and j respectively and w_{ij} is the weight connecting them. This formula is derived from probability theory and estimates the co-occurrence probability. Each unit has a bias equal to

$$-ln(P(x_i=0)/P(x_i=1))$$

This measures the degree to which a unit is on; if it is often on, this number is negative; if often off, it is positive.

They performed a Hopfield energy-minimizing relaxation on the network (see section 2.8) by clamping the value of one of the forty descriptors. Out of the 2^{40} possible states of this (binary) system, they found that the system always settled to one of five states corresponding to the room that is most associated with that descriptor. None of these five schemata is explicitly represented in memory; they are emerge as patterns in the correlations between pairs of microfeatures.

There were also subschemata within these schemas: smaller bits of related microfeatures, such as floor lamp and easy chair, desk and desk chair, window and drapes. If one of these pairs is present in the network, but not the other, the Hopfield energy is higher than if both are present. Rumelhart and his co-workers describe gradient descent in terms of a function, the goodness-of-fit function, that is the Hopfield energy function inverted; it is high when the Hopfield energy is low and vice versa. They plotted this goodness-of-fit function for those states in the intersection of a plane formed by three maxima (rooms) in the state space and the forty-dimensional state space of the network. If the "goodness" function sagged deeply between the maxima, this meant that rooms in between these maxima were not very good rooms at all, whereas if the goodness function looked more like a plateau, this meant that intermediate rooms were plausible. Explorations of goodness "landscapes" in this fashion indicated, for instance, that intermediate rooms between bathroom and office were not very good rooms, but intermediate rooms between bedroom, living room, and office are much better, as one might expect.

This implementation of schemata differs from that of Touretzky (see section 4.3) and Dolan and Dyer (section 4.4) which more explicitly treat schemata like Minsky's frames, each of which is as a collection of slot/filler pairs. The schemas of rooms in Rumelhart and co-workers' work are more simply collections of microfeatures.

4.3. Storing Frames in Neural Networks

Touretzky (1987) in his paper "Representing Conceptual Structures in a Neural Network", tackles some of the issues involved in connectionist approaches to knowledge representation. A classic knowledge structure in AI, the frame, consists of a series of slot names and slot fillers. For instance, Touretzky gives as an example the frame representation of the sentence "Down by the henhouse, John threw a rock at the fox." which is:

Agent: John
Verb: Throw
Object:Rock
Destination:Fox
Location: Hen House

In his scheme, both slots and slot fillers are represented as bit vectors. Each bit in the vector represents a microfeature. Touretzky does not go into the semantics of these microfeatures, except to say that they are primitive, but he notes that similar slot names and fillers should have similar patterns of microfeatures.

His scheme is called DUCS, for Dynamically Updateable Conceptual Structures. It allows one to store multiple slot–filler relationships in a structure called the concept buffer. The architecture of DUCS is shown in Figure 4.1.

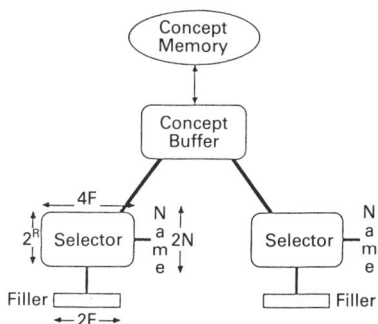

Figure 4.1 The architecture of DUCS (Touretzky 1987). Reprinted by Permission.

Traditional approaches to knowledge representation in the connectionist paradigm involve local representations for each slot and filler; the relationships are given by the weights of the connections between local nodes. In order to retrieve several slot–filler relationships, copies of the entire network have to be made.

DUCS gets around this by having concepts be patterns of activity in a structure called a "concept buffer". Multiple selectors can be attached to this buffer to pull different slot–filler relationships from it.

Concepts, in DUCS, can have an arbitrary number of slots. Performance degrades as slots are added and the available units become saturated.

In addition to concept buffers, which hold individual concepts, DUCS also contains a concept memory, which can hold several concepts at the same time. Individual concepts are retrieved from the concept memory by activating several of the concept's slots at the same time so as to uniquely identify the concept.

The selectors perform a dual purpose: they allow you to store and remove additional slot–filler associations, and also retrieve associations—that is, if you give one of a slot–filler pair, the network will supply the other.

Slot names are $2N$–bit vectors, the first N bits being the values of N binary-valued microfeatures (one means the microfeature is present, zero means it is absent), and the second N bits being the complement of the first N. This is to allow for some redundancy in the representation, since in DUCS's storage scheme there is the possibility that two or more patterns may try to use the same node.

The slot fillers are $2F$ bits long, F being the number of microfeatures in the fillers. They are represented in the same way as the slot names. The selectors are $4Fx2^R$ rectangular arrays of units, where R is a parameter of the system ranging between 0 and N. The degree of overlap between associations and thus the rate of errors in making associations is dependent on R and on the number of associations that are stored. To record the association between filler v (expressed as a bit vector) and slot name a, a pattern is stored in the selector units. For each bit v_i in v, one bit is turned on in the same column in the selector array, and also a bit is turned on in column $i+2F$. Which bit—k—in a given column is turned on is based on a randomly selected R-bit subset of the slot name vector a. The subsets are randomly chosen, but wired into the selector, one subset per column. Each subset can be interpreted as an R-bit binary number, to determine k. Positive connections are then made between the R-bit subsets and the kth bit in the column. All the bits in a given column inhibit one another, to form a winner-take-all network.

DUCS uses non-linear Hopfield-Tank units with symmetric connections. (see section 2.9) These units have variable gain, so that they do not initially rise very much in activation, but the gain rises after they receive some activation, and they become saturated after 20 activation updates.

The creation of a slot–name–filler association creates a pattern in the selector. All the bits in the selector are then copied to the concept buffer in the same places; the concept buffer is the same size as the selector. The concept buffer's contents is then used as input to the concept memory. The concept buffer serves as a connector between the concept memory and the selectors.

The concept memory is an associative memory following Willshaw (1981). (see section 2.7). Willshaw's net is useful for storing associations between binary vectors. In this case, each concept is viewed as a one-dimensional vector of length $4Fx2^R$ and Willshaw's memory is used as an auto-associator to complete incomplete patterns. Incomplete patterns are created in the selector units by presentation of one or more slot name/filler pairs. These patterns are copied to the concept buffer, which in turn uses the concept memory to retrieve the concept.

When a particular pattern is clamped into the slot name units, the combination of the activation from these units and from the concept buffer causes the selector units to become activated. This process works even if there is not exactly correct input on the slot name, because there is redundancy in the representation of the slot filler. Since each bit is redundantly represented four times in the code for the filler, and since each of these bits is associated with a different R-bit subset of the slot name, and since these subsets, if $R<<N$, are likely to be disjoint, an error in the slot name will probably not affect more than one of the subsets. Since each column unit in the selector array that is activated by a particular bit in the slot filler is connected positively to all the other three bits that are also activated by that slot filler, if one of the bits is not turned on, and another bit in its column is turned on instead, due to an error, the other three bits will activate it to such an extent so that that the original bit will win out over the other activated bit in the column.

For instance, Touretzky gives the example of trying to retrieve the value of an elephant's "trunk" slot using the pattern for "nose". The slot name pattern "trunk" will most likely replace the name "nose", because there is no slot for nose, and so trunk's filler will be retrieved, and it will reinforce the pattern for trunk.

Of course, the weights have to be set in such a way so that this works properly. All the weights in DUCS are set in advance, and are based on various parameters of the model, such as F, R, and N. Thus updates involve only changes in activation. Connections are symmetric; that is, if node a is connected to node b, a reverse connection exists as well. There are inhibatory connections between a slot filler bit v_i and the bit v_{i+f} which represents its complement; similiarly, there are inhibatory connections between a slot name bit a_i and a_{i+N}. There are exhitatory connections between a bit in the selector and the corresponding bit in the concept buffer. Each bit in the selector is also, as mentioned above, positively connected to R bits in the slot name. Each selector bit in column i is positively connected to the slot filler bit in that column as well as the redundant representation of that bit in column $i+2F$, and negatively connected to the complementary bits in columns $i+F$ and $i+3F$. All the selector bits in a particular column inhibit one another, since only one of them should be activated after relaxation. Relaxation leads to the multiple satisfaction of all the constraints embodied in the foregoing connections.

DUCS is, as a Touretzky points out, a two level architecture. At the bottom level, slot names are used to retrieve fillers; at the top level, slot name/filler pairs are used to retrieve concepts, consisting of whole frames. Both of these processes are basic to a frame-based view of cognition. Touretzky contrasts his approach to that of Derthick (1987), in which constraints between microfeatures composing filler or names are built-in; for instance, the presence of the microfeature "human" would imply the presence of the microfeatures animate and mammal. In DUCS, these constraints are implicit in the connections to the selector units.

4.4. Storing Schemata with a
Complex Neural Architecture

Dolan and Dyer (1987) propose a scheme for implementing schemata in a connectionist network. They adopt a structured, functional approach to implementing connectionist models. They model a system with a complex architecture, and replace functional parts of the architecture with neural networks that perform the function in question.

They note that connectionist models can be classified along the dimension of the degree to which they are are decomposed into functionally differentiated parts. On the one hand we have systems of units, like those of Hopfield, which are relatively homogeneous with respect to connection patterns and neuron behavior. Other models, such as that of Hinton (1986), allow for differentiation of the larger network into groups of units, which each have their own purposes. Dolan and Dyer argue that these more structured systems lose none of the emergent properties associated with the less structured systems, but gain some capabilities. These capabilities are gained, I might add, at the cost of designing a network to be specific to a particular task.

Dolan and Dyer's system is called CRAM, and its goal is to understand fables (short stories). It performs recognition and instantiation of schemata and binding of roles in these schemata. The schemata that they use are similar to the scripts used by Schank and Abelson (1977) in their story-understanding efforts.

When a character in a story is recognized as playing some role in a schema, then the rest of the schema must be instantiated in order to fill other roles and comprehend the rest of the story.

Their system is divided into four components: schema memory, working memory, procedural memory, and a role binder (see Figure 4.2). The procedural memory, which resembles Touretzky and Hinton's (1988) production system (see

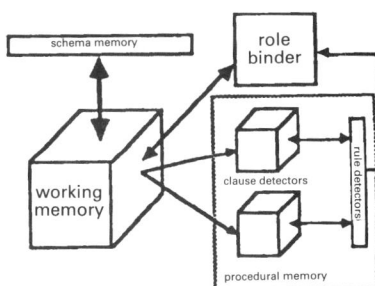

Figure 4.2 The architecture of CRAM (Dolan and Dyer 1987). Reprinted by permission.

section 3.2), is divided into 2 components, the clause detectors and the rule detectors.

The schema memory contains many winner-take-all subnetworks. Each of the subnetworks is connected to the others. Each node in the memory represents an entire schema. Inheritance is implemented by strong positive weights on connections between nodes representing superclasses and nodes representing subclasses. All of the subclasses of a given superclass are in the same winner-take-all network, since they are mutually exclusive. For instance, if a mammal is a dog, it is not also a cat. Exceptions in inheritance are implemented as strong negative connections between schema nodes.

Dolan and Dyer use a feature representation of symbols as bit strings, similar to that used by McClelland and Kawamoto (1986b). In this scheme, each concept is represented by a string of bits indicating, for each of a series of features, whether or not that feature is present in the concept. They initialize their schemata with prototype tokens filling the roles. The idea behind this is to allow for default information to fill roles until more specific information comes in. When the actual role–filler replaces the prototype, some of the prototype's subfeatures—those that do not conflict with the new token—are retained.

They borrow the concept of the unit cube from Hinton and his co-workers (1986a). The unit cube is useful for representing binary relations. In this scheme, a cube is created of units having, in each of its three dimensions, respectively, the number of bits found in the representation for the relation and its two operands, each of which is a symbol represented as described above. Each unit in the cube has a value that is a three-way conjunction of the value found on the respective bits for the three-bit vectors in the relation. This allows for the storage of many relations in a single cube of units. This is the design that they used to store relations in their working memory.

When new assertions enter the working memory, they are also put into a set of units that hold the input relation. These units are input to a unit cube called the probe network. The purpose of the probe network is to retrieve whatever was previously bound to the particular role whose value is being input.

For instance, if we have, for a particular restaurant schema, the role customer, filled by John, this may be expressed as the triple (restaurant customer John), and the first two places (restaurant customer) are input to the probe network. The probe network is represented by conjunctive coding in a unit cube as described above. The old binding, say man, for the customer role, may be readily extracted as a bit vector, because, looking along the dimension of the third symbol of the triple, the unit cube will contain the two dimensional conjunctive coding of the first two two symbols in each relation at each layer of the unit cube in which the third symbol's value is one.

This old binding is used as a key to look up in the working memory all the relations in which it is contained. These relations are stored, one at a time as they are extracted, in a unit cube called the 3-d probe network. They are projected into a two-dimensional image that represents conjunctively the first two symbols in each relation; this is then projected into a 3-d network using the new binding, to represent the new relation. This relation is then inserted into the working memory in place of the one containing the old binding.

Queries to the working memory work basically as follows; bit k in the third symbol will be on if bits i and j are on and bit ijk in the cube is on. This design for a working memory differs from that of Touretzky and Hinton (1985) (see section 3.2), in which triples representing relations are represented by randomly selected receptive fields in a set of units.

There are exhitatory connections between nodes in the schema memory and nodes in the working memory that represent relations that form part of the schema represented by a given schema node. This allows the insertion of assertions into the working memory to trigger a particular schema, and vice versa.

Dolan and Dyer note that this type of treatment of symbolic representation in schemata goes against two dearly-held assumptions of the physical symbol system hypothesis (PSSH) (Newell 1980). The first assumption is that it is possible to make arbitrarily finely graded distinctions between symbols. This is not possible in their system, since everything that could distinguish between two symbols must be encoded in the symbols' representations. Secondly, contrary to the PSSH, variables can no longer be abstract entities used merely to show relationships between slots in a schema, but must be represented in the same way as their values. Thus the type/token distinction disappears.

Another important difference between the connectionist implementation of schemata and the conventional implementation is the absence of pointers in the neural network. One solution to this, Dolan and Dyer note, is to represent pointers by symbols, as Touretzky does in BoltzCONS (see section 2.32). For instance, the list (A (B C)) would be represented by (x A y) (y B C), where x and y are symbols representing pointers. The other alternative that Dolan and Dyer suggest is to use intermediate names for structures. For instance, the recursive frame

> (family-1 mother Sue
>   father Bob
>   mother's-family (family-2 mother alice
>   father joe
>   son herb
>   daughter sue)
>
>   etc.

would be represented as

> (family-1 mother sue)
> (family-1 father Bob)
> (family-1 mother's-family family-2)
> (family-2 mother alice)
> (family-2 father joe)
> (family-2 son herb)
> (family-2 daughter sue)
> etc.

This allows the decomposition of arbitrarily complex frame structures into triples so that they can be represented in a connectionist working memory, like that used by Dolan and Dyer, or Touretzky and Hinton.

4.5. Learning Microfeatures for
Knowledge Representation

Mikkulainen and Dyer (1988) approach the problem of how to represent concepts in a neural network. They contrast their work with that of McClelland and Kawamoto (1986b), in which semantic microfeatures, chosen in advance, were used to represent concepts (see section 7.6). The problem with this approach is that it is difficult to see a principled way of choosing which microfeatures one should use. Often the microfeatures chosen are themselves complex concepts that need to be decomposed, such as "human" or "animate".

Another way to encode concepts is the five layer back-propagation network of Hinton (1986), in which there are is a layer of output units, a layer of input units, a layer of units that represent the output, a layer that represents the input, and a layer of hidden units in the middle (see Figure 4.3). A single unit is on in each of the input and output layers, that is, a local representation is used. This is transformed to a distributed representation by using back-propagation to force layers 2 and 4 in the system to encode the input and output patterns respectively. There are many fewer units doing the encoding than are in the input and output layers—in fact there can be as few as log_2n if the units are all binary-valued. This has the advantage over McClelland and Kawamoto's scheme in that this allows compact representations without having to choose what the semantic microfeatures are before the fact.

Mikkulainen and Dyer extend this by allowing their architecture (which they call FGREP, for Forming Global Representations) to remember what these representations are while they are being learned. They do

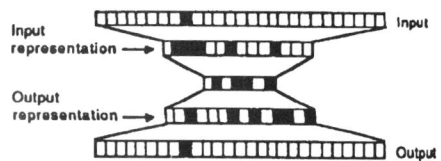

Figure 4.3 The five-layer network of Hinton (1986). Reprinted by permission from Mikkulainen and Dyer (1988).

this by adding a module to their network called the lexicon. The lexicon stores particular input and output patterns. For instance, in a language processing task, each word in the system is represented by a pattern in the lexicon. However, the pattern that is used changes over the course of the learning.

Their system has a network consisting of three layers: a layer of input units, a layer of output units, and a layer of hidden units, completely connected in a feed-forward fashion. Each of these units has a real-valued activation ranging from 0 to 1; the weights range between -1 and 1, and are also real-valued. Both the layer of input units and the output units can hold several "words" (patterns) from the lexicon, which is the other component of their system. The system uses back-propagation. The error signals, however, are back-propagated an additional step to *change the input pattern*. This change in the input pattern changes the representations of the patterns in the lexicon that formed the input pattern. The next time the (now altered) input pattern is presented, it will be closer to the old target output pattern. Of course, the output pattern itself will have changed, since it is also composed of patterns from the lexicon. Thus back-propagation is "shooting at a moving target", as the authors put it.

They applied this system to the problem of assigning roles to the sentence constituents that McClelland and Kawamoto used (see section 7.6). They used a subset of the sentences used in McClelland and Kawamoto's work, with the roles agent, act, patient, instrument, and modifier-of-patient, and the syntactic categories subject, verb, object, and object-of-with. There were 19 sentence generators of the type "the human ate", "the animal broke the fragile-object", etc.

The nouns in the system were classified into groups for the purpose of generating sentences; for instance, "plate" was classified as a "fragile-object", and "dog" as an animal, so the sentence "the dog broke the plate" was one of the sentences that was generated. In this sentence, the dog was assigned to the agent role, and the plate the patient role. In order to learn this role assignment, the patterns corresponding to "dog", "broke", and "plate" were concatenated on the input units in the slots reserved for subject, verb, and object (the object-of-"with" category is empty, in this case). At the same time, the patterns for "dog", "broke", and "plate" were put in the output units in the slots for "agent", "act", and "patient" (the output slots for "instrument" and "modifier" were empty.) Back-propagation was applied, changing the patterns for "dog", "broke", and "plate". The new patterns were then stored in the lexicon.

Each word was initially encoded with a random pattern of 12 units. Over time, nouns that fell into the same class tended to evolve similar patterns. Of the 1553 sentences created by their sentence generators, using a small set of nouns, the system was trained on 1515 sentences, and the remaining 38 were used to test the performance of the network.

They tested the network both on these 38 novel sentences and on sentences that the network had seen before. Performance was good, resulting in correct role assignment in most cases, with role assignment being ambiguous in those cases in which words have more than one role assignment. For instance, they cite the word "bat", which can either be, as the kind of bat that is a flying animal, the agent of an action or, as the kind of bat used in baseball, the instrument of a "hitting" action. In this case, the role units are activated to the extent that this object tends to play one or the other role in the sentences given in learning. For instance, if "bat" is more frequently an instrument than an agent, the pattern for bat would tend to be dominated by the characteristics of the baseball bat. In this case, the system would not perform well with the bat used as agent.

There is little difference in performance between the novel and previously seen sentences. Because of the distributed nature of the representations, the system also exhibits graceful performance degradation with loss of units. Mikkulainen and Dyer refer to their representations as "holographic" because they do a reasonable job of classifying the words if some or even most of the units comprising the representation are omitted. Even a single unit exhibits the classification of the words nicely. They attempted to interpret each unit semantically as a microfeature, but were unable to do so—the units, most likely, were functioning as complex disjunctions and conjunctions of many of the microfeatures that are useful in partitioning the space of nouns.

They applied a merge clustering algorithm to the representations (Kohonen 1982), in which, at each time step, representations that were most similar to each other on a Euclidean distance metric were merged. The results confirmed the expected classifications; for instance, words representing food—e.g. "pasta" and "cheese" were merged early. They also got a feeling for the topological arrangement of the representations by reducing each representation, viewed as a 12-dimensional vector, to a two-dimensional vector using Kohonen's (1988) self-organizing feature map (see section 2.18). This showed them that ambiguous words such as bat and chicken (the latter viewed as food and as a live animal) are intermediate in representation between their two meanings. The exact distance between the word and its two meanings is distorted in the two-dimensional "collapsing" of the vector, but the topological relationships between representations are preserved.

The main advantage of this system is its lexicon. However, the lexicon is a non-connectionist system as it stands, although it could probably be implemented in a connectionist system. In this work it acts more like just a conventional memory.

Because of this lexicon, this system—and other systems built using the FGREP architecture—can communicate with one another and become parts of a larger modular system. For instance, Mikkulainen and Dyer suggest that there could be another FGREP system that relates sequences of actions to causal relations, and that this system could take its "lexical" entries from the states of the hidden units in the case role system, thus encoding the "shallow semantics" (role semantics) compactly for the purposes of understanding the semantics of causation. On a lower level, the sentence-role system could communicate with syntactic/phonetic systems, to create a modular language understanding system. Building such systems is essential for performing comprehensive AI tasks.

4.6. Implementing Evidential Reasoning and Inheritance Hierarchies

Shastri (1988) has adopted ideas from semantic nets, evidential reasoning, and inheritance hierarchies to develop "A Connectionist Approach to Knowledge Representation". His goals are to eliminate the need for an external homunculus for responding to queries; instead he wants to have queries, which are expressed as patterns of activation in the network, directly elicit other concepts.

He wants to constrain the possible set of inferences that the network can form to those inferences that people seem to make automatically. These inferences include inheritance of class properties to instances of those classes, and recognition of class membership.

He wants, also, in his model, to incorporate knowledge about how things are correlated, to deal with things like exceptions. For instance, Shastri gives the example of the facts that Dick (Nixon) is a Quaker, Quakers tend to be pacifists, Dick is a Republican, and Republicans tend to be non-pacifists. If the facts "Quakers tend to be pacifists" and "Republicans tend to be non-pacifists" are expressed as all-or-none entailments, that is, "Quakers are pacifists" and "Republicans are non-pacifists", then there are conflicting ideas about Dick. If, however, the relationships are expressed as statistical correlations, based on experience, then the probability of Dick being a pacifist can be estimated by using rules to combine statistical evidence. This does not preclude the existence of some necessary truths, in which a proposition A implies another proposition B in all cases.

He defines his conceptual structure formally. A concept is similar to a frame, that is, it is a set of (attribute, value) pairs (Minsky 1975). There are two kinds of attributes: properties and structural links. Examples of properties are color, dimensions, and weight. Structural links are such relations as "is-a" (class membership), "is-a-part-of", and "occurs-during". The values of attributes are themselves concepts. Thus, in terms of logic, attributes correspond to 2-place predicates. N-place predicates can always be decomposed into 2-place predicates, in order to express arbitrarily complex relations.

He divides concepts into tokens and types—tokens correspond to perceptual instances of types (classes). His model also stores, for each attribute/value pair in a concept, the number of times that pair has been observed, so, for instance, for the concept "apple", the attribute/value pair color/red might have been observed 30 times and the pair color/green might have been observed 20 times. (More precisely, the ratios of the frequencies to the actual number of observations are stored.)

This frequency information is used in the probabilistic inference methods of the system. Is-a links are viewed as special in his system; they are relations between concepts, and are all-or-none; his system does not deal with fuzzy set membership (Zadeh 1973).

The frequency information can also be used to determine the most likely value for a property: it is simply the value with the highest frequency. Given a set of concepts, and the description of a concept in terms of attribute/value pairs, the frequency information can also be utilized to determine which of the concepts best fits the set of pairs.

The frequency distribution of the independent properties does not fully constrain the frequencies of combined properties. For instance, to use one of Shastri's examples, if we know that 30% of apples are sour, 70% are sweet, 60% are red, and 40% green, this does not determine what percentage are red and sweet, for instance. This may be formalized by having all the values of one property on one dimension of a matrix, and the values of the other on the other dimension, so that the cells in the matrix a_{ij} represent co-occurrence frequencies. Only the sums of the rows and columns are known, not the a_{ij} themselves. The a_{ij} matrix is referred to by Shastri as a macroconfiguration. Given no other information, it is most logical to assume the most likely macroconfiguration meeting the constraints on row and column sums. Shastri uses probability theory and a mathematical technique called Lagrange multipliers to show that $a_{ij} = R_i C_j$, where R_i and C_j are the row and column sums of the row and column in question. Shastri points out that this formula, which he calls the maximum entropy configuration, is equivalent to Bayesian inference theory if it is assumed that the probabilities of two attribute/value pairs are independent, because this means, for instance, that

$$P((red,sweet)/apple)=P(red/apple)P(sweet/apple)$$

If additional information about co-occurrence frequencies is known, then it can be incorporated as additional constraints to the maximum entropy method, which can still arrive at a solution.

Inheritance is used to determine the frequency distribution of values of a property for a subset if no better information is available. For instance, if we know that 20% of cars are blue, and we have no other information about the color distribution of Toyotas, then it is reasonable to assume that 20% of Toyotas are blue. Given an inheritance hierarchy, it is most reasonable to inherit this distribution information about a particular attribute/value pair for a concept A from that category which contains A most immediately; for instance if A is a Toyota, and 30% of Japanese cars are blue, but only 20% of cars in general are blue, then it makes more sense to assume that 30% of Toyotas are blue, since Toyotas are more similar to Japanese cars than they are to cars in general (one presumes). This is what Shastri calls the principle of relevance, that is, that the most relevant category is selected.

If a particular concept C is a member of a series of concepts $B_1,...,B_N$ such that none of the B_i are subsets of any of the others, and each of the B_i has a particular incidence of a property/value pair P (for instance, 20% of the members of B_1 are red in color, in B_2, 30% are, etc.), the question is how to determine the property/value incidence for that value in C, e.g., how many of C are red. The set B_i of concepts relevant to C on concept P is referred to as $\Gamma(C, P)$. He shows that the best estimate for the incidence of a particular attribute/value pair is estimated by combining values upwards in the conceptual hierarchy to determine the incidence of that property/value pair in the category Ω that is the most specific and includes all the $B_i's$. This is recursively computed from the tree of categories whose root is Ω and whose leaves are the B_i. Without going into the specifics, the incidence values amount to a form of weighted geometric average of all the frequency values for the given property/value pair for all the $B_i's$ and the categories that subsume them, up to Ω.

Given this formal theory of concepts and evidential reasoning, Shastri goes on to implement it in a connectionist network. He uses six kinds of nodes: (1-3) nodes representing concepts, properties and values, (4) binder nodes that bind concept, property, and value nodes together, (5) enable nodes (which allow the network to distinguish between recognition and inheritance queries, the two main types of queries that the system is designed to deal with), and (6) relay-nodes, which implement links between subset and superset nodes. (Shastri did this work at the University of Rochester, the home of complex nodes.)

Each of the concept nodes has six connection sites. The first site, which he calls the *RELAY* site, has connections to parents and children of the concept in the is-a hierarchy; each is-a relationship is represented by two links, one in each direction, between the parent and child nodes. The strength of the parent to child link is given by the ratio of the parent's frequency of occurrence divided by the child's. The weight of the child to parent link is the reciprocal of the parent to child link.

Binder nodes function in associating property/value pairs with concepts and concept/property pairs with values. The first kind of binder node has a special site where a property/value pair gives input, as well as a special site called *inherit*. All three of these inputs must be present in order for the binder node to give output to the relevant concept. Another set of binder nodes work similarly in associating concept/property pairs with values; they receive input from a special node called recognize. Inheritance is implemented in the following manner: if B is a superset of A that has property P, and there is no superset of A that is more specific than B that also has property P, then there is a connection between the binder node for the B-P relationship and the binder node for the A-P relationship, with a weight equal to the ratio of the incidence of the properties in the two nodes. The concept nodes combine evidence, from the various concepts from which they are inheriting it, in the geometric fashion that was mentioned above; the ratios serve to make the incidences relative to one another so as to use them as fractions in computing the total evidence. The potential of a given node is the product of these fractions.

As well as having a potential, each node in his network has a binary state, inactive or active, so that only some nodes are active at any given time. Binding nodes are active only if they receive input from all three inputs mentioned above; concept nodes are active if they receive any input at all. The potential of a binding node reflects the incidence of the (concept, property, value) triple it represents; the potential of a concept node indicates to what degree that concept is present in the particular situation given to the network.

Shastri translated his "Quaker" example given above into a network. There are concept nodes corresponding to pacifist, non-pacifist, belief, person, Quaker, Republican, and Dick. Dick is a subset (an instance is equivalent to a subset in this model) of Quaker and Republican to some degree; these categories are in turn subsets of person. Pacifist and non-pacifist are both subsets of the concept belief. Person, Quaker, Republican, and Dick are all connected to the nodes pacifist and non-pacifist, via a binder node which is also connected to the property node "has belief".

Thus, for concept Dick (as well as the other three concepts just mentioned), there is a property "has belief" which has the possible values pacifist and non-pacifist. The network is initialized by clamping (fixing as active) the nodes inherit, Dick, and "has belief". This is a query as to what Dick's belief is. Because of the connections, after a short time the pacifist node settles to a potential of

$$\frac{(number\ of\ pacifist\ Quakers)(number\ of\ pacifist\ Republicans)}{(number\ of\ persons\ with\ beliefs)(number\ of\ pacifists)}$$

due to the various connections I have described above. The pacifist node receives input from the person node, which receives input from the Republican and Quaker nodes, which receives input from the Dick node. The connections are set up so that the pacifist node receives activation corresponding to the probability that a person is a Quaker Republican pacifist. A similar formula holds for the node corresponding to non-pacifism.

He also applied his network formalism to problems involving inheritance from multiple categories.   He built a system that represented fruits and   vegetables as are edible things with the properties color and taste.   Various things are known about the distribution of properties with respect both to instances of fruits and vegetables such as apples and carrots and the more general categories themselves. Shastri's system could answer questions about the frequency distribution of properties for entities such as a red sweet fruit or vegetable.   The system utilizes local and inherited information in arriving at the frequency distribution of entities it settles on.

Since Shastri's nodes are so complex, it is hard to see how they could be biologically implemented as single neurons; more likely they would have to be small clusters of neurons.   It is also unclear how binding nodes, which effectively implement ternary relations, could come to have this function among a set of nodes that have come to represent concepts.   There is a biologically plausible learning rule for the strength of connections between concept nodes: a Hebbian rule that strengthens the association between pairs of nodes that co-occur. Since Shastri's weights are based on relative frequency of occurrence, these are roughly compatible with such a rule.

5

Speech Recognition and Synthesis

5.1. Introduction

Speech recognition and synthesis are problems that naturally lend themselves to a connectionist analysis. For one thing, speech naturally is hierarchically structured, with different aspects of the speech signal combining to form phonemes, which in turn combine to form words. Speech is context- and speaker-dependent; phonemes and words sound different in different contexts and when spoken by different people. All of these characteristics of speech indicate that it is well suited to processing in a highly parallel, interactive and hierarchical fashion, all of which can be accomplished in a multi-layer connectionist network.

There are at least two ways that speech can be processed in a connectionist network. One is to lay the speech signal out spatially across a layer of input units, and allow different parts of the speech signal to interact via connections to units higher up in the network. This approach is taken by the TRACE system (McClelland & Elman, 1986a), which is discussed in this chapter. The other method is to present only a time slice of the speech signal to the input units, and present subsequent slices in their turn to the same set of input units. In order to combine information from different time slices, it is necessary to build some sort of memory into the network, such as self-loops that allow internal units to retain older patterns of activation, or additional input units that duplicate the old activation pattern in the hidden units and recycle it through the network.

This second approach is taken by the work of Hopfield and Tank (1987) and that of Watrous and Shastri (1987). Hopfield and Tank view a speech signal as a sequence of states. State detectors, which are their input units, output based on the probability that that state is present at a given point in time. These signals are integrated over time to accomplish word recognition. Watrous and Shastri took an approach that is similar in spirit. Their input layer was comprised of 16 units, which represented the amplitudes of 16 bandpass filters applied to the speech signal. Units above the input layer had self-links that allow temporal integration of the speech signal. Similar work was also done by Lang (1987).

Speech synthesis is an easier problem for computers than speech recognition is. This is because many different sequences of sounds can be interpreted as the same sequence of words, so speech production is relatively unconstrained, unlike recognition, which must give a single interpretation to its input. We consider two approaches to speech production in a connectionist network, that of Reggia and his co-workers (1988) and Sejnowski and Rosenberg's NETtalk (1986). These two systems take sharply different approaches to the production of speech from text. Reggia and his co-workers' system is based on the analysis of the process of reading aloud. Reggia and his co-workers model two complementary pathways for this process, one that maps strings of letters, called graphemes, to phonemes, and the other, which maps whole written words to their entire stored speech patterns. They built a system that employs both of these pathways in parallel.

Sejnowski and Rosenberg's NETtalk takes a more naive (or at least agnostic) approach to speech production. They allow the back-propagation algorithm to learn the relationship between text and speech, using a feed-forward perceptron consisting of input (text), hidden, and output (speech) layers. After the network had been trained, they analyzed its behavior to determine what it was paying attention to in the text in determining how it was pronounced, and discovered some interesting rules implicit in the network's behavior.

5.2. Comparing Algorithms for Speech Recognition

Lippmann and Gold (1987) compared the performance of several different algorithms for speech recognition. They note that the best current algorithms use hidden Markov models (HMMs) (Rabiner & Juang 1986, Bahl, Jelinek & Mercer 1983) and they consider a neural network implementation of a particular HMM. HMMs are still considerably worse than people at speech recognition.

Lippmann and Gold note that the best speech recognizers can typically be trained to recognize 100 words spoken in isolation with 99% accuracy, and 2000 words spoken with pauses in between them, drawn from office memos (a constrained domain), with up to 95% accuracy. More advances need to be made before a machine will be able to successfully process connected speech from a variety of speakers. They note that neural networks offer hope of improving recognition performance, because they compute in parallel, and because they can learn from experience.

Speech recognition, as currently conceived, is basically a matching problem. Speech waveforms are broken down into chunks or segments, and each of these is spectrally analyzed using a fast Fourier transform, bandpass filters, or the like. These spectra are then compared to examplar word spectra, and a distance metric is computed. These spectra sequences have to be aligned temporally with the exemplar, because of variations in speaking rate between different people. The word is selected that receives the best matching score.

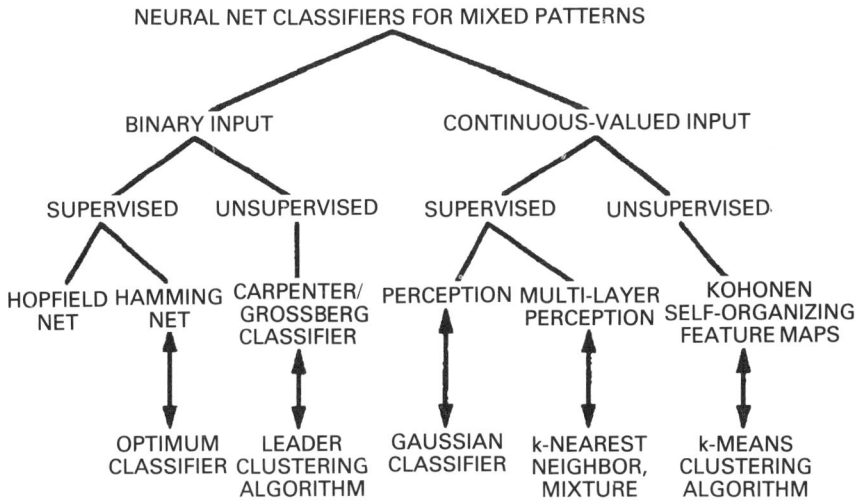

NEURAL NET CLASSIFIERS FOR MIXED PATTERNS

BINARY INPUT   CONTINUOUS-VALUED INPUT

SUPERVISED   UNSUPERVISED   SUPERVISED   UNSUPERVISED

HOPFIELD HAMMING   CARPENTER/   PERCEPTION   MULTI-LAYER   KOHONEN
NET   NET   GROSSBERG   PERCEPTION SELF-ORGANIZING
                    CLASSIFIER   FEATURE MAPS

OPTIMUM   LEADER   GAUSSIAN   k-NEAREST   k-MEANS
CLASSIFIER CLUSTERING   CLASSIFIER   NEIGHBOR,   CLUSTERING
            ALGORITHM   MIXTURE   ALGORITHM

Figure 5.1. Taxonomy of neural networks used in speech recognition (Lippmann and Gold 1987). Reprinted by permission.

Lippmann and Gold organize six neural network algorithms that are useful for this word classification task in a taxonomy (see Figure 5.1) They note that five of the six networks are close to algorithms that were used in earlier approaches to speech recognition, except that they are explicitly parallelized and adaptive.

They compare the performance of a two-, three-, and four-layer perceptron with a standard k-nearest neighbor classifier on the speech recognition task (Duda & Hart 1973). They used the back-propagation algorithm to train the perceptrons.

They used the Texas Instruments Isolated Word Data Base (Doddington & Shalk 1981). The five classifiers were trained on the spoken versions of the first seven monosyllabic numbers (one, two, three, four, five, six, and eight), each repeated ten times during training, and for each of the 16 individuals whose speech was digitized in the TI database. They used perceptron classifiers with a variety of different numbers of hidden units.

The k-nearest neighbor classifier performed best (6.0% classification error rate), then the best three layer perceptron (7.7%), then the Gaussian classifier (8.7%), and finally the two layer perceptron (14.4%). The addition of hidden units beyond 16 per layer did not prove necessary, since no significant improvements in performance were achieved with this addition. Although the four layer perceptrons performed only about as well as the three-layer ones after their weights converged (using the back-propagation algorithm), the convergence was much faster, less than 2000 trials in all cases. The three layer nets having a large number of hidden units took over 6000 trials to converge, and the two layer perceptron took more than 29,000 trials to converge. If the classification process is viewed as a process of placing stimuli into regions in an n-dimensional feature space, the four layer perceptrons have a clear advantage in convergence, since they can more readily construct the required boundary surfaces in this space, apparently because the four layer perceptrons tend to start out with surfaces near the required ones.

5.3. Speech Recognition as Sequence Comparison

Hopfield and Tank (1987) designed an analog neural network that is capable of recognizing sequences of states. This problem is common to the analysis of visual motion, of speech, and of DNA sequences. It is the problem of interpreting sequences of stimuli by grouping them into adjacent sets which can be interpreted as a single category. For instance, if the word "hello" is one of the categories that one wants to recognize, then the problem is recognizing the individual phonemes in "hello" and then recognizing the series of phonemes as the word. Two instances of a particular word can vary in many ways; phonemes can be missing, they can be replaced by other, similar phonemes, or extra phonemes can be inserted.

Hopfield and Tank ground their work in the theory of sequence comparison (Sankoof & Kruskal 1983). If a, b, and g are the stimulus states forming a category (in the case of speech, phonemes or shorter speech chunks), and s_1, s_2, and s_3 are the categories (words in speech), composed of sequences of states, then there exists a probability distribution $p_a(t)$ defining the probability that state a is found a time t before the end of the sequence comprising a particular category, say s_1. These probability distributions are of a Gaussian form, with their peaks being in the middle of the time interval in which the particular state is most likely to be found.

Hopfield and Tank's sequence recognition network is based on the fact that once we detect a particular state in the sequence, we know the probability distribution that describes when the sequence of states is going to end. This is because we know (from our detector) when the state ends, since we know when it began and how long it is, and we know the probability distribution of how long before the end of the sequence a state is supposed to occur, we can look at it the other way around, and that gives us the probability distribution of when the whole category is going to end.

If the sequence of states does in fact form an instance of a particular category s_1, then all the probability distributions should add in phase, peaking at the time when s_1 is supposed to end. No other category should receive as high a peak, because no other category will have its probability distributions add in phase. Thus the correct category should "win" a competition between all the categories.

Hopfield and Tank implement such a competition in a layered, feed-forward neural network in which input units that are state detectors are connected to output units that detect sequences (categories). The time-layered probability distribution is handled by having each state detector unit output, to those sequence units representing sequences in which that state is found, a signal that varies temporally according to the aforementioned probability distribution. The sequence recognition units are organized in a winner-take-all network, so that only one of them can become fully activated at once, the one receiving the most input.

Hopfield and Tank's hardware implementation of this network was limited to the problem of recognizing a few words as spoken by a single speaker. They were forced to make certain approximations to an ideal network, such as the fact that they did not allow arbitrary temporal probability distributions in their circuits, but used a fixed set of time delay functions.

During the operation of Hopfield and Tank's machine, many of the input detector units are active but only a single output word characterization unit is active. The inputs were the results of measurements of signal strength at various frequencies along the audible frequency spectrum, along with an input representing the rate of change in the sound volume. The inputs are passed through a linear programming circuit which passes them all through to the output if they are all small, but if the inputs are large, it selects only one of them. Thus it acts as a winner-take-all network only for a strong input, allowing it to defeat other inputs. This makes sense, because a strong input represents a high degree of certainty. In any given time period, the linear programming circuit selects the input that corresponds to the strongest formant in the speech. (A formant is a single frequency-band component of a speech signal.) Hopfield and Tank note that their system is not very robust with respect to changes in pronunciation by the speaker which cause certain formants to be de-emphasized and others to be emphasized.

They hand-wired the connections in their circuit by measuring the outputs of the detectors as the words were input. If detector P_i was active at time t during the utterance of a word, a positive (time-delayed, according to the probability distribution) connection was made between it and the output unit corresponding to the word. All the other detectors were connected with inhibitory connections to the word, so that other words would inhibit this word, since they would excite the other detectors.

Hopfield and Tank achieved good performance on the eight words that their circuit was wired to handle. Their circuit was able to tolerate a 30% variation in the speed with which words were spoken.

They suggested the use of a modified Hebbian learning rule in order to improve network performance. The difference between their rule and the classical Hebb rule is that instead of changing the weight $T_{i\text{-}o}$ of the connection between input and output based on their cross-correlated activation strength V, with the formula

$$\partial T_{i\text{-}o} = <V_i(t)V_o(t)>$$

the input response is replaced with the immediate time-delayed response of the input unit, *effect(i)* (the probability distribution function). Thus we have

$$\partial T_{i\text{-}o} = <effect_i(t)V_o(t)>$$

Hopfield and Tank suggest that the network can adapt to a particular speaker's variation, or possibly the variation between speakers, in the production of utterances, using this formula.

They note that their model is asynchronous; that is, it operates without a system clock. The analog circuitry of the machine allows irregularly spaced temporal events to contribute to the recognition of a word.

A model such as this could be made of other recognition processes that involve interpretation of a stream of data, notably natural language understanding. Provision would have to be handle recursive embedding in a sentence and long-distance relationships between constituents of sentences.

5.4. The Temporal Flow Model

Watrous and Shastri (1987) trained a connectionist model to learn phonetic features from sampled speech. Their first goal was to train the model to discriminate between the word pair "no" and "go", which are called a minimal pair since the two words differ on only one phonetic feature. They used one male and one female voice.

A three-layer connectionist network was used, which they call their temporal flow model. There were 16 input units, used to input the strength of the speech signal at various frequencies, produced by multiple bandpass filters. They called it the temporal flow model because the values presented at the input units change over time. Thus earlier input values were "remembered" by units higher up in the network because activation has flowed up from the input units. They used units with a sigmoid output function. Units in the second and third layers had links to themselves so that their values are maintained by positive self-feedback. This allows earlier activation flows to be "remembered" so that they can be integrated with later ones.

Watrous and Shastri used a modified form of the back-propagation algorithm to train their network, in order to handle the self-links (which a strictly feed-forward network does not have.)

In their first experiment, they had only two output units, which were all that were necessary for the "no"-"go" minimal pair discrimination. They trained the network using an output function that was linearly increasing in time; for instance, for "go", one unit was supposed to increase from 0.5 to 1.0, and the other to decrease from 0.5 to 0. This corresponded to the gradual integration of evidence over time. In the case of "no", the units were trained to have the opposite behavior.

When Watrous and Shastri trained their network, they did not get a monotonically decreasing error function, because the back-propagation algorithm was not devised to deal with continuously changing input conditions. Although the back-propagation algorithm did not proceed monotonically to a minimal error value, it did reach such a value, and the weights in the minimal network were the ones that they selected for further study. This network was able to clearly distinguish between the "go" and "no" stimuli; in the case of each one, one of the units had its activation driven down and the other one had it driven up, over the temporal course of the stimulus. The response was not the simple ramp that the network was trained on, but it clearly distinguished between the two stimuli, without needing to be told where in the temporal sequence of the stimulus to look for a distinguishing feature. Effectively, it had learned to detect the burst of sound that comes at the beginning of a "g" sound that distinguishes it from an "n"; thus the n was the default.

The logical extension of this experiment would be to a network that could distinguish between *n* stimuli using *n-1* features. Their next experiment was to discriminate between three consonants (b, d and g) in one network with three output units, and six vowels (i,e,a,u,U,¡) in another network with six output units. One wonders if they would have been able to achieve the same results with a binary encoding of the output on the output units, instead of a localist representation. Both networks used 16 hidden units.

They used as stimuli the 18 combinations of the consonants (b,d,g) with the vowels (i,e,a,u,U,¡). They selected the transitional portion of each syllable, and used it alone as input, to reduce processing load.

In this experiment, they used a second-order optimization algorithm called the Broyden–Fletcher–Goldfard–Shanno algorithm (Fletcher 1980), which uses both the first and second derivatives of the error surface to achieve more rapid convergence to a minimum. Instead of a linear target function, such as that chosen in the "no"/"go" experiment, they used a Gaussian function shaped like a hump. This allowed unit response to decay back to a value of 0.5 (neutral response) after each speech event, so that the network could readily be presented with a series of events.

Because of the second order optimization, they were able to achieve uniform gradient descent, along the error surface, to a minimum. They got network responses that were similar to the target functions presented during training. For each vowel and consonant, they were able to train each network so that one of the output units (in either the vowel or the consonant network) would respond to that sound.

Watrous and Shastri make three conclusions about their work: (1) The networks were able to learn the discrimination task without having to be shown both stimuli at once. (2) The consonant network was able to discriminate between three different consonants in the context of six different vowels, which is surprising given that these sounds look different in those different contexts. This bodes well for the ability to extend this approach to more complex stimuli. (3) The temporal-flow model is workable (which was not at all obvious at the outset).

5.5. The TRACE model

The TRACE model of speech understanding (McClelland & Elman 1986a) contains three levels of units, corresponding to words, phonemes, and features of speech. The model, in its feature units, represents a time slice of speech. For each feature, and each quantized time unit in the slice, there is an array of units representing the possible values of that feature. Thus, each feature has a two dimensional array of units associated with it. Three of the features are vocalization, diffuseness, and acuteness, each of which, at any point of the speech stream, can range from a low to a high value; there are other features as well. For each phoneme, and for every three time slices, there is also a unit, again forming a rectangular array with time on one dimension and the phonemes on the other. The phoneme detector units span six time slices, so they overlap with each other. This is also the case with the word detectors; the model is not very economical, especially because of the necessity for duplication of the word detectors.

McClelland and Elman refer to their entire network of units as the TRACE, because it is a trace of the analysis of the speech input. All units are active at all time slices, not just the units that directly respond to the current time slice; processing of previous time slices continues in parallel with the initial processing of the current time slice.

Excitatory connections exist between units within a level and in different levels that are mutually compatible. For instance, if a particular phoneme has a high value on a particular feature, say the vocalization, units representing high values on that feature have bi-directional excitatory connections to the unit for that feature at each time slice. Features, words or phonemes that are mutually incompatible have bi-directional inhibitory connections between them; for instance, at each time slice the units representing all the phonemes that are centered at that time slice inhibit one another in a winner-take-all network.

Context-sensitive effects are modeled by the use of multiplicative "gating" connections. They give the example of the fact that the phonemic features of a /t/ are altered when it is then followed by an /i/; the unit for an /i/ at a given time slice therefore multiplicatively gates connections between feature detectors and the unit for /t/ at the previous time slice.

McClelland and Elman developed two versions of their model, TRACE I and TRACE II. TRACE I processed real speech, consonant-vowel pairs spoken by a male. It contained detectors for each of 15 input features; the input was divided into 5 millisecond time slices.

TRACE II was not concerned with feature detection and how features vary between phonemes and within a given phoneme depending on its context. Rather, they used "mock speech" which had the proper values for the features of each phoneme already set. TRACE II wanted to account for the way words influence phoneme perception top-down. TRACE II simplifies speech in that it only uses 7 input features at each time slice instead of 15. Each phoneme has a set (relative) value on each of these 7 features. Each phoneme takes 11 time slices, and its characteristic feature pattern grows in strength and then fades. The peaks of adjacent phonemes are six time slices apart. The phonemes that were supported are a subset of the full set of phonemes found in English; the system could detect 211 words composed only of this subset.

The TRACE II model accounted well for psycholinguistic findings on phoneme perception. They did an experiment in which they presented a phoneme intermediate between "b" and "p", followed by the phonemes /l/, /u/, and /g/ as in plug. After the "u" phoneme is presented, the words "plug", "plus", "blush", and "blood" become activated, which are the only words that the system knows about that fit this pattern. When the "g" enters the system, "plug" wins the competition between these four words, and top-down reinforcement flows to the "b" phoneme, which wins the competition with the "p". Until then, the phoneme remains ambiguous. This winner-take-all behavior on the phoneme and word level models the categorical perception characteristic of people.

The TRACE model exhibits several other properties of human word perception. For instance, the model can perceive a word better if it is preceded by a valid word, so that it knows better where the boundary is between the two words. It cannot tell that a word has ended until somewhat into the next word, in the case when one word is the beginning of another (for example, bell and bellows). It is able to recover from a badly specified beginning of a word, even though the model is heavily dependent on word beginnings to start to activate words.

The major deficiency of the TRACE model, which McClelland and Elman admit, is the local nature of the model and the enormous number of units and connections that this entails. If connections and weights are learned such as the multiplicative, gating connections between a phoneme's features and the following phoneme mentioned earlier, it is difficult to find a mechanism to generalize this learning across the entire network. This problem is common to a lot of connectionist networks that use local representations; most handle it by doing the learning in some sort of central network, which then distributes it, in the manner of McClelland's (1985) Connection Information Distributor (CID). McClelland and Elman conclude that some combination of a central representation and local, temporally specific representation are required.

5.6. A Model of the Print-to-speech Transformation Process

Reggia, Marsland, and Berndt (1988) developed a connectionist model of the transformation of text to speech. There are two competing theories of how people do this. In one, each grapheme—one or more letters in written text that correspond to a phoneme—is mapped onto a phoneme, and the phonemes are then concatenated together in the speech stream. In the other, the entire word is read, and then its entire sound pattern, stored as part of lexical memory, is uttered. Evidence for the former method is that people have no trouble pronouncing non-words that look like words, e.g., "kint"; evidence for the latter is that people have no trouble pronouncing words with irregular spellings. These two methods need not be exclusive of one another; in fact, many people believe that both operate in parallel in the process of reading aloud.

Reggia and his co-workers embodied such a two-process model of reading in a network. The network has three types of nodes; grapheme nodes, word nodes, and phoneme nodes. Activation flows both directly from grapheme to phoneme nodes (which they call the grapheme–phoneme correspondence (GRC) route) and through word nodes (which they call the lexical route), that is, from grapheme to word to phoneme nodes. For each letter and phoneme position in the input or output stream, they had to represent all the possible values that each of these could take on. They used a study by Hanna and co-workers (1966) to arrive at a set of 168 graphemes and 48 phonemes for English. They also used this study to determine the possible grapheme-to-phoneme mappings. Each grapheme was connected to all the phoneme nodes in the same position that represented possible pronunciations for it. The weights on these connections were set to observed probabilities of each grapheme–phoneme pair, given the grapheme. Thus the weights on connections coming out of each grapheme node summed to one.

Grapheme group k in the input represented all those graphemes that participate in letter position k of a word. Each grapheme in group k was connected to all the words in which that grapheme was found in position k. If a given grapheme was connected in such a manner to n words, the strength of each connection was set to $1/n$.

Thus the network is feed-forward, with all positive connections, and two distinct pathways for activation. This is what

Reggia and his co-workers refer to as indirect competition, unlike other competitive schemes, such as in competitive learning (see sections 2.15-2.17), in which there is lateral inhibition between alternative nodes/pathways. This is more akin to integration of information from parallel sources. Their network is designed explicitly for this kind of competition.

They used the following activation update rule:

$$a_i' = k_i(in_i - 2a_i(1-in_i))(1-a_i)$$

where a_i is the prior activation of the *ith* node, a_i' is the activation after the update, and in_i is the total input received at the node. This rule causes a winner-take-all behavior, as simulation demonstrates. When all the a_i are initialized to zero, the a_i always stay between 0 and 1, because of the behavior of the above rule, and converge over time to one or the other extreme.

In the case of grapheme and phoneme nodes, the constant k_i was set to 1; in the case of word nodes it was set to a logarithmic function of the prior probability of the word being present at all (based on the word's frequency in English), thus it takes more evidence and more time for a less frequent word to be recognized and activated. The model was initialized with the grapheme nodes that were present in the input receiving an input of one and all others receiving zero input. The output of a given node along a given path is based on what proportion of activation should be sent to that node based on the competitive strength of that node. The competitive strength c_{ik} of a path from node i to node k is defined as

$$c_{ik} = \frac{w_{ik}a_i(t)}{\sum_m w_{mk}a_m(t)}$$

where m ranges over all the nodes to which node k is connected. Thus node k receives input based on not only the activation flow of the path from i to k, but also the relative strength of the path from i to k compared to all the other paths, from m to k. The output from i to k is: $out_{ik}(t) = c_{ik}(t)a_k(t)$. The input at each node is set based on all the outputs that it receives: $in_i(t) = 1 - \Pi_k (1-out_{ik}(t))$. Reggia and his co-workers devised this numerical version of the "or" function, because it increases with an increase in any one of the out_{ik}.

They contrast this approach with that of ordinary feed-forward neural networks, in which the input to a node is almost always a weighted sum of the activations of the nodes inputting to it, which remains stable in time. Here nodes compete to receive input, those with activation tend to get more, and those with less tend to get less. Thus the system evolves—relaxes—to a stable state.

Each word receives input from each of n graphemes in it. The input from the grapheme number p at node i is given by $in_{ip}(t) = 1 - \Pi_k(1 - out_{ik})$, where k ranges over the input nodes. This simulates the "or" function, since, ideally, only one of these input graphemes should be contributing, at each letter position. In order to combine the input from graphemes at different positions in a word, a product of all the in_{ip} for all values of p is used, because this simulates the "and" function—all graphemes must be present for a word to be present.

There is also the question of how the inputs to the phoneme (output) units should be combined. Each phoneme unit at each position receives input from grapheme units at the same position, as well as word units. Initially they combined these as simply the product ("and" function), but this did not account for the partial "or" nature of the print-to-sound transformation process mentioned earlier, like the ability to pronounce non-words such as "hink". Therefore, they changed the function that combines information from the two sources to:

$$in_i = in_iAND(1-a_i) + in_iORa_i$$

where $in_iAND = in_iWin_iG$ and $in_iOR = \backslash 1 - \Pi_R(1 - in_iR)$. Here a_i is the activation of the ith phoneme unit, in_{iw} is the input from the word units (calculated using the "or" function given above), in_iG is the corresponding value from the grapheme units, in_iOR is the "or" component, where R is either W or G—that is, in_iOR is the "or" of the two values. The total formula emphasizes the "and" component when a_i is relatively de-activated and the "or" component otherwise. This modification allows the correct phonemes to saturate when the information coming from either the lexical route or the grapheme route is weak.

Reggia and his co-workers point out that the normal way that parallel sources of information "advise" one another is via top-down

connections.   In their model, it is done somewhat differently.
Information is passed backward, but only in terms of the relative
activation of different output and hidden units, which determines the
forward flow of input.   For instance, in a standard top-down
implementation, word nodes might influence phoneme nodes, which
then—top-down—would influence grapheme nodes.   And vice
versa.   In their model, the fact that a phoneme node is receiving
more activation from a word node will cause it to get more input
and thus activation from a grapheme node as well.   But because
there are no explicit top-down connections, Reggia and his co-
workers refer to their model as "indirectly interactive".

They develop a metric of word regularity that is based on the
frequency of grapheme–phoneme mappings in a word.   They define
the regularity of a word as

$$R = \frac{\sum\limits_{i=1}^{n} (1.05 - p_i) p_i}{\sum\limits_{i=1}^{n} (1.05 - p_i)}$$

where p_i is the proportion of times that the grapheme in the ith
position of the word represents the given phoneme (and n is the
number of graphemes in the word).   Thus R ranges between 0 and
about 1; values close to 1 are highly regular and values close to zero
are highly irregular.   Reggia and his co-workers used a value of
1.05 rather than 1 in the formula so that the cases in which p equals
1 would be counted.

They gave the example of presenting the network with the
word "onion", in which each letter was a grapheme (in many words,
more than one letter may form a grapheme).   Initially, the word
node corresponding to "union" was more strongly activated than that
for "onion"; this was because "union" occurs more frequently in
English than "onion".   After relaxation, only the phonemes
corresponding to the correct pronunciation of "onion" all became
saturated.   They ran their model with 64 words of varying
frequency and regularity; in all these cases exactly the right set of
phonemes became saturated after relaxation.   As might be expected,
this occurred most quickly with high-frequency regular words, and
least quickly with low-frequency irregular words, with high-
frequency irregular words, and then low-frequency regular words,

coming in between. Frequency and regularity, as well as the two of them combined, all produced statistically highly significant differences in the time required to reach saturation, based on analysis of variance.

Reggia and his co-workers experimented with presenting non-words to the model. Often not all the phonemes in the output were saturated. Moreover, these non-words were subject to interferences in their pronunciation from orthographically similar words which would not have occurred if the model had only performed the grapheme-to-phoneme mapping.

A theory of some forms of dyslexia is that one of the two routes from printed text to speech is disrupted. Reggia and his co-workers tested the implications of this by turning off the grapheme-to-phoneme portion of their model, leaving only the lexical component. They presented the same 64 words as before, and again all the correct phonemes were activated. As one might expect in this case, only word frequency played a role in the speed at which the system converged to a solution, not word regularity. Also, as might be expected, this network had much more trouble with non-words.

When they turned off the word portion of the model, many irregular words were pronounced in a regular manner. This "over-regularization" is typical of surface dyslexia.

Reggia and his co-workers feel that their work is significant in two ways: (1) It provides a mechanism for competitive activation along multiple pathways that does not explicitly involve inhibitory links and (2) It provides a detailed, localist model of the print-to-sound transformation that accounts for dyslexia, unlike NETtalk (see the next section), which is a distributed model and uses back-propagation learning.

5.7. NETtalk: Reading Aloud with a Three-Layer Perceptron

One of the earliest and best-known applications of the error back-propagation algorithm (see section 2.12) was to the problem of pronouncing printed text. Sejnowski and Rosenberg (1987) developed their NETtalk system for this problem.

The NETtalk system consists of three layers of units in a feed-forward network. The bottom layer consists of units that represent seven letters. Each letter is represented by a group of 29 units in which exactly one unit is activated. 26 of the units in this group constitute a local (unary) representation for the alphabet, and 3 designate punctuation and word boundaries. There are 203 (7*29) input units.

The goal of the network is to output the correct representation for the phoneme corresponding to the central letter of the seven being presented. The other six surrounding letters provide clues to its pronunciation. Sejnowski and Rosenberg observe that most of the information as to the pronunciation of a letter can be found in its immediate context. They would have used a larger window than 7 letters if computational resources had been sufficient, but they found that 7 was sufficient to capture most context information.

While they use a local representation for their input, they use a distributed representation for their output. Each phoneme is represented by a set of 26 articulatory feature units, as well as three units to denote stress and syllable boundaries. Thus there are 29 output units.

There are also 80 hidden units. Each of the 203 input units is connected to each of the 80 hidden units. Each of these, in its turn, is connected to the 29 output units. They used back-propagation and a sigmoid activation function for their units.

As learning proceeded, the seven letters represented in the input units functioned as a sliding "window" into the text that was used for training. Sejnowski and Rosenberg used two corpuses of text for the training. The first was a phonetically transcribed speech of a child in first grade; the second was drawn from Webster's Pocket Dictionary. Each of these corpuses contained paired text–phoneme information for use during learning.

The first corpus contained 1024 words. Performance improved rapidly at the beginning of training, and then leveled off. Early on, the system distinguished between vowels and consonants, and then made more subtle distinctions. The system performed better at placing stress than at finding the exact phoneme. Errors often resulted from the confusion of similar phonemes. The system had a learning curve that followed the power law characteristic of human subjects (Rosenbloom & Newell 1986). After 50 passes through the corpus, the system achieved 95% correct performance.

To gauge generalization performance, the trained network was tested on an additional 439 words from the same speaker. It achieved 78% correct performance. They found that the more words the system was trained on, the better generalization performance it achieved.

They introduced noise into the weights; they produced degradation in performance commensurate with the amount of noise introduced. The degradation was gradual. The network recovers quickly upon retraining if the noise introduced is not too great.

They used the second corpus, from Webster's Pocket Dictionary, to test the effect on performance of the number of hidden units. 1000 of the most frequently occurring (and thus also the most irregular in pronunciation) words in English were selected from this dictionary and used for training. With no hidden units, just direct connections between the input and output units, performance reached a plateau at 82% correct. With 120 hidden units, 98% performance was achieved; varying the number of hidden units between 0 and 120 led to performance between 82% and 98%. They also tried systems with more than one hidden layer of units. For instance, a four-layer system with two hidden layers of 80 units each, which had about as many weights as the system with one hidden layer of 120 hidden units, had asymptotic performance on the training set which was about equal to the 120-unit system.

They compare NETtalk with non-connectionist approaches to speech synthesis, which typically use a look-up table, which is a dictionary that contains the pronunciation of each word. NETtalk, functioning with 80 hidden units, requires 18,629 weights. If each weight is allocated 4 bits, this is a total of about 80,000 bits. The dictionary of 20,012 words requires about two million bits of storage. The reason NETtalk can achieve such a reduction is because of the substantial redundancy in the pronunciation of English.

They do not claim that NETtalk represents a good model of speech production in people. People learn to speak and then to read; NETtalk learns both at once. Also, the 7-letter "window" for establishing context does not accurately model the wider range of information available to the human reader (including information drawn from linguistic sources other than phonetics.)

Rosenberg (1987) took a close look at NETTalk's internal representations in order to determine exactly what features of the input it was detecting in effecting the transformation from text to speech. One of the first things that Rosenberg wanted to find out was whether NETTalk divided its internal knowledge into two sources: a source of lexical pronunciation knowledge and source of grapheme pronunciation knowledge, like that done by the system of Reggia and his co-workers (see the last section)

He used factor analysis, which attempts to account for variables in terms of a linear combination of underlying variables, and cluster analysis, which iteratively groups items into continually more general clusters, in his investigation of the model.

NETtalk, in its 80 hidden unit version, has about 20% of its hidden units highly activated, and the rest relatively inactivated, at any given time.

Rosenberg wanted to classify the patterns of hidden unit activation that resulted in each output phoneme. To do this, he averaged the activation of these units over many occurrences—those found in 1000 words—for each phoneme. He then had a good representation of the average hidden unit pattern of that phoneme. This hidden unit vector was computed for each of 48 phonemes. Correlation coefficients were computed for each pair of phonemes, to create a 48x48 matrix.

These coefficients were then used in a hierarchical clustering analysis in which the most similar pairs of phonemes, judged by the correlations, were grouped together first, then progressively less similar ones. These led to different results with respect to the vowels and consonants. Vowels were classified mainly on the basis of their place of articulation. For instance, vowels were divided first on the basis of whether the tongue is toward the front or the back of the mouth when they are pronounced. Within these divisions, they were further divided into those for which the tongue is high in the mouth, and those for which it is low.

The consonant phoneme groupings were more related to the way they are written than their place of articulation. For instance, one cluster is around the possible pronunciations of the letter t: /T/, /D/, /C/, and /S/. Other groupings are around the possible pronunciations of x, of m, of s, of n, of p, and of g.

Rosenberg was able to account for 68% of the total variance in ten vowels using three factors from factor analysis. Two of these factors roughly correspond to the place of articulation in the mouth, in that /I/ and /i/ have high values on one of the factors and they are articulated near the back. The third factor accounts for the height of the vowel; the low vowels /c/, /a/, and /@/ have high values on this factor. Thus his results from factor analysis basically duplicated the results from hierarchical clustering.

These analyses revealed an important fact about NETtalk; that it uses its hidden units in distinctively different manner for vowels and consonants; patterns for vowels are similar if they have similar heights or places of articulation, whereas patterns for consonants are similar if they correspond to alternative pronunciations of input letters.

6
Visual Perception and Pattern Recognition

6.1. Introduction

Approaches to visual perception in the connectionist paradigm have been very eclectic. There are two basic ways one can recognize objects, depending on how the object is represented. One way objects can be represented is as line drawings. Recognition of line drawings of various types has long been an active area of research in AI; for some examples, see Huffman (1971), Clowes (1971), and Waltz (1975). Sabbah (1985) extended this work into the connectionist research paradigm, using large numbers of local units to represent objects at various levels of complexity, such as lines, angles, and faces.

The other main way object recognition can be accomplished is by using input that is much like a photograph, that is, that is represented as an array of gray-level values. (Of course, there is a whole range of possible inputs between a line drawing and a photograph.) Machine vision using photographic input is most realistic, as such an input is similar to what people have to deal within their visual field. As in the case of line drawings, the most successful approaches to scene understanding has been hierarchical; simple features detected at the lowest level are then combined into more complex features. This is the approach taken by Honavar and Uhr (1987) with their *recognition cones*. These structures are roughly cone-shaped networks of several layers; they have fewer units and detect more complex features as one goes up in the network from the input. Since the number of units tapers off as you get further from the input, these networks are cone-shaped. Each unit in the network has a receptive field consisting of connections to units below it; the weights are learned through back-propagation. Honavar and Uhr also introduce a technique they call generation, whereby units can change their receptive fields adaptively to improve performance. Generation is a form of learning. By combining hierarchy, generation, and learning of weights, Honavar and Uhr are able to recognize a variety of simple two dimensional objects.

Beyond general object recognition, another area to which connectionist systems have been applied is the modeling of human visual perceptual phenomena. Two of the most important such phenomena are: (1) The separation of a visual field into figure and ground, when one has a simple visual field consisting of a dark continuous "field" against a light "ground". (2) The perception of an object in a position-independent manner, coupled with its position. The primate perceptual system appears to separate the tasks of determining what an object is and where it is in the visual field. Kienker and his co-workers (1986) attacked the problem of devising a connectionist system to separate figure and ground. Rueckl and his co-workers (1988) devised a neural network to explain why primates process where an object is, and what it is, separately.

Finally, as a transition to chapter 7, which is on language understanding, we discuss the work of Lakoff (1988) and that of Regier (1988) on linking visual and verbal semantics. In the development of a child, he or she learns to recognize the objects in the visual world at the same time as he or she is learning their names.

Central to Lakoff's conception of the linkage between the world of objects and language is the concept of cognitive topology; topological relationships between objects in the world is central to understanding the meaning of simple prepositions such as *in*, *around*, and *towards*. Also, the concept of motion is central to the semantics of many verbs. For example the phrase "Nadia got over Tomas" refers to Tomas as a metaphorical "obstacle" on Nadia's life "path". Regier shows how these simple concepts can be detected by a neural network.

6.2. Interpreting Origami Figures

Sabbah (1985) applied a connectionist model to a famous problem domain in computer vision, "origami world", originally studied by Kanade (Kanade 1980). Origami world is a generalization of the famous blocks-world made famous by Huffman (1971), Clowes (1971), and Waltz (1975). An object in Origami world is composed of surfaces expressed as line drawings such as in Figure 6.1; blocks-world consists only of solid objects, as in Figure 6.2. Thus the line that the arrow points to in, Figure 6.1, would not be allowed in blocks world, since it cannot be interpreted in terms of solid objects alone. Objects in origami world, although they must be formed out of flat surfaces, include complex objects such as the Origami duck (Figure 6.3).

Sabbah uses a set of parameter spaces to represent the different levels of object recognition in his model. A parameter space is simply a set of local units that each corresponds to a particular value of a vector of parameters. At the lowest level, edge segments are represented. Edge extraction is not included in Sabbah's model, but has been the object of considerable study (Rosenfeld & Kak 1976).

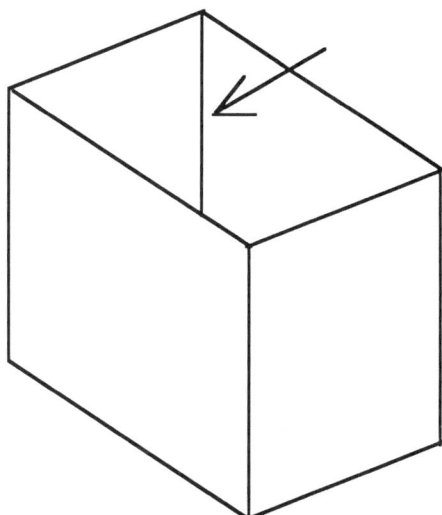

Figure 6.1. An object in Origami world.

There are relaxation methods for detecting edges, which can readily be adapted to neural network implementations.

At a higher level, lines are represented as collections of edges that line up with one another. In order to be noise-tolerant, Sabbah allows lines to be composed of edges that have gaps between them. Rays are half-lines. Rays are critical in defining the various joints in an origami figure.

Sabbah has two kinds of joints in his scheme, l-joints and t-joints. L-joints (so called because two rays come together at such a joint to make an "L") represent corners of a face. T-joints represent points of possible occlusion, that is, where there is one face blocking another. In Figure 6.4, an l-joint and a t-joint are shown. Sabbah also has a parameter space for c-joints, which are present when two or more partially visible faces meet. He also has a parameter space for skewed faces.

In each parameter space, each particular entity is represented by a set of parameters which uniquely characterize it. Thus, for example, an l-joint is defined by its location (two parameters), the angle of one of its rays relative to a coordinate axis in the image plane, and the angle between the rays of the l-joint. Thus this parameter space is four-dimensional. The parameter space for skewed faces (which are parallelograms) is six-dimensional, since a skewed face can be represented by one l-joint and the length of each of the l-joint's rays.

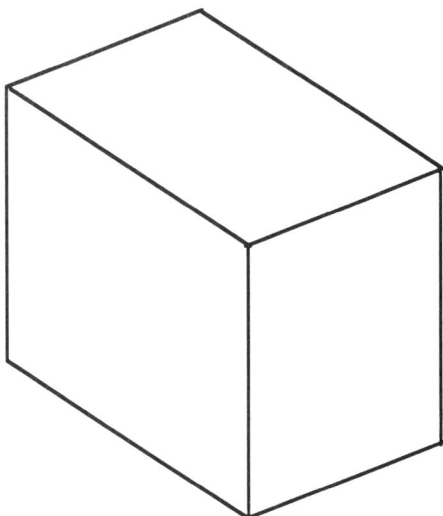

Figure 6.2 An object in blocks world.

Sabbah's representations are local, not distributed. Since each parameter space has an infinite number of points, there are potentially an infinite number of nodes. Thus in any real implementation, the parameter must be partitioned into *n*-dimensional regions formed by a grid in *n* dimensions, and any feature in the input must activate a node corresponding to the interval in which it falls. Because of the high dimensionality of several of Sabbah's parameter spaces, large numbers of units are required.

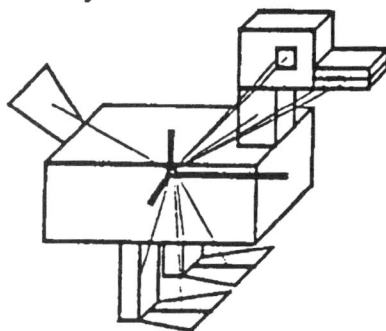

Figure 6.3. The Origami Duck. Its quacks are flat, too.

Sabbah's parameter spaces are organized into a hierarchy. Nodes in a lower-level parameter space are connected with positive weights to higher-level nodes with which they are compatible. For instance, a particular l-joint node is connected positively to all the nodes for all the skewed faces that are compatible with it, that is, that could possibly have it as a corner.

His model incorporates both bottom-up and top-down connections. An l-joint reinforces all the skewed faces that are compatible with it, and a skewed face reinforces the specific four l-joints that compose it. This top-down reinforcement is necessary because there are cases in which component features are obscured by occlusion or noise, yet the system still needs to infer their presence.

Sabbah's scheme was inspired by the Hough transform (Rosenfeld & Kak 1976), which is used for edge detection. In this transform, each point in the image space "votes" for all the edges with which it is compatible. Those edges receiving many votes are inferred to be in the image. A particular point is considered to be consistent with all of the edges that could pass through it.

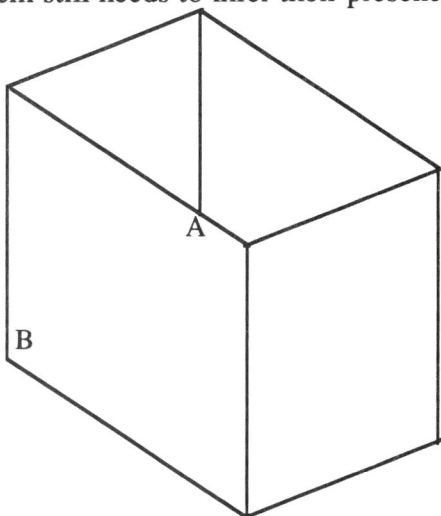

Figure 6.4. Vertices A and B marked on the Origami world box.

The Hough transform is similar to Sabbah's hierarchy of units, in that units in Sabbah's scheme also "vote" for the higher level units with which they are compatible. Sabbah's is one of many connectionist systems which have borrowed ideas from earlier, non-connectionist, work in computer science and artificial intelligence.

Each of Sabbah's units has an activation level (al) which ranges from 0 to 10 (the maximum is arbitrary). The initial rule that Sabbah used for each unit was

$$al_{n+1}=al_n+(E_{n+1})-(I_{n+1})$$

This formula was applied iteratively, in the manner of a relaxation; al_n was the activation level of a given unit in the system on the nth iteration. Initially nothing was activated except the lowest level nodes, which corresponded to perceived features.

All the connections between nodes are either excitatory or inhibitory. E_{n+1} is the mean activation input of all the units that are connected to the unit in question by excitatory connections. I_{n+1} is the largest activation of any unit that is connected in an inhibitory fashion.

Sabbah's units had a tendency to saturate quickly, since any small amount of activation that they received accumulated over a series of iterations. To handle this, Sabbah added a noise threshold term, *NT*, to his equation:

$$al_{n+1}=al_n+(E_{n+1})-(I_{n+1})-NT$$

This problem, Sabbah notes, could also have been handled by inhibitory connections between all the incompatible units on a particular level in his hierarchy (winner-take-all), but this was impractical to implement. Instead, he allows only units representing similar features to inhibit one another.

Sabbah's other problem stemmed from poor input. Under conditions of poor input, some units reach maximum activation while others lag behind. Sabbah fixed this by forcing the activation level to remain at maximum for a certain amount of time. In addition to this, he added normalization factors to E_{n+1} and I_{n+1} to increase the amount of time over which evidence can accumulate. Now his formula became:

$$al_{n+1}=al_n+(E_{n+1}/k_{time})-(I_{n+1}/kinh_{time})-NT$$

k_{time} and $kinh_{time}$ were both large.

Finally, he modified his last term *(NT)* to provide fast decay of a node's activation after saturation in the absence of top-down feedback and the presence of inhibition from other nodes, slow decay with no feedback and no inhibition, and no decay in the presence of feedback.

Sabbah tested his network with four examples. The first was with a complex object, the origami chair. Since the input is perfect, and only correct features are evoked at the lowest level, the network reaches the correct interpretation quickly; effectively it is functioning as a look-up table.

The next stimulus Sabbah presented to his system was a square with a corner obscured by a black noisy blotch (see Figure 6.6). In addition to detecting the three unobscured corners, the system detected several corners within the blotch. In the absence of top-down feedback from the higher-level node representing the face as a whole, these corners within the blotch decay. Initially, the system made a wrong decision as to what corner is present in the blotch, but this decision was inhibited by the correct choice, which was activated by top-down feedback.

Sabbah's third and fourth examples have to do with occlusion. In the third example, a solid is occluded by a rectangle; in the fourth, a box is occluded by itself (see Figures 6.5 and 6.7). The network reacts by activating all the possible faces that could be the occluded face in a "winner-take-all" network; the face that "wins" will get activation from t-joints (occlusion points) and l-joints, and consideration will be given to the extent of the occlusion (candidate faces extending beyond the occlusion must be ruled out).

(left) Figure 6.5, box occluded by face. (center) Figure 6.6, face with noisy corner. (right) Figure 6.7, self-occluding box.

6.3. Recognition Cones

Honavar and Uhr (1988) propose a system for object recognition and classification that is unusual because the neural network topology varies as the learning proceeds; units and links are generated. They use a system with multiple layers wherein each neuron has a relatively small and local receptive field. They start with their concept of *recognition cones* (Uhr 1987, Honavar & Uhr 1987).

Recognition cones are inspired by both the human visual system and other hierarchical architectures in computer vision, such as pyramids (Uhr 1983, Burt 1984). They are composed of several layers of units; the number of units in a particular layer is a logarithmic function of the layer number. The resolution of the layers decreases logarithmically as one moves from the input layer upwards.

Typically each unit in a particular layer is connected to some local neighborhood of units in the layer below, and typically in a regular fashion; for instance, a 2x2 layer of units might be connected to a 4x4 layer below it by connecting each of the four units in the upper left corner of the 4x4 array to the upper left unit in the 2x2 array. Or, the arrays might have overlapping receptive fields, which would create a form of coarse coding.

Honavar and Uhr's simulations involve both upward and downward connectivity. Because of the local receptive fields, units in a recognition cone system can compute a large variety of possible local image transforms (functions), such as traditional edge-detectors, and create a complex multi-resolution representation of an image. As you go up in the cone, more complex features are represented. They have been applied, using pre-designed architectures, to recognize noisy handwritten letters, place settings consisting of hand-drawn knives, plates, spoons, and forks and complex features (windows) in photographs of houses.

Each unit is viewed by Honavar and Uhr as a *transform* of its inputting units. Transforms are re-weighted using a variation of Rumelhart and co-workers' back-propagation algorithm. Honavar and Uhr suggest a heuristic to guide this process, which they call the minimal complexity heuristic. This is as follows: in order to perform a given pattern classification task, choose the simplest structure that is necessary to perform the classification, by minimizing the number of nodes, links, and/or layers.

In their simulation, they used a 32x32 bottom input layer; each layer above it reduced each dimension by two, to give five layers. Each unit computes a set of transforms. When a transform is selected for use in a particular layer, it is provided to all the units in that layer. The bottom input layer's units are each presented with the outputs of eight edge detectors, spaced 45° apart.

Honavar and Uhr evaluate the performance of their network by keeping track of the percentage of correct responses for each pattern class, for the recent performance of the network. Transforms are randomly selected from a set of non-linear functions with the constraint that each transform should only draw on the receptive field of the unit it is associated with.

As the error is propagated back, from top to bottom, through the layers, we see which transforms are performing well at each layer. If the transforms at a particular level are performing badly, some of them may be pruned, and new random ones generation. Thus a sort of "natural selection" process occurs with the transforms (not unlike the NGS theory of Reeke and Edelman; see section 2.19).

Generation of transforms is an independent learning method which can be used either by itself or in combination with a variety of learning rules-- supervised or unsupervised. (Honavar 1989)

Honavar and Uhr ran their simulation to recognize two classes of stimuli—letters (T,D, & E were used) and simple objects (an apple, a banana and a cup were used). Several versions of each stimulus were used, hand-drawn by different people. Their program achieved 100% classification accuracy after training when generation of new transforms was used, but only about 60–80% accuracy when it was not used. Their data seems to indicate that the generation of links in a selective fashion in a neural network can be a powerful technique in improving network performance. The question is, is generation of links, rather than simple weight change in a more highly connected network, a biologically plausible process? Recent neurophysical evidence has suggested that it is (Greenough & Bailey 1988, Honavar 1989).

6.4. Separating Figure from Ground

Kienker, Sejnowski, Hinton, and Schumacher (1986) applied connectionism to the classic perceptual problem of separating figure from ground, using connectionist ideas. This perceptual process is illustrated by Rubin's famous illustration, containing two faces which form a vase, in which figure and ground are reversed (see Figure 6.8). In one interpretation the black vase is in the foreground (the "figure" in "figure and ground) against a white field ("ground"); in the other interpretation, the two faces are the figures and the black field is ground. Kienker and his co-workers cite psychological experiments (Ullman 1984) which show that subjects can quickly (within a few tenths of a second) determine whether or not a dot shown in conjunction with a closed figure, is inside or outside of a the figure. This leads one to believe that figure–ground discrimination is a fairly basic perceptual process.

Kienker and his co-workers start not with literal image data but with slightly higher level information. The units are in several planes; each plane consists of a grid of units. One plane consists of "edge" units, that is, units representing edges in the image. Another plane consists of figure units, an array of units that determine whether or not a particular pixel in the image is in the figure. The determination of whether or not a particular pixel is in the figure is a function not only of the image itself but of "attention"; that is, some higher-level process will clamp some of the figure units to *on*, so as to attend to that particular part of the image, and bias the system into arriving at a figure containing those units. Shifting attention is what accounts for the shifting perception of the faces and the vase in the Rubin illustration.

The figure units were arranged in a 20x20 grid in their simulations. Weights ranged from -15 to +15, in integer values. Each unit is connected to its eight neighbors by excitatory connections, with a weight of +10. Each location in the image has an edge unit for each orientation that is represented; in their simulation only horizontal and vertical orientations were supported. Each edge unit has connections to the figure units in its immediate neighborhood. The orientation of the edge unit does not represent the orientation of the edge itself, but rather represents the direction in which the figure can be found.

Figure 6.8. A famous illustration by Rubin, in which figure and ground are reversed between one interpretation and another. Form Kienker et al. (1986). Reprinted by permission.

An edge unit reinforces (with a connection strength of +12) the figure unit it is immediately pointing towards, as well as the two units immediately flanking that unit (+10); it has negative connections with the unit it is pointing away from (-12) as well as the two units immediately flanking it (-10). All connections in their network are reciprocal.

Each edge unit inhibits (-10) the unit with the opposite orientation. Making edge units excite flanking units as well as the units that they directly point to allows edge gaps to exist in the image, without disrupting the figure/ground discrimination. They also connected pairs of edge units that could represent corners; units representing possible corners were connected with a positive weight (+5), and units representing impossible corners with a negative weight (-5) (see Figure 6.9).

Attention was implemented by training a Gaussian "spotlight" on a region in the figure units. A figure unit is distance d from the center of the attention received an excitatory input equal to

$$A e^{-(d/s)^2}$$

where A is the amplitude of the spotlight and σ the width of the spotlight.

Kienker and his co-workers use the Boltzmann machine update rule to perform relaxation in the network (see section 2.10). In the Boltzmann machine, the weights are fixed. They use simulated annealing on their Boltzmann machine, whereby the temperature T (which corresponds to the amount of noise that is allowed to affect the network) is initially high and is reduced gradually over

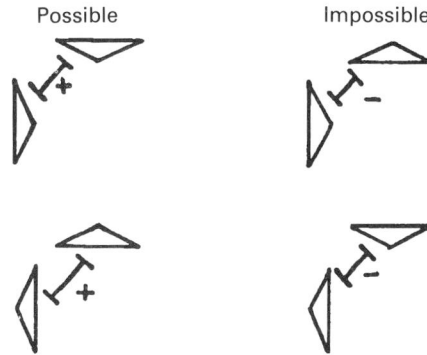

Figure 6.9 Impossible and possible combinations of edge units. From Kienker et al. (1988), reprinted by permission.

the course of the relaxation. The result of the relaxation is to establish a stable pattern in the figure units, so as to establish the discrimination between figure and ground.

Kienker and his co-workers tried their network out on a variety of shapes, ranging, in complexity, from a rectangle to a spiral. They performed 2000 random unit updates per iteration, since their system consists of 400 edge units in each of the four orientations, plus 400 figure units, for a total of 2000 units. Each unit can expect to be updated once, although due to the stochastic nature of the algorithm, some units will be updated more than once per iteration and some will not be updated at all. They carried out a maximum of 148 iterations over the course of the simulated annealing, over which the temperature was gradually reduced from 1 to 0. However, most of the trials reached stable states long before 148 iterations.

For a simple rectangle with all the edges specified, most of the trials resulted in convergence to a correct final state in under 40 iterations. If only the corner edge units of this rectangle were specified, then most trials reached a correct final state within 60 iterations. The increased time is required for the activation to spread properly and the border between figure and ground become properly established, in the absence of edge units. The ability of the network to create the correct interpretation of the figure, with only corners present, reflects human performance nicely. For a third input, a C-shaped closed figure, convergence to a solution occurred more slowly, because of the concave region on the inside of the C, which is reinforced by neighboring figure units, but not by neighboring edge units. For this figure, most trials stabilized before 100 trials.

Kienker and his co-workers compared their stochastic algorithm with a deterministic (Hopfield) algorithm, with a strict binary threshold rule. The deterministic algorithm is only guaranteed to converge to a local minimum energy (see section 2.8). not a global minimum If there are no holes in the edges, then the deterministic algorithm is equivalent to a "spreading ink" algorithm; activation in the figure units spreads and is contained by the edge units. If there are holes in the edges, or the width of the Gaussian spotlight of attention is too large, activation will "leak" out of the contained figure. Thus, for a closed figure, the spotlight has to be finely focused on the figure itself, in order for the deterministic algorithm to work.

Kienker and his co-workers' attempt to find the correct solution for an enclosed spiral failed in a majority of trials, using simulated annealing. If the cooling proceeds more slowly, they can anneal to the correct solution; one trial proceeded to a correct solution after 961 iterations.

They tried to introduce variability into the temperature distribution by introducing random factors, one per unit, that multiplied the global temperature to create a local temperature for each unit. This was closer to the behavior of a true physical system. However, this did not affect the network's performance to a significant extent.

6.5. Determining "What" and "Where" in a Visual Scene

Rueckl, Cave, and Kosslyn (1988) consider a classic problem in visual perception from a connectionist standpoint. This is the separation of the information about an object into (1) the location-independent description of the object, and (2) where it is in the visual field (and what view is given,, that is, as they term it, "what and where". The question that they address in this work is whether the methods of determining "what" and "where" are consolidated in a single mechanism ,or in two parallel mechanisms.

They constructed two systems to address this question. Both systems received input from a 5x5 array of binary-valued inputs.

The different "objects" that could be formed each consisted of a pattern in a 3x3 grid. Each of these patterns could be centered on any of the 9 units in the 5x5 grid that were not on its edge. Only one pattern was present in the input at any given time. Thus the state of the input units could be completely described by a pair of numbers each having a value between 1 and 9, the first describing the shape of the stimulus and the second describing its location.

Rueckl and his co-workers used a three layer feed-forward system, in which the bottom layer consisted of the 25 input units, and in which there was a middle layer of 18 hidden units, and an output layer of 18 units. Nine of the output units described "where" and nine described "what", that is, one of the output units corresponded to each position and one corresponded to each shape. Thus a correct output pattern had exactly two output units activated, one of the "where" units and one of the "what" units, in a local representation.

The authors refer to their two systems as the "split" and "unsplit" systems. In both systems, all of the input units are connected to all of the hidden units. In the unsplit system, all the hidden units are connected to all of the output units as well. In the split system, the hidden units are divided into two groups of nine each, one group being completely connected to the 9 "where" output units, and the other group completely connected to the 9 "what" output units. Thus the number of connections in the split system was half that of the unsplit system. The split system, above the input units, was effectively two parallel systems

Rueckl and his co-workers trained both models on random sequences of input patterns in which all valid inputs were presented, using back-propagation to teach the model to arrive at the correct output. Both models learned the task, but the unsplit model learned it faster. After 300 learning cycles, the unsplit model was producing significantly less error than the split model. They suspected that this was due to the differences in the difficulty of learning the "what" and "where" tasks, so they looked at the sum-squared error in each of the two subsets of the output units, in each of the two models. It turned out that both models exhibited rapid and similar convergence on the units representing location, and the difference between the two models is mainly in the speed of convergence to the correct pattern on the output units signifying the shape of the stimulus. This led Rueckl and his co-workers to conclude that location was easier to learn, because the input patterns representing a given location were more similar to one another (in terms of shared activation) than the input patterns representing a given shape were to one another.

This in turn led them to consider dividing the hidden units between the two tasks in an asymmetrical way, so as to allocate more of the hidden units to determining shape. The "12-6" split model allocated 12 of the hidden units to shape and the remaining 6 to location. They tested this model against the original (9-9) model and 15-3 and 14-4 models. They found that the 14-4 and 12-6 models converged to a solution significantly faster than the unsplit model, while the 9-9 and 15-3 models did worse. This clearly shows that a correct allocation of units to the two problems is critical; too few units allocated to either task leads to degraded performance.

They noticed that the unsplit model did better than any of the split models in the early phases of learning, although the 14-4 and 12-6 models did better asymptotically. They attributed this to the fact that the unsplit model has more connections.

They explored the nature of the receptive fields of the hidden nodes. There were hidden nodes whose connections to the input units detected alternating stripes of activation and inhibition, in either a horizontal, diagonal, or vertical direction. These were useful in detecting shapes in a position-independent manner. Another group detected activation along the borders of the input array. Yet another group were sensitive to a single strip of input activation at some orientation Some nodes seemed to have no particular rime or reason to their receptive fields, and some were specialized to detect a localized configuration of features. All these types of hidden nodes, taken together, were able to provide the output units with information about "what".

The "where" hidden nodes included "border nodes", as above, as well as nodes with excitatory areas in the receptive fields. With few hidden nodes devoted to the "where" task, the size of these excitatory areas was large, because relatively coarse coding was necessitated. As more hidden units are assigned to the "where" task, eventually each node comes to represent only a single location in the input.

In the unsplit network, the hidden nodes had strong output connections to both the "what" nodes and the "where" nodes. The unsplit network did not spontaneously develop the specialization required by the split network. There were similar types of nodes, in terms of their receptive fields, in both the split and unsplit networks, but their frequency distribution differed.   There are more continuous-region detecting nodes in the unsplit system, suggesting to Rueckl and his co-workers that location was more important in the unsplit system.

They made a classification of the shapes by various properties. Does a shape have a single vertical or horizontal stripe? Is it skewed to the right, left, top or bottom borders of the visual field? Is it strongly horizontal or vertical (that is, does it have more than one horizontal or vertical stripe)? These classifications were based on the response specificities of particular hidden nodes. They used multi-dimensional scaling analysis of the weights (Shepard 1962) to show that single-stripe and border patterns are more important in the unsplit system compared to multiple stripes, which were more important in the split system. Thus they quantitatively showed the effect that they observed just by looking at the network itself directly.

The multiple stripe detectors were position-independent. Thus, their added importance in the split model indicated that the split model was more able to incorporate position-independent factors in the determination of what the shape of the stimulus was. The unsplit model was unable to do this because the hidden nodes were involved in computing both "what" and "where" spontaneously.

Rueckl and his co-workers argue that, in the unsplit model, the computational resources (hidden units) that could be allocated to improve performance on the shape task are, in the unsplit model, instead allocated to improve location performance, even though the shape task needs them more. This prevents the unsplit system from arriving at the solution arrived at by the best of the split systems, that it could have in principle arrived at, since it had all the connections of the split system, plus more.

Their experiments support their hypothesis that a neural system will more readily adapt to computing shape and position if it uses separate computational resources for each of these tasks, and provides a plausible explanation for why the brain does so. It also provides a plausible account of why the primate visual system devotes many more nerve cells to areas that compute shape than those that compute position.

They note that the requirement that shape and location information be available separately for later processing in other systems places no constraints on how these separate pieces of information are computed; they note that both the split and unsplit systems satisfy this criterion. Thus this criterion alone is no explanation as to why the brain devotes separate regions to the two tasks.

They note that the primate visual system is enormously more complex than their system, presumably because it has much more complex recognition tasks—many more shapes at many more positions. This raises the question: does their model "scale up" to this larger size? Further experiments may answer this question.

6.6. Linking Visual and Verbal Semantics

Lakoff (1988) makes an analogy between connectionist models and a variety of linguistic theory that he and others have been advocating, cognitive linguistics (Lakoff 1987, Langacker 1987). A central concept of cognitive linguistics is the idea of cognitive topology. Cognitive topology relates linguistic concepts—such as simple prepositions like over, under, in, and through—to spatial concepts in topology. For instance, Lakoff gives the example of people watching a game of ping-pong. The ball is described as going over, under, or into the net, and people are able to make these descriptions despite that there are literally an infinite number of trajectories that the ball can take. (In ping-pong, of course, the ball rarely goes under the net; but it is possible; volleyball might have been a better choice.)

The explanation that Lakoff gives is that people use topological descriptions of space in forming these concepts. These concepts include BOUNDED, REGION, PATH, OBSTACLE, etc. Lakoff claims that, since much of our experience of the visual world is universal, these are universal concepts in human language. He notes that "in" and "out" use the concept of a BOUNDED REGION, that "across" uses the concept of PATH, etc. This spatial reasoning underlies much of language and explains much metaphor, according to Lakoff. For instance, he gives the example of a couple whose relationship has "hit a dead-end street". This is a pervasive spatial metaphor which, Lakoff claims, is used with all sorts of actions. In this metaphor, according to Lakoff, "TRAVELLERS correspond to LOVERS, THE VEHICLE corresponds to THE LOVE RELATIONSHIP, ... THE PATH corresponds to THE COURSE OF THE RELATIONSHIP, etc.". Because of the pervasiveness of this metaphor, Lakoff sees cognitive topology as central to a theory of language.

Preliminary work has been done in linking cognitive topology to visual data using a connectionist paradigm (Regier 1988) (see the next section). The hope is that a natural bridge can be built between cognitive topological concepts such as prepositions, and images, as each is represented in a neural network.

Lakoff presents a series of convergences between the ideas of cognitive linguistics and connectionism. The basic analogy is that a pattern of weights in a neural network corresponds to a linguistic pattern, which is a meaningful symbol because of its causal relation to stimuli. Both cognitive linguistics and connectionism view semantics and phonetics as "autonomous", because they are based, respectively, in the sensory and motor systems; syntax and morphology are patterns of connections between semantics and phonetics. This is in sharp contrast to generative grammar, which relies on recursive rules and manipulation of symbols. It also denies Chomsky's (1980) concept of "autonomous syntax", whereby syntax is viewed as the product of a module in the brain employing a generative grammar, and cut off from semantics and phonology. Lakoff also, in a quite general manner, draws analogies between the two theories in regards to how patterns of activation are combined, how patterns vary and inherit properties, how they express partial activation of a concept, how concepts are defined, how metaphor is expressed, etc. He then goes on to outline how the basic concepts of cognitive linguistics could be defined in connectionist terms.

6.7. Recognizing Image-schemas

Regier (1988) attacks the problem of recognizing image-schemas, which are cognitive models of an image-based situation; that is, topological descriptions of the spatial relationships in an image. Image schemas are not static, but may contain descriptions of motion. His system handles images containing objects, represented by a binary array of pixels. His system uses Ullman's (1984) concept of "visual routines", which consist of simple procedures for performing simple visual tasks, such as detecting enclosed spaces, completing a boundary, etc., as well as rules for combining primitives to form more complex ones.

His system consists of an image net, two object nets, a closed object net, and three working image nets. The user manually selects two objects out of the image stored in the image net, and these are placed in the two object nets. The object in the first object net, called A, is in some relation to the second object—B, e.g. "in", "into", "outside", "out-of", and "over"—these are the five prepositions that his system was designed to handle.

After object B is copied to its object net, it is copied to the closed object net. There it is closed by detecting its endpoints and connecting them, using a connectionist version of standard algorithms for doing this (Rosenfeld & Kak 1976). He then copies object A into the working image nets, and performs what he calls "bounded spreading activation" on it. That is, when he is testing whether object A is *in* B, activation spreads out from object A, but is not allowed across the boundary of B (now closed). If activation ever reaches the edge of the net, then A is not in B, otherwise it is (B has contained the spreading activation). When he is testing whether A is *over* B, activation "rains down" from A to cells in the net below it. If there is activation on both sides of B on the bottom of the working net, then A is over B, in the sense of being above B and having either moved over or extended across B. (The sense of over as "above" alone is handled more simply.) He handles the concepts of "into" and "out of" as transitions from being in the state of being outside to the state of being inside, and vice versa, respectively The three working nets are needed for the spreading of activation in multiple time frames. He performs two types of "focusing" in these working nets; (1) path-focusing, in which the entire path of an object is stored in one of the working nets and (2) end-point focusing, in which the object is shown at an endpoint of its path.

The system Regier has implemented has more of the flavor of a procedural array processor rather than a connectionist system. It would be interesting to see it implemented into a more strictly connectionist implementation that does not depend on outside control (which Regier implements as a sequencer network, after Jordan 1986b, that controls the activation function of the other networks!) This is rather unorthodox connectionist work.

7

Language Understanding

7.1. Introduction

Natural language is one of the most challenging areas for connectionists, since it contains a good deal of recursive structure that is readily handled by recursive symbol-manipulating languages such as LISP and PROLOG. How to handle language in a connectionist network is not as apparent.

As in the case of speech understanding, the words of a sentence can be input to a neural network in two ways; one word at a time in serial succession to the same set of input units, or each word to its own whereupon all the words are processed in parallel. Both of these approaches have been taken in the various pieces of research discussed in this chapter.

The first work we discuss, that of Servan-Schreiber and his co-workers (1988), investigated the processing of linguistic data serially in a recurrent network. Their linguistic data was generated by a finite-state grammar. Finite-state grammars are among the simplest known, but they have the property, which is also characteristic of natural language, that which symbol appears at any point of a valid string of symbols is a function of the symbols that preceded it. Thus any system that can distinguish between strings that are in the language specified by the finite state grammar, and those that are not, must have some memory of the previous symbols encountered. In this system, this is handled by the recurrent network of Elman (1988). This work illustrates the usefulness of recurrent networks for serial processing, but for realistic natural language processing, finite-state grammars are insufficient. Below we discuss systems that parse context-free grammars based on production rules. These systems are more relevant for natural language processing.

Before doing this, though, we discuss systems that attempt sentence understanding. Some of the first work done on sentence interpretation with connectionist systems was done by Waltz and Pollack (1985). Their system, like several of the others discussed in this chapter, is not completely connectionist, because they used a conventional chart parser (Kay 1973) to create the parse trees that were used as input to their system.

The purpose of their system is to resolve lexical ambiguity. They do this by creating a network in which there is one (local) node for each interpretation of each word, and all compatible interpretations of different words reinforce one another; all incompatible interpretations inhibit one another. each parse tree of a given sentence reinforces the particular semantic node that is compatible with their interpretation of the syntactic category that a word belongs to, in the case of words that have multiple syntactic categories, depending on their use Relaxation brings the semantic network into a state reflecting a consistent sentence interpretation.

Like Waltz and Pollack, Cottrell and Small also developed a model of sentence interpretation and word-sense disambiguation. Instead of having an intensional semantics based on reinforcing and inhibiting connections, Cottrell and Small use a representation for each verb in terms of a case frame, which plays an important role in determining the interpretation of words and sentences via connections between word sense nodes and case role nodes. A case frame is a data structure that is associated with a verb that has slots for all the noun phrases involved in the action. Again, compatible nodes reinforce one another, and incompatible nodes inhibit one another, and again, relaxation creates a consistent sentence interpretation.

We also consider another system that does case semantics, that of McClelland and Kawamoto (1986b). The systems of Cottrell, and of Waltz and Pollack, do lexical semantics; that is, they resolve ambiguities in the interpretation of words in a sentence. McClelland and Kawamoto's system fills in all the slots of the case frame of a verb: for instance, for the verb "to rent", these might be the lessor, the lessee, the thing rented, the period of time, and the amount of money charged.

They use a microfeature representation of words. Their input is a sentence, and their output is a series of case fillers, in a particular order. They use rather complex distributed representations of these. The network is trained using sentence/case filler pairs using a simple two-layer perceptron with no hidden units and the perceptron convergence procedure. The system was able to learn the training set and to generalize on it; it even formed defaults for missing case fillers. Because of their emphasis on compositional semantics, McClelland and Kawamoto's work is closely related to the work on knowledge representation along these lines that was discussed in Chapter 4.

We consider five approaches to parsing with networks, those of Hanson and Kegl (1987), Li and Chun (1987), Charniak and Santos (1987), Selman and Hirst (1987), and Fanty (1985).In all of these except Hanson and Kegl's work, the system creates in the network structures that contain or resemble parse trees.

Hanson and Kegl's work on PARSNIP is similar to Sejnowski and Rosenberg's NETtalk (see section 5.7), except that it is applied to parsing sentences instead of turning them into speech. Like NETtalk, PARSNIP uses a three-layer feed-forward network composed of input, hidden, and output layers. Unlike NETtalk, and like Cottrell and co-workers' image compression system (see section 2.31), PARSNIP is auto-associative. The "parse" is built up in the hidden units. There are fewer hidden units than there are input units, so the hidden units act as a bottleneck that must compress the information inherent in the structure of the input sentence. They succeeded in training their network in auto-associative manner. Their network was able to perform a sentence completion task in which a word category left out of the input was inserted in the output by the system. They did not completely analyze the behavior of the hidden units, but they found that there were certain units that learned to respond to constituents such as noun phrases or verb phrases.

Both Charniak and Santos, and Li and Chun, developed approaches to parsing that were not strictly connectionist, but remained roughly so in flavor. Both systems have connections between nodes in a network, but allow the execution of local programs associated with each node to enforce rules or constraints. Charniak and Santos represent a parse tree in a set of nodes arranged in a table, and allow connections between nodes which contain symbols for the various constituents of a sentence. Rules in each node control the kinds of connections each can make with neighboring nodes.

In Li and Chun's system, there is a network which embodies the entire context-free grammar that the system is set up to understand. There is a node for the left side of each grammar rule, which is connected to nodes for each constituent on the right side of the rule, below it. The system operates by passing markers, which represent sentence constituents, upwards, and constructing parse trees with programs associated with each node which access global data structures. At the bottom level nodes for terminal symbols all receive any input appropriate to them; nodes above them need to receive all necessary markers to make up a rule, in the proper order. Part of each marker is the location of that constituent in terms of which words in the sentence it encompasses; higher-level constituents must be made up of markers (constituents) that are adjacent in the sentence. By passing this location information, Li and Chun avoid the approach taken by Fanty, which is to have a large number of units to represent each possible rule in every sentence position. Unfortunately, Li and Chun are forced to augment connectionism with symbol passing and complex operations in each node, in order to accomplish this.

Fanty (1985), like Li and Chun, and Charniak and Santos, developed a connectionist system to parse context-free grammars. His is a multilayer system in which there is a node for every rule, at every sentence position, connected to every set of symbols which could compose the right-hand side of the rule. This leads to a very large number of units. Like many other connectionist parsing systems, Fanty's system is hierarchical; rules containing more complex constituents are higher up in the network. His system parses in two "waves", a bottom-up one and a top-down one. Activation is sent up the network to the start symbol at the top, and this symbol then sends another wave of activation down. At the end, the only fully activated units in the network comprise a parse tree for the sentence; all partially activated sub-trees that did not receive top-down activation are not included.

We conclude the chapter with a discussion of two models of human processing of language that attempt to account for psychological data.. The first is Rueckl's (1986) model of letter and word identification in reading; the second is Rumelhart and McClelland's (1986a) model of learning the past tense by children. We review an elaborate critique of this latter model by Pinker and Prince (1988).

Rueckl's work was partly motivated by a desire to explain the word repetition effect, which is that subjects recognize words that they have recently seen better than those they have not. In order to explain this phenomenon and related phenomena in reading, Rueckl developed a three-level model. The first level extracts features from the visual field; the second level expresses these features in object-centered coordinates, and the third level performs object identification. In order to account for people's ability to give the same representation to visually disjoint objects, such as "a" and "A", he adds a fourth module, which stores these correspondences, and passes them to the object identification module. The word repetition effect is accounted for by the hypothesis that the system comes to recognize an object by relaxation; if an object has recently been activated, relaxation proceeds faster, since the network is closer to its representation in weight space than it would otherwise have been.

Rumelhart and McClelland's model of the development of the formation of the past tense in English parallels the behavior of children. The model proceeds, over the course of learning, from no knowledge of how to form the past tense to the ability to form it using "-ed". This rule (in both their system and in children) is over-generalized, forming non-words such as "taked". Both children and the system learn to correct this over-generalization, and even learn rules applying only to the formation of the past tense in specific classes of irregular verbs (for example, take becomes took, shake becomes shook, etc.)

Both the input and output of their system use distributed representations of the phonological features of the words in question. Each word is represented by a sequence of wickelphones, which are phoneme symbols surrounded by the symbols of the phonemes immediately to their left and right. These wickelphones are represented as patterns of activation across a set of units called wickelfeatures. The system consists of a layer of wickelfeatures for the input word completely connected to a layer of wickelfeatures for the output. Because the system has no hidden units, like McClelland and Kawamoto's model of the comprehension of verbs, it was trained using the perceptron convergence rule. It learned the past tense formation task in the manner described above. The rules it learned were implicit in the connections and weights. The distributed representations made feature detectors in the form of hidden units unnecessary, since the wickelfeatures already represented various conjunctions of wickelphones.

Pinker and Prince (1988) developed an elaborate critique of Rumelhart and McClelland's model. They criticize the wickelfeature representation as being inadequate to all the possible phonetic transformations that are found in human languages.

Pinker and Prince's main point is that many linguistic and morphological transformations, such the addition of an "s" at the end of a word, are used in many contexts in English and other languages. An associationist approach to the creation of these inflections does not allow an independent rule system to be generalized across a series of different contexts. Yet the fact that the rule is applied uniformly across a variety of contexts leads one to believe that each inflection does not have its own representation of the rule. Of course, much of this criticism is due to the limited nature of Rumelhart and McClelland's model. It must be kept in mind that a larger scale linguistic model, that would handle parsing, semantics, and morphology in parallel, would not treat each inflection independently, but would integrate linguistic information from various domains. Thus, for instance, some units might be devoted to the "s" inflection, but would perform this inflection in a variety of contexts, depending on information received from other subsystems, including one that does parsing.

7.2. Processing Finite State Grammars Sequentially

Servan-Schreiber and his co-workers (1988) discuss an algorithm for dealing with sequential data such as that given in natural language. They investigate a proposal by Elman (1988) whereby a connectionist system can "remember" earlier stimuli given to it. He starts with the usual three layer system of input, hidden, and output units, and adds a fourth set of units, the context units (see Figure 7.1). At each time slice the contents of the hidden units are copied into the context units, and they in turn feed back into the hidden units during the next time slice (that is, when the next input is given).

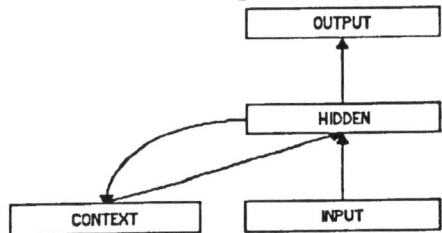

Figure 7.1 Architecture of the system of Servan-Schreiber et al. (1988) Reprinted by permission.

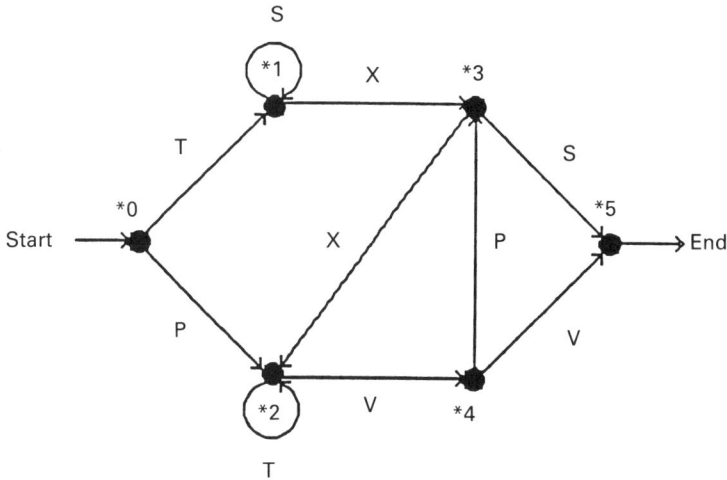

Figure 7.2 The finite-state machine of Reber (1967). From Servan-Screiber et al. (1988). Reprinted by permission.

Servan-Schreiber and his co-workers apply this model to learning the grammar specified by the finite-state machine devised by Reber (1967) for his language learning experiments (see Figure 7.2). There were five symbols in the alphabet of the language specified by this machine. There were seven input units corresponding to the five symbols, and a start and finish symbol. The output units were used to predict the next element in a (legal) sequence representing the language. Thus there were seven output units. There were also three hidden units and three context units, which functioned as described above. The network was trained using back-propagation, with 200,000 strings of varying length as stimuli.

Since there are two alternatives at each juncture in the finite-state machine, except at the final symbol, the best performance that could be achieved would activate each of the two output nodes corresponding to these two symbols equally when the system reached that juncture in its input, and no other nodes at all.

Servan-Schreiber and his co-workers' network does this, roughly, although there is some stray activation seeping to the other nodes, and the ratio of the activation of the two nodes varied somewhat from one. A string was considered "rejected" if no output node was more than 30% activated after presentation of any of the symbols in the string. The system was presented with 20,000 randomly generated strings that were in the grammar, and it accepted all 20,000 of them. It was also presented with 130,000 randomly generated strings of the five symbols, of which 0.2% were in the language. All of them were rejected except for this 0.2%.

Servan-Schreiber and his co-workers analyzed the internal representations that the network used, starting from the assumption that these patterns must encode the position of the current input in the total string. In fact, analysis of the activation patterns showed that the system grouped together—that is, had similar patterns of hidden unit activation—for all those string prefixes that arrived at the same position in the finite-state machine. (String prefixes are beginnings of strings.) There were five such clusters in the patterns of activation, corresponding to the five nodes in the automation other than the start node. Within each cluster, the patterns were further divided into those whose corresponding input string had a similar "history" with respect to which nodes in the finite state machine had been previously visited.

They note that the network is readily interpretable because of the fact that there are only three hidden units. More hidden units would have resulted in more redundancy and more distribution of information. If insufficient hidden units are provided, then the network may not achieve adequate performance—inadequate performance occurs even with three units under some initial configurations of weights and timing sequences.

The machine described above basically functions in the same fashion as the "memory-less" finite-state automaton—it represents mainly information about the current node, and information about the path to that node that is needed in order for the system to function correctly.

In their second training experiment, Servan-Schreiber and his co-workers trained the network on the set of grammatical strings with lengths less than or equal to eight. There are 43 such strings generated by Reber's automaton. They used 21 of these strings to train the network, and the remaining 22 to test its performance. They presented the 21 training strings repeatedly until no improvement in performance was noted; this took 2,000 training cycles. After training, the network was tested on the remaining 22 strings, which contained a total of 165 symbols. It incorrectly predicted the successor of ten of these symbols. There were also ten cases where the symbol had two legal successors, and the system predicted only one of them.

The representation learned in the hidden units differs somewhat from the first training set, because now the system "knows" that the strings must be of a limited length. Thus, for instance, if the network sees an X in position 7 of a string, it knows that an S must follow (this should be clear if you look at the automaton).

The cluster analysis of the hidden unit patterns produced in this second experiment revealed that the network clustered together partial sequences that led to the same prediction, partial sequences that ended in the same letter, and partial sequences that ended in the same node by taking similar paths. Thus path information, as well as node information, is incorporated in the representation, which was not the case in their first training experiment. This results directly from the fact that string length information is useful for the network to perform well in this task, and the best way to do this is to encode information on the path taken, which amounts to much the same thing.

Servan-Schreiber and his co-workers analyzed the learning process for a slightly simpler machine, and discovered that it divides, roughly, into phases. In the first phase, little learning has occurred, but the network produces different responses to different symbol inputs. In the second phase, the individual letters presented are grouped by what prediction (output) they make. Here the network is ignoring the context units. Then the network learns to pay attention to the context, which basically encodes what letter preceded the one that is currently being presented. At this point, it is learning associations between pairs of letters—the input letter and the one that preceded it—and the desired successor. In the final stage of learning, it learns to "remember" farther into the past, beyond the immediate predecessor, to find clues about what should follow. It is able, in the case of the first learning experiment, to use this information about the past to effectively determine the node in the finite-state machine at which it finds itself at any given point in its input stream.

The network has more difficulty "remembering" the further back in the input that the relevant information is. For instance, Servan-Schreiber and his co-workers consider the two sequences "PSSS" and "TSSS", which require the successors "P" and "T" respectively. When of the final "S" in each sequence is presented, the two networks (one processing each string) would have to have different internal representations (in the hidden units). The only way this could occur is if a discrepancy is retained from the initial letter, since all the S's are the same in both cases and could not have caused the difference. They observed that the amount of time needed to train the network was an exponential function of how far, in terms of the number of symbols, into the past it was being trained to remember.

Language processing requires the listener to remember constituents across arbitrarily long sentences of words. One example of this is in embedded clauses. For instance, in the sentence "the man who ran for governor sang a song", the listener must remember, when he or she hears the word "sang", that the subject of this sentence is "the man" despite the fact that there is an intervening clause. This problem is a generalization of the problem of a repeating letter discussed above. They studied it by using a more elaborate finite machine in which the strings in the language generated by the original (Reber's) machine was surrounded by either P's or T's (see Figure 7.3).

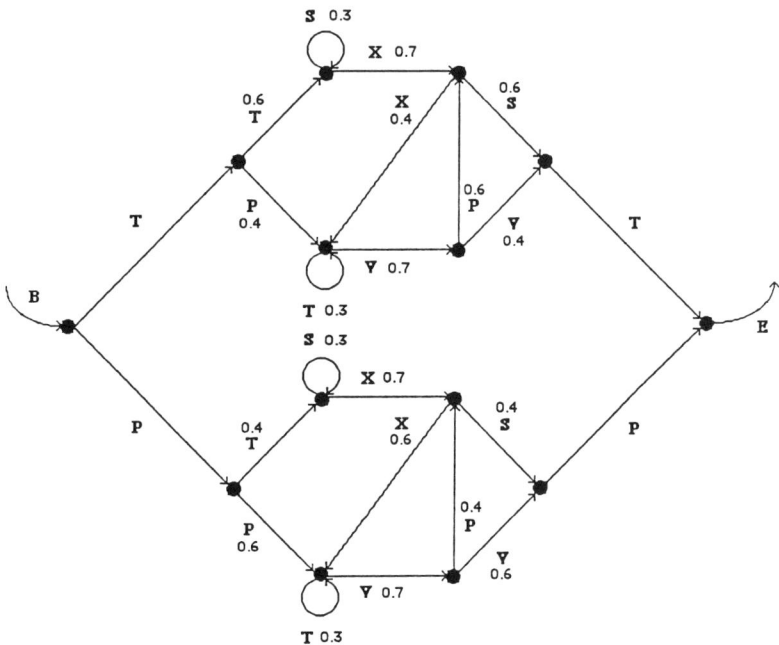

Figure 7.3. An elaboration on Reber's original automaton. From Servan-Schreiber et al. (1988); reprinted by permission.

If the transition probabilities are all equal to 0.5 in this machine (since there are two choices at each junction), when the training set of strings is generated, the network is unable to correctly predict a final T from an initial T or a final P from an initial P. Only if the strings surrounded by P's have a different statistical sample size from those surrounded by T's in the training set is the system able to learn to complete a string correctly. In other words, the initial symbol must be somehow encoded in the embedded sequence in the training set, which is what the network is quite poor at doing.

Thus this particular implementation of the embedding problem as a network was not very successful. The authors take an optimistic view of this, noting that small statistical differences in the training set are sufficient to create differences in performance on the completion task. They note that these simple recurrent networks are limited to "paying attention" to what immediately preceded a given symbol in the input; thus they are not applicable to context-free and more complex grammars in which totally independent sequences may be embedded in a certain string. Nevertheless, they have modeled an important aspect of language processing, to a limited extent: the speaker's expectations at any given point of the flow of speech.

7.3. Sentence Interpretation

Waltz and Pollack (1985) combine knowledge from a variety of sources in their connectionist model of sentence interpretation. Their approach is reminiscent of the HEARSAY II speech recognition system (Fennel & Lesser 1977).

They use a chart parser (Kay 1973) to create a parse represented as a network which contains several parse trees corresponding to syntactically valid readings of the sentences. Two non-terminals in the grammar that, at the same level in the network, ultimately contain the same words as constituents, inhibit one another; all child–parent connections are excitatory. Thus relaxation will result in a single unambiguous interpretation of a given sentence.

Waltz and Pollack view the resolution of lexical ambiguity as concurrent with parsing. When a word is activated, their system activates a network that represents all of its meanings; a set of nodes representing the word's alternate senses and lexical categories. All of the meanings inhibit one another, each meaning excites the lexical category the word is a member of, given that meaning, and inhibits all the rest of the lexical categories in the network. Finally, all the lexical categories inhibit one another. For instance, the word "shot" has four meanings, and so there are nodes corresponding to "tired", "bullet", "fired", and "wasted". "Tired" is an adjective; "fired" and "wasted" are verbs (in these meanings), and "bullet" is a noun (as in "buckshot"). There are nodes corresponding to "noun", "verb", and "adjective '; the "tired" node excites the "adjective" node and inhibits the "verb" and "noun" (the same connections are made in the reverse direction), etc.

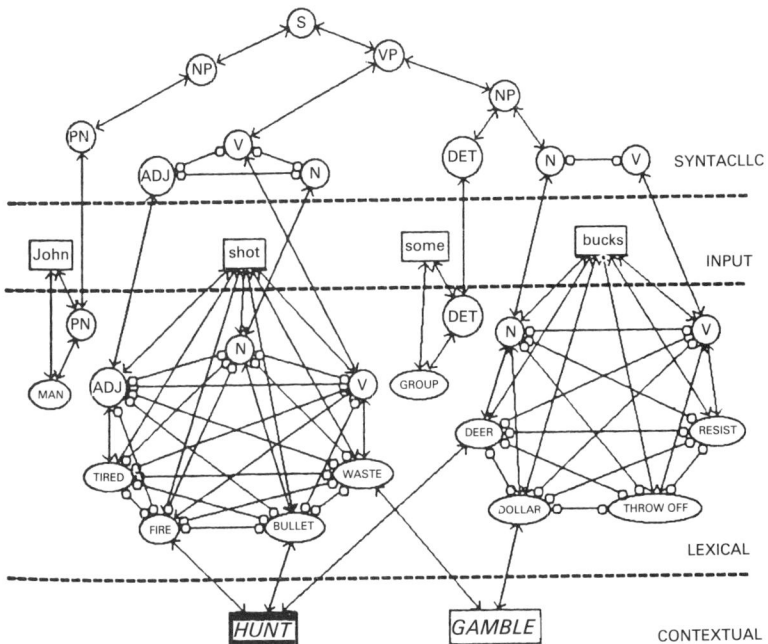

Figure 7.4. A network from Waltz and Pollack (1985) for interpreting the sentence "John shot some bucks" in the two contexts of hunting and gambling. Reprinted by permission.

A network for the sentence "John shot some bucks" is shown in Figure 7.4. This network is shown in the context of the node representing hunting being activated, as opposed to the node representing gambling being activated, that is, the sentence is taken to mean "John fired at some male deer" rather than "John wasted some money". When the node for the hunting context and the active syntactic categories are clamped at high activation, the network relaxes to a state which reflects the correct interpretation of the words "shot" and "bucks" in hunting. Nodes representing lexical categories that are the same in the lexical and syntactic portions of the tree activate one another as one can see by looking at the figure.

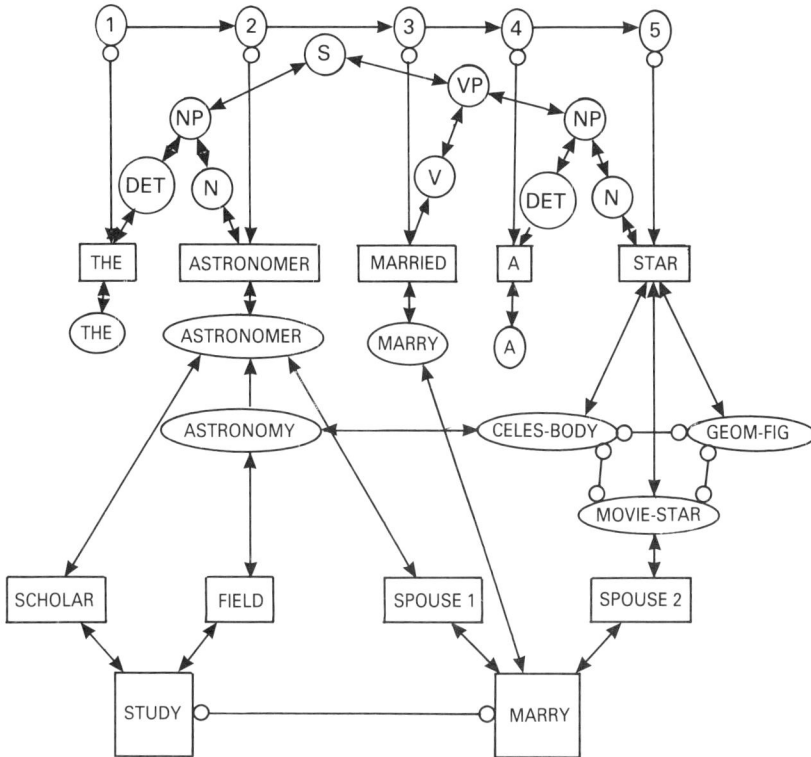

Figure 7.5. Network for disambiguating "The astronomer married a star." At this point, early in the relaxation, the incorrect interpretation ("star" as celestial body) is winning (dark nodes), but it soon will be defeated by the correct one ("star" as celebrity). From Waltz and Pollack (1985); reprinted by Permission

Waltz and Pollack's system exhibits the same sorts of "double-takes" as people do with sentences such as "the astronomer married a star". Many people upon hearing this sentence, briefly think that the astronomer married a celestial body, but then realized that s/he married a movie star, since one can't marry a celestial body (bad puns aside). This is modeled by their network's performance in Figure 7.5. Initially, the meaning of "celestial body" for "star" is highly activated by both the word "star" and the node for "astronomy" which has been activated by "astronomer". The node for "movie star" is not highly activated, since activation has not yet propagated through the node for "marry" to the "spouse 2" node and then to "movie star" as a plausible candidate for spouse 2. Eventually "movie star" wins out, as activation from "marry" beats activation from "astronomy". Of course this is dependent on the assignment of weights: This raises the question of whether weights alone are sufficient to convey the information that spouse 2 is necessary to the marriage.

In Waltz and Pollack's system, context and semantics play a major role in disambiguating syntactically and semantically ambiguous sentences. "An astronomer married a star" is an example of semantic ambiguity that their system handles well; their system can also handle sentences like "John ate up the street", in which one interpretation is wildly implausible, by using the semantic network to render implausible the interpretation that what was eaten is the street. Thus the syntactic and semantic/lexical parts of the network, although each is localized, have connections which allow them to work together at arriving at a plausible interpretation of a sentence.

Waltz and Pollack advocate a knowledge representation scheme in which the system's knowledge would be encoded in up to hundreds of thousands of nodes, and there would be a large set of microfeatures, on the order of a thousand. Each concept should be associated with a set of microfeatures, which would be a subset of the total set of microfeatures. These microfeatures, according to Waltz and Pollack, should represent concepts that are broadly used by people in dealing with a wide variety of situations. Their microfeatures are not based on logical decomposition, but simply on commonness and ecological usefulness. Waltz and Pollack note that any hierarchies and sets that exist emerge as a result of concepts that utilize the same subset of microfeatures. Since microfeatures are shared by many concepts, they can serve as a context.

For instance, in the earlier example of "John shot some bucks", they posit that the node for "hunt" might be connected to a node for the microfeature "outdoors". If the sentence "John shot some bucks" was preceded by "John and Mary drove to the cabin" and the node for "cabin" was connected to the "outdoors" node as well, then the "outdoors" node would be activated prior to the system seeing "John shot some bucks", and then the "hunting" node would be activated preferentially to the "gambling" node. If a number of other microfeatures also reinforced the "hunting" node (and possibly inhibited the "gambling" node), then the bias would be even stronger for the system to settle on the interpretation in the context of hunting.

The microfeatures would make it possible to quickly converge on the correct interpretation without necessitating a connection between every pair of nodes in the system, since two concepts can be connected indirectly, via one or more microfeatures. Waltz and Pollack note that the microfeatures should be chosen in such a fashion so as to discriminate any concept from all others. Connections would be strongly positive between a concept and microfeature (weight = 1), weakly positive (0.5), neutral (0.0), or weakly negative (-0.5). It would be rare that a concept and a microfeature to not be associated with one another. The set of microfeatures that two concepts share can be viewed as encoding a relation between them, so the association is not simple, as it would be in an ordinary (unlabeled) semantic network.

Waltz and Pollack note that since the world tends to have clusters of microfeatures that co-occur, the patterns of microfeatures would not be uniformly and randomly distributed, but would tend to cluster. They do not propose an adequate solution to the type/token problem; if there is only one set of microfeature nodes, then only one (or slightly more than one) concept can be active at a given time. One would think that the microfeature nodes would have to be duplicated in some way to handle complex thought patterns involving the simultaneous activation of several concepts.

Waltz and Pollack discuss how the weights and connections might come into being, and how they might be dynamically generated. It would be interesting to see how any of the various connectionist learning algorithms might be used to generate a network like that used by Waltz and Pollack.

Bookman (1988) developed a model, MICON (Microfeature Context), which extends Waltz and Pollack's work. Like Waltz and Pollack's model, MICON consists of nodes for word meanings, words, syntactic categories, and semantic microfeatures. He also adds a layer of timing nodes which delay the processing of the next word until the current word has been fully processed. His system performs word node relaxation followed by microfeature relaxation in a cycle, and thus establishes a shifting context in which new sentences can be interpreted.

7.4. Word Sense Disambiguation

Cottrell and Small (1983) approached the problem of disambiguating the meaning of a word with a connectionist model. Their model consists of four levels (see Figure 7.6); the lexical level, the word sense level, the case level, and the syntax level. At the lexical level, there is a unit for each word in the system. Each word has one or more nodes at the

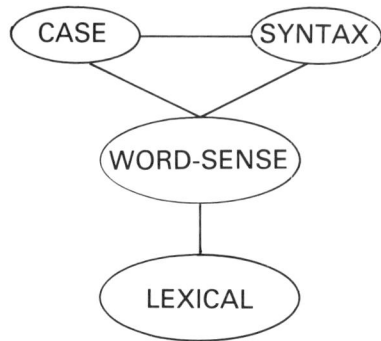

Figure 7.6. Architecture of the model of Cottrell and Small (1983). Reprinted by permission.

word sense level, corresponding to each of the meanings of the word, as in Waltz and Pollack's model. Each word on the lexical level is connected to each of its meanings on the word sense level. Each of the senses of a word, embodied in a node, inhibits all the other senses of that word.

Case theory, as advocated by Fillmore (1968), holds that the roles played by the various constituents in a sentence are critical to its comprehension. Word order gives cues to the roles played by the different noun phrases, as does the form of the verb. For instance, in the sentence "The boy ate the banana", we know from word order that the boy is the agent of the action of eating and the banana is the patient (thing eaten). If the form of the verb changes, as in "the boy was eaten by the lion", now word order gives us opposite information: the boy is the patient, the lion the agent. Prepositions like "by" also give clues to the role played, as do the semantic properties of a noun. For instance, only nouns with the property "animal" can (in non-idiomatic uses) be the agent of the verb "to eat".

Cottrell and Small's system's case level contains nodes representing cases; the authors use what they call an "exploded case representation" in which there are hundreds of semantic case roles rather than the dozen or so that are commonly mentioned (agent, instrument, etc.). The syntax level acts to enable or disable connections between various case rules; for instance, a particular word might take on a particular one of its senses, and a particular case role, if it is in a particular syntactic position (e.g., subject noun).

Cottrell and Small use the complex "and-of-or" units introduced by Feldman and Ballard (1982) (see section 2.2). Such a unit has multiple input sites, each of which has one or more inputs. Each site computes an "or" of all the inputs impinging on that site, or, in the case in which the inputs are real-valued, the maximum of the inputs (which is an extension of the "or" function to the real-valued case). The results computed at all the sites are then added together.

Cottrell and Small define cases as binary relations between predicates and arguments, for instance: Agent(run)=John, in the sentence "John ran home". They explode the case representations by encoding a single node for each predicate-role combination; thus there is a "buy–agent" node which denotes agents of the act of buying. The buy–agent node would be connected to all the nodes at the word sense level that are capable of being the agent of an act of buying. This specificity allows the system to embody a good deal of knowledge about which words can play which roles in a given action.

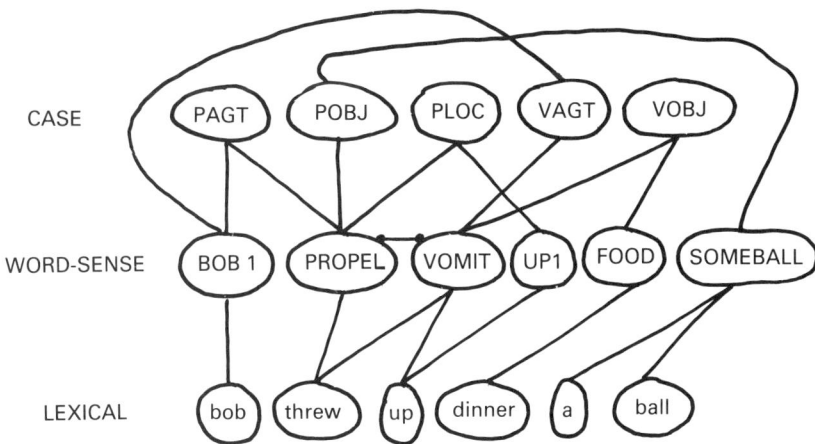

Figure 7.7. Subset of the network needed to distinguish "John threw up dinner" from "John threw up a ball." From Cottell and Small (1983); reprinted by permission.

Cottrell and Small give an example of a network that successfully disambiguates the various meanings of "threw", as in "Bob threw a ball for charity" (GAVE), "Bob threw the fight"

(THREW1), "Bob threw a ball to the dog" (PROPEL), and "Bob threw up dinner" (VOMIT). The four meanings are represented by 4 nodes denoted by GAVE, THREW1, PROPEL, and VOMIT. There are three case nodes denoting the agent, object, and location of the PROPEL action—PAGT, POBJ, and PLOC; and two nodes denoting the agent and object of the VOMITing—VAGT and VOBJ (why Cottrell and Small chose this particular unappetizing verb to disambiguate is beyond me!)

The subset of the entire network needed to distinguish "John threw up dinner" from "John threw up a ball" is shown in Figure 7.7. In the case of the former sentence (referring to the figure), we see that "dinner" has primed "food", which in its turn has primed "VOBJ", which primes "vomit". "Bob" primes "Bob1" (its sense node), which in its turn primes both "PAGT" and "VAGT". Thus the word "Bob" alone does not help in the disambiguation. Originally, when the system starts processing, the meanings PROBEL and VOMIT both get activated, but the inhibition between them insures that one of them will win out. In the case of the former sentence, it is "vomit", since it is receiving more activation (from the "up", "threw", "VAGT" and "VOBJ") than is propel (which is getting activation from "PAGT", "threw", and "PLOC"). The critical word "dinner" makes the difference, via "VOBJ". If it is replaced by "ball", then VOBJ becomes deactivated and POBJ becomes activated, and thus the "propel" meaning of "threw" wins out.

The connections between nodes can reflect the statistical frequencies of correlation between them. This way, if a word is heard, the system will assume the most common meaning of it.

Without large amounts of lateral inhibition, activation will "bleed" through Cottrell and Small's network. A theory is needed which tells where inhibiting links must be placed in order to lead to stable coalitions of nodes that represent a consistent sentence interpretation.

7.5. Making Case Role Assignments

McClelland and Kawamoto (1986b), like Cottrell and Small, developed a connectionist system for making case role assignments. Case role assignments are also sometimes ambiguous, as in "the boy saw the girl with the binoculars". Here, depending on the context, either the boy or the girl have the binoculars. McClelland and

Kawamoto's goal was to develop a model which simultaneously accounts for the multiple constraints on role assignment. This model was to select the proper verb case frame, to account for the effects of context, to select default values for missing constituents, and to generalize, guessing properties of a previously unseen word based on the role it is playing in a sentence.

The model has two sets of units—one representing the constituent structure of the sentence and the other representing the role assignments of the sentence. The model learns by being presented with associations between activation patterns in the two sets of units, using the perceptron convergence procedure.

Each word is represented by a set of semantic microfeatures. They chose those microfeatures based on important divisions in human perception, such as "soft/hard", "male/female/neuter". Verbs have microfeatures such as "touch/no touch" which tells whether the agent touches the patient during the course of the action, or "cause, no-cause, no-change" corresponding, respectively, to conditions in which the verb causes something to happen, or in which there is no cause specified, or in which the verb doesn't cause any change at all. There are eight dimensions describing nouns and seven describing verbs. Each microfeature is specified by the minimum number of bits needed to specify all of its values. Each noun and verb is therefore represented by a bit vector which is a concatenation of the bit values on each microfeature. If a word is ambiguous, then it is represented by the average of its possible patterns.

The "bits" are real-valued; a word that had a 1 on one bit in one meaning and a 0 on it in the other meaning would have a value of 0.5 on that bit. The model uses top-down constraints to resolve such ambiguities, forcing the bit value to either 0 or 1.

Both verbs and nouns have more than one meaning. The model separates the different uses of a verb into different bit vectors; for instance, the use of "broke" when no instrument is specified indicates that the agent manually broke the patient whereas a use such as "the hammer broke the glass" specifies no agent, and there is contact between the instrument and the patient. The microfeature pattern for "touch" has a different bit for each role that could touch the patient. This representation is subject to criticism from the point of view of Fodor and Pylyshyn (see section 1.9), who argue that connectionist models that do not have the ability to manipulate combinatorially combined symbolic expressions face the necessity of using a different node to represent each combination, as

McClelland and Kawamoto do, using separate nodes for each pair agent/touch, instrument/touch, both-instrument-and-agent/touch, etc. Of course, in their system the number of roles is rather low, so the number of combinations is low.

The simple sentence input they use is preprocessed with the use of a standard, non-connectionist parser into its four constituents; the verb, subject, noun phrase (NP), object NP. These constituents are each represented redundantly by an array of units called sentence structure (SS) units. There is an SS unit for every pair of microfeature bits; for instance for the nouns there is a unit corresponding to human=yes/ gender=male. If both of these bits are on, the conjoined unit is on (value 1) with a probability of 0.85; if only one is on, the conjoined unit is on with a probability of 0.5, and if both are off, the conjoined unit is on with a probability of 0.15. The units are thus stochastic.

Cottrell and Small view case slot fillers as relations of the form (A R B), e.g., (Broke Agent Boy) denotes the fact that the agent of the verb "broke" is "boy". A localist representation would require that each combination of three features would have its own node. McClelland and Kawamoto use a distributed representation composed of the case structure units. There is an array of units corresponding to each of the agent, patient, instrument, and modifier in their simplified case structure. Each unit in each array represents the conjunction of a microfeature from the representation of the verb, that is the first operand in the relation, with a microfeature from the noun, that is the second operand. The main difference between the sentence structure and case structure units is: in the sentence structure units an entity's microfeatures are conjoined in a cross product with each other, whereas in the case structure units the microfeatures of one operand are conjoined with those of the other.

Each of the sentence structure units is connected to each of the case structure units via weighted connections. Each unit has a variable bias. The system, since it has no hidden units, was trained using the perceptron convergence procedure. The patterns in the two sets of units were set during the training by a conventional computer program. There are about 2500 units total in the case role representation, and approximately 100 of these should be activated by any given sentence. Their model, after 50 training cycles, turns on about 85 of these accurately, and 15 of them incorrectly.

McClelland and Kawamoto interpreted the model's ability to generalize case role properties of different verbs. For instance, if the model learns that the role "patient" of the verb "to break" is always filled by a "fragile object", it should be biased toward assuming this when a novel sentence is presented. It should be able to use this to arrive at the correct interpretation of "the dog broke the plate" and "the window broke". In the former case, "dog" should be assigned to the role "agent", whereas in the latter case, "window" should be assigned the role "patient". This is exactly the behavior the model exhibits, after being trained on a number of examples in which a fragile object is the object of "broke". This behavior is due to the complete connectivity between the case structure and the sentence structure units, which allows the model to pick up the microfeatures of a particular slot filler no matter where it may be found in the sentence.

Conversely, the model is able to use word order information to make the correct role assignments for "the girl hit the boy" and "the boy hit the girl", although boy and girl, in their model, differ only on a single microfeature. This is because the model is able to form strong correlations between patterns in particular role constituents and patterns in particular sentence constituents.

The model exhibits the automatic generation of defaults. A default represents a weighted average of all the arguments that have been presented in training in the place taken by the missing argument. The model also is able to use case frame information and context to resolve lexical ambiguity, as in "the chicken ate the carrot", where chicken is correctly assigned the role of eater despite the fact that it normally plays the role of the thing eaten. This is because the carrot can play the role of the thing eaten, and the word order makes the chicken preferentially play the role of eater.

The model is also able to make "errors" that reflect context. In the case when a soft ball breaks something the model incorrectly labels the ball as hard, because normally hard objects are needed to break other objects.

7.6. The MPNP Parsing System

Li and Chun (1987) developed a connectionist system for parsing natural language. Their work is unorthodox from a connectionist point of view, since it uses both a connectionist network, and the passing of explicit symbolic markers. In their system, the nodes can themselves contain symbolic tokens. They refer to parsing their system as the MPNP (Massively Parallel Network-based Parsing) system.

They have three modules in their system, the dictionary interface, the MPNP network, and the inference network. The dictionary interface processes the input sentence, creating a sequence of markers indicating the syntactic category of each word. The MPNP network represents an entire context-free grammar. The bottom of the network has one node for each terminal symbol in the grammar. Grammatical rules are represented by connections to nodes lower down in the network.

For each non-terminal symbol, there are as many nodes in the MPNP network as there are instances of that symbol on the left-hand side (LHS) of a rewrite rule. The LHS symbol is connected to all the symbols, below it in the network, that are on the right-hand side (RHS) of the rule. Figure 7.8 shows a sample grammar and the MPNP network that is constructed from it. Note that recursive rules imply self-links in the network. The links are labeled A, B, C, ... according to their order on the RHS of the role, giving the ordering for use by a homunculus internal to the LHS node.

Each of the nodes in their system has its own local memory. In order for a node to become active, it must receive all of its inputs in the order given by the labels on the links. Only after this can a marker pass across the link. The markers represent phrases; each of them contains the start position of the phrase in the input sentence, a value one greater than the end position, and a pointer to a data structure representing the syntactic or semantic structure of the phrase.

(1) S -> S1
(2) S1 -> NP VP peri
(3) S1 -> VP excl
(4) VP -> Vnt [adv]
(5) VP -> Vtr [adv] NP
(6) VP -> Vdo NP NP
(7) VP -> VP PP

(8) PP -> pre NP
(9) NP -> det NP1
(10) NP -> NP1
(11) NP -> NP PP
(12) NP1 -> non
(13) NP1 -> adj NP1

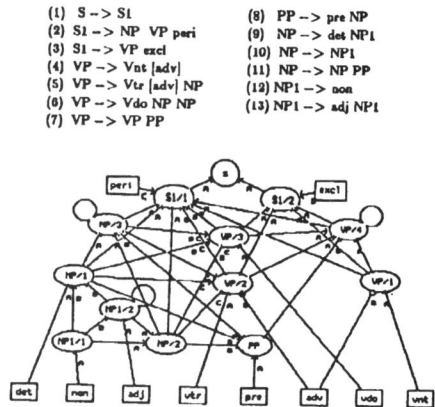

Figure 7.8 A grammar and a network representing it. From Li and Chun (1987); reprinted by permission.

Each node in the network runs an independent version of a program called the housekeeper. The housekeeper makes sure that the markers that are passed into the node arrive in the proper order, and rejects any that arrive out of order. It also makes sure that the starting position is correct. When all the required markers of a given node are received in the proper order, a new marker is constructed out of them that has as its starting position that starting position of the first marker comprising the phrase, and as its ending position the ending position of the last. This new marker is then passed upward to all the nodes that the node in question is connected to (in that direction.) This results, ultimately, in a left-to-right parse of the input sentence, but it avoids the duplication of resources required by a more strictly connectionist implementation such as that of Fanty (see the next section), while retaining the same amount of parallelism.

Like Fanty's system, Li and Chun's system implements top-down expectations by using two levels of activation. They propagate this top-down expectation from the start symbol S, which is at the top of the network. As this expectation is propagated downwards, nodes below the S symbol are placed into a semi-activated state. Only semi-activated nodes can receive input from below; when they have received one of their required marker inputs, they can move into a fully activated state. If nodes do not receive any bottom-up input, they are deactivated. The system therefore starts with very broad expectation, which is gradually narrowed down over the course of parsing.

The system also contains, within each node, procedures which Li and Chun call demons. The function of these demons is to construct a parse tree out of the smaller trees passed up in the grammatical network with the markers that come from the phrase constituents below. Each marker, you may recall, contains a pointer to such a parse tree; the demon need only combine these trees left to right. It may also perform associated tasks, such as filling in semantic roles in a case frame, or perform semantic inferences by accessing a knowledge base.

The system is able to deal with recursive syntax rules naturally enough, via self-links. Nodes pass markers to themselves which then get included in larger markers.

Li and Chun used their system to parse both English and Chinese sentences. The system extends nicely to handle a problem found in understanding Chinese, that one or more characters may correspond to a word. A character occurring alone may denote one thing, whereas in combination with another character it may mean something different. It is difficult to ascertain which one is intended without the aid of syntactic or semantic information. In Li and Chun's system, these character combination rules are naturally added at the lowest level of the MPNP system, and thus syntactic and word combination information are integrated naturally.

The main advantage of the MPNP system over conventional serial mechanisms of parsing that utilize backtracking are its parallelism and its mechanism of passing phrase markers to all the nodes that might need them. A promising line of research might be to figure out a way to implement the marker passing used in MPNP in a more strictly connectionist manner.

7.7. Parsing Strings from Context-Free Grammars

Fanty (1985) developed a connectionist model that parses sentences that are formed from arbitrary context-free grammars (CFGs). Given a CFG that contains no e-productions (rewrite rules that replace symbols with nothing), Fanty constructed a connectionist network that parses strings of some maximum length, and creates a parse tree that is implicit in the activations of nodes in the network. His model is purely syntactic. In contrast to the work of Selman and Hirst and others, who typically have the network relax to only one valid parse, Fanty's system computes all the possible parses of an input sentence in parallel.

Fanty based his network on the CYK parsing scheme (Hopcroft & Ullman 1979). Like many other schemes, Fanty's involves a hierarchy of units. On the bottom level is a set of units representing the input string, which Fanty refers to as the terminal units. There is one unit on this level for each symbol position in the input string, and then, within each symbol position, for each terminal symbol in the grammar. So, for each symbol position that is active in the input string, exactly one input unit is active.

The other two types of units in his network are the non-terminal units and the match units. Each of the three kinds of units has two sites, one for top-down and the other for bottom-up input. There is a non-terminal units for each combination of a non-terminal unit and a possible length (length of the substring that the non-terminal stands for, that is, the length of the substring is found in the leaves of the parse tree below that non-terminal), starting at every possible position of this substring. Thus the representation is highly local, requiring a large number of units.

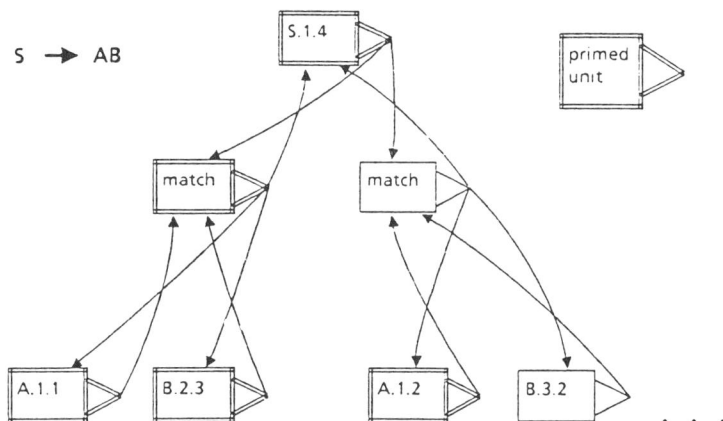

Figure 7.9. A sub-network of match units representing a grammar rule. One of the match units happens to be primed by input. From Fanty (198); reprinted by permission.

The match units are used to represent the production rules. Each production rule in the grammar has a number of match units associated with it. There is a match unit for each set of non-terminal units that can logically come together in a position and length-specific instantiation of a rule. So for instance, if there is, as on the left side of Figure 7.9, a unit for the non-terminal A starting at string position 1 and of length 2 (thus occupying positions 1 and 2 of the string) and there is a unit for the non-terminal B starting at position 3, also of length 2 (thus occupying positions 3 and 4), since these two non-terminals are adjacent (in terms of what they represent), the rule S->AB applies to them. Thus there is a match unit which receives input from these A and B units, as well as from an S unit which represents strings of length 4 starting at position 1. The former connections are bottom up, and the latter ones are top-down. All the links are weighted.

There are also match units for rules containing terminal symbols; the only difference is that each terminal symbol represents a substring of length one, while non-terminals usually represent longer substrings.

A parse takes place in two phases, a bottom-up phase and a top-down phase. Units in the terminal layer are initially activated by being "primed", which, in Fanty's implementation, gives them an activation value of 5, out of a possible 10. The weights are set so that, as this priming activation flows upwards, match units will become primed if all the units below them are primed. Non-terminal units are primed if any of the match units that give input to them are primed, since the priming of any one of these match units represents an instance of that non-terminal.

A parse is effected when a unit representing the start symbol is primed. There is such a unit for every possible length of the sentence; in the case of a sentence of length n, there is a special symbol in symbol position $n+1$ that provides input to the start symbol for a sentence of length n, causing it to turn "on". "On" and "primed" are the two states of a unit in Fanty's system. This start unit now provides top-down input to those units below it in the network. Every bottom-up connection has a corresponding top-down connection. Non-terminal units turn on if they are primed and the unit giving them the maximal top-down input is on. Terminal units turn on if they receive top-down input from a unit that is primed. Thus all the valid parse trees of the given input sentence come to be embodied in the network, each comprised of units that are on.

The network, as it has been described above, requires somewhat complex units, since they have three discrete levels of activation: off, primed, and on. Fanty shows that each of these three-state units can be easily replaced with two binary-state units, one for the bottom-up pass of activation, and one for the top-down pass.

Fanty modified the network so that it automatically disambiguated syntactically ambiguous sentences. He did this by making a winner-take-all network out of each set of match units corresponding to a given non-terminal unit, so that each sentence constituent can only participate in a parse in a single way, and thus only a single parse can be represented in the network. It was necessary to introduce some randomness into the network so that one of the match units would win out over the others, since the way the network was initially programmed, all valid match units would receive an equal amount of activation.

In order to learn new productions, or more specifically, instances of productions at particular locations in the sentence, Fanty created a new class of match units, which he called *free match units*. The network goes into "learn" mode when an attempt is made to turn on a nonterminal that is not primed. This indicates that a production instance exists that has not been detected and therefore should be learned. Each free match unit can respond to at most two local units below it, each representing a specific constituent at a specific position and a specific length. If a free match unit responds strongly after the system enters learn mode, it is recruited as a fixed match unit for the non-terminal that was missing a match, and the system leaves learn mode. (Learn mode is entered when a special unit called the learn unit is activated.)

Fanty also devised a quite elaborate mechanism to generalize these locally learned production instances throughout all the positions of the network. The basic idea behind this, taken from McClelland's (1985) Connection Information Distributor (CID), is that there is a global representation of each production, which is distributed throughout the network in the form of instances. I will not go into the details of this here.

There is room for substantially more work on natural language parsing to follow up this work. Fanty suggests learning and parsing more complex grammars, such as augmented phrase structure grammars, as a possible avenue of attack

7.8. PARSNIP: A Parsing System
Based on Back-propagation

Hanson and Kegl (1987) developed PARSNIP (a "snippet" of a parser), a connectionist model that learns to categorize the words in sentences into syntactic categories. They use the auto-associative version of back-propagation, in which the input and the teaching output are the same. They chose, as a training set of sentences, the Brown Corpus of text (Francis & Kucera 1979), which has about a million words. Each word in this corpus has an associated syntactic tag (noun, verb, etc.), which was chosen by human judges with a knowledge of linguistics.

They used a feed-forward network with 270 input units, 270 output units, and 45 hidden units, for a total of 585 units in the system. Thus their system, like Cottrell and co-workers' image compression system (see section 2.31), must record in the hidden units a representation of the input that is more compact than the surface structure of the input sentence.

Only the syntactic categories of each word were input to the system, not the words themselves. A 9-bit string carried the syntactic information about each word; this string was formed by combining information about part of speech, inflection, punctuation, and whether a word is a function word, to result in 467 unique syntactic codes. They limited the length of the sentences shown to the network to 15 or less, padding out the input with zeros if necessary in order to use all 270 units. There were 25,000 such sentences in the Brown corpus. They also included codes for word boundaries in the input.

When they presented 10 sentences repeatedly in training, it took about 100 cycles through the data—that is, about 1,000 sentence presentations in total—until 95% of the codes for syntactic categories passed from input to output, unaltered. After the network was trained to this degree, they increased the number of training sentences to 100. Performance quickly plummeted to about 50% correct; it took about another 160 epoches of training on the new data—16,000 presentations—before the performance returned to 95%. Finally, another 900 sentences were added to the training set, for a total of 1,000 sentences. Even after 180 epoches of 1,000 presentations each, the network achieved no better than 85% correct performance, and performance fluctuated chaotically in the short term. Thus the network apparently reached its capacity.

They observed that word boundaries tend to be learned first, then mass nouns and personal pronouns, and then other forms. Generalization was tested by showing each of the three networks 1,000 novel sentences. The network trained on 10 sentences gave about 50% correct performance, the network trained on 100 sentences gave about 60% correct performance, and the network trained on 1,000 sentences gave about 85% correct performance (the same as on the training set).

PARSNIP is able to complete sentences with missing words, indicating in its output the syntactic category of the missing word. It is also not fooled by classic "garden path" sentences, such as "the horse raced past the barn fell". This is demonstrated by the fact that if the incorrect part of speech is inserted in the input sentence—for example, if "past" is characterized as an adverb, the system replaces it, in its output, with the correct category—in this case a preposition.

The system is also able to correctly auto-associate center embedded sentences, such as "The rat the cat chased died", but is unable to handle doubly embedded sentences. This behavior is similar that of people.

Hanson and Kegl do not feel that PARSNIP provides an adequate model of language acquisition, yet it has shown that it has acquired some of the important aspects of linguistic structure by its performance on the garden path and missing word tasks. They note that the system exhibits behavior that cannot be explained by simple finite-state grammars or matrices of transition probabilities. For instance, they point out that when faced with the sentence completion task "the destruction of the city ____", PARSNIP indicated that the blank should be filled by a conjunction, even though a conjunction is not the most likely word to follow a noun. Like a standard context-free parser, PARSNIP is able to remember "long-distance" relationships.

An analysis of PARSNIP's hidden units needs to be done in order to determine precisely what constituents the system understands. Hanson and Kegl do have evidence that clusters of hidden units respond either to noun phrases or verb phrases.

7.9. A Quasi-Context-Free Parsing System

Charniak and Santos (1987) devised a connectionist system for parsing sentences drawn from a context-free grammar. They point out that connectionist parsers, insofar as they do not contain unlimited numbers of units, cannot be truly context-free, since they cannot represent sentences with arbitrary amounts of recursive embedding. Yet, since a connectionist parser can be devised which has, as its limit, a context-free parser, as the number of units goes to infinity, Charniak and Santos argue that we ought to consider it context-free

They represent the parse tree of a sentence by a two-dimensional array of units, each of which holds a terminal or non-terminal symbol of the grammar. The bottom row of units contains the terminal symbols in a sentence.

Above each terminal symbol, in each column, is the complete path to the start symbol. Thus the parse tree in Figure 7.10 is represented by the table in Figure 7.11.

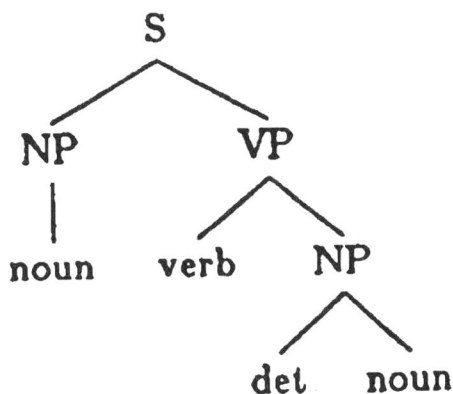

7.10. Parse tree used by Charniak and Santos (1987). Reprinted by permission.

Links are made in the table between tokens in adjacent columns that represent the same constituent.

The parser works by taking in new word categories in the lower right corner of the table and shifting them to the left as it parses. Each time a new word category is moved into the table, all the cells in the table recompute their values, using rules that will be described shortly, and then the entire table is shifted one column to the left, to prepare for the input of the next word category.

The system has a number of rules that it attempts to enforce at every location in its parsing table. Each location has a number of non-terminal symbols associated with it, each with a probability of being present. Rules are used to raise and lower the probabilities of location-non-terminal combinations. The first such rule enforces the equality

	S		
NP	VP		
		NP	
noun	verb	det	noun

Figure 7.11. Table representing parse tree from Charniak and Santos (1987); reprinted by permission.

of non-terminals that are linked together, left to right. Another rule states that if the non-terminal in table position *(i,j)* is connected by a link to a non-terminal in position *(i-1,k)*, then a non-terminal in position *(i,j+1)* should be connected to a non-terminal in position *(i,k+1)*. This makes sure that none of the connections in the table cross; any chain of connections, as in Figure 7.12, is strictly above or below any other chain. This is a property of a parse tree as it is represented in this kind of table.

Grammatical rules are embodied in more such constraints. Charniak and Santos give as an example the grammatical rule S←NP VP, which implies that an NP at location *(i,j)* leads to an S at *(i, j+1)*, leading to a vertical representation of the parse tree. This is the case for

			S	S
S	S	VP	VP
NP	VP	NP	NP
noun	verb	det	noun

Figure 7.13. Charniak and Santos' (1987) representation of a parse. Reprinted by permission.

every constituent of a rule such as A ←... B ...: A is placed in the slot above B in the table. Moreover, as rules start and end, constraints make sure that no units to the left and right of the start and end respectively of a rule are connected to the start or end symbols. (This is necessary because every slot in the table, whether it is empty or not, contains a pointer value.) Another constraint says that if a rule such as S<-NP VP has its VP inserted in the table, which is finishing (that is, it has "gobbled up" its the constituents which it represents), then it should encourage the S above it to finish, and vice versa. "Finishing," in this use, denotes terminating the chain of left-to-right connections between symbols representing the same constituent.

Because of the limitations of the size of the table, the system is limited in the lengths of sentences that it can parse. The table can be made arbitrarily big, at the expense of resources, to parse larger and larger sentences. The system handles right-embedded sentences fine, but it cannot handle center-embedded sentences, because new constituents moving into the table that are center-embedded have nothing in the parse tree to be connected to. This is somewhat consistent with psychological results that indicate that parsing center-embedded sentences is more difficult for people; nevertheless, the parser needs to be improved so that it can handle them, because people can.

7.10. Parsing Using a Boltzmann Machine

Selman and Hirst (1987) use a Boltzmann machine and simulated annealing to accomplish parsing in a context-free network. They do this using a network with two layers. The input layer contains units that represent the terminal symbol of a context-free grammar. The parsing layer

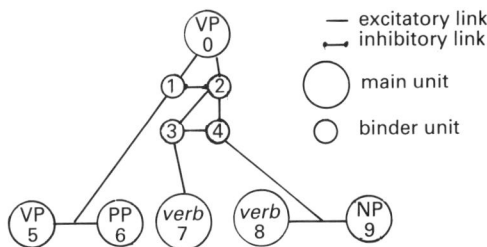

Figure 7.13. Selman and Hirst's (1987) represenation of grammatical rules. Reprinted by permission.

consists of small groups of units that represent context-free rules. A rewrite rule such as S←NP VP is represented by three nodes, one for each symbol, connected together in a clique. Selman and Hirst refer to such a rule clique as a connectionist *primitive*. Connectionist primitives are linked together by special units referred to as binder units. For instance, if there are three rewrite rules for VP, these are linked to one another via binder nodes, which inhibit one another (see Figure 7.13). All nodes other than binder nodes are referred to as main nodes.

The input layer is divided into groups, one for each word in the input. Each group has a unit for each of the lexical categories—that is, the terminal symbols supported by the grammar. There are enough input groups to deal with every word in the longest sentence that the system supports. Exactly one unit is activated in each group; the rest are de-activated. Selman and Hirst use the two output values -1 and +1, as opposed to other work that uses simulated annealing, which uses 0 and 1. This entails slight modification of the simulated annealing equations. After simulated annealing, when the system has reached low temperature, the units outputting +1 represent the parse tree.

In their simulations, Selman and Hirst only had grammar rules with one or two symbols on the right-hand side (RHS). In order not to bias the choice of which rule is incorporated into the parse tree, they use a weight of +2 in the excitatory connections between units in one-symbol RHS primitives and connections of +1 in the two-symbol RHS primitive. The inhibitory weights (between pairs of adjacent binder units) were set to -3. If a main unit was connected only to binder nodes, its threshold was set to -2, otherwise it was set to 0. The binder units had a threshold of +2 (since they compete with one another, only the one receiving the most input should be activated).

Selman and Hirst were concerned that their stable states might not lead to states representing parses. As a possible solution to this problem, they proposed a scheme in which the energy is measured on the basis of whether all the units in the system have reached stable states. They built a sample network based on a sample CFG with 11 rules taken from Winograd's textbook (1983). After simulated annealing, the units that were active embodied the parse tree of the sample sentence that was used. The temperature sequence used was $T = 10,000, 4, 2, 1.8, 1.6, 1.4, 1.2, 1.0, 0.8,$ and 0.6 Each temperature involved 2,000 updates per unit. Thus, simulated annealing, as usual, was a slow process; if realized in hardware it would be much faster.

Selman and Hirst tested the effects of changing the weights and thresholds to incorrect values. The setting of one of the thresholds to an incorrect value led the system to fluctuate between two states, one of which was the correct parse. The stochastic nature of this algorithm led to this fluctuation; when the temperature was lowered to zero the system settled into one state or the other.

7.11. Learning the Past Tense

Rumelhart and McClelland (1986a) offer a connectionist theory that attempts to explain how the past tenses of English verbs are learned, as an alternative to the traditional approach of rule-learning that is exemplified by the work of Pinker (1984). In this letter approach, unconscious rules are acquired by a special language acquisition device (LAD) in the mind, following Chomsky's theory (1980). Rumelhart and McClelland argue that processes that appear to be rule-governed are in fact governed by other processes; they give the example of a honeycomb, whose characteristic hexagonal form is a result of the interaction of lower-level actions taken by the bees. They claim that a connectionist model can substitute for explicit rules.

They note that children typically go through three stages in the learning of the past tense. In stage 1, children know a small set of past forms, such as came, got, gave, looked, needed, took, and went, of which only two are regular (looked and needed). In stage 2, children are able to form past tenses using -ed, but they over-generalize to form charming errors like "taked". In stage 3, this over-generalization is corrected. The movement from stage 1 through stage 2 to stage 3 is continuous and gradual, like many human learning processes.

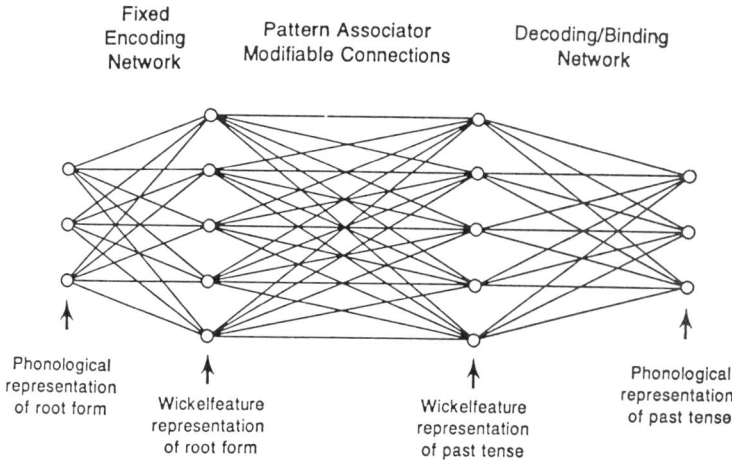

Figure 7.14. Architecture of Rumelhart and McClelland's (1986d) verb learning model. Reprinted by permission.

Their model consists of units phonologically representing the root forms and units phonologically representing the past tense forms. These are connected to each other in a pattern associator network. Two layers of units lie between these two sets of units, to form a four-layer network. The root form phonological units (layer 1) are connected to "wickelfeature" units (see below) representing the root form (layer 2) These latter units are connected to wickelfeature units representing the past tense form (layer 3), which are connected to the phonetic units for the past tense. (layer 4) The idea is that a phonological representation of the root form given as input will cause a phonological representation of the past tense form to appear as output (see Figure 7.14).

They use binary threshold units with a logistic probability of becoming activated; this probability depends on the amount a unit's input exceeds the threshold. In their first example, they trained a simple pattern associator, using only a two-layer perceptron and the perceptron convergence procedure to recognize associations. They then extended their model so as to account for the representations of words, using the four-layer associator mentioned above.

Each sound is represented phonetically by its sound and the sounds of the two sounds surrounding it. These are called wickelphones, since this scheme was first suggested by Wickelgren (1969). For instance, tthe wickelphone representation of the word "cat" is #k$_a$, k^{a}t at#. (# denotes a word boundary.) The trouble is that there are too many wickelphones, about 42,000. Therefore, Rumelhat and McClelland do not explicitly represent wickelphones.

Instead, wickelphones are coarse-coded; each wickelphone is represented as a pattern across another set of units (layers two and three in the description above), called the "wickelfeatures". Eleven bits are used to classify each sound in terms of whether or not it is a stop, fricative, a nasal stop, etc.; thus 33 bits are needed to represent the three sounds in a wickelphone. Each wickelfeature unit corresponds to a triple of features; one drawn from each phoneme participating in the wickelphone, in the *nth* place out of 11 features. For instance, a particular wickelfeature might represent all those phonemes that have a left context that is a nasal, a right context that is a stop, and whose central phoneme is voiced. They did not use all possible wickelfeatures, just about half, which "covered" the wickelphone territory sufficiently with their receptive fields. They also "blurred" the representation of wickelphones by randomly turning on some wickelfeature units that were similar to the wickelfeatures in given wickelphone's receptive field. This permitted the system to generalize based on limited experience.

Thus in the four layer system described above, only the inner two layers actually exist in the system: wickelfeature units for representing the base form of the verb (the input units) and wickelfeature units for representing the past tense. There were 460 units on each side, and learning proceeded using binary threshold units, a logistic activation rule, and the perceptron convergence rule. Their model reflected the three stage performance of children, and was able to generalize to verbs it had not previously seen.

The model was first trained on 10 high-frequency verbs, then on 420 medium-frequency verbs. Then its responses to a set of low-frequency verbs was recorded. Performance on irregular verbs originally rose at the same rate as regular verbs (stage 1), then fell off as the regular verb performance continued to improve (stage 2). Irregular verb performance then started to improve again (stage 3), but never reached the level of regular verbs. In children, the error of over-generalizing was more likely to be made earlier in the learning process.

Their simulation can be criticized on the basis that it does not accurately simulate the actual data that children receive. It would be more accurate to simply train the network on all the verbs at the frequency that they occur naturally, and let the system simply attend to the more high-frequency ones in its behavior; this is what children have to do.

They show that the model correctly captures children's performance on a variety of different irregular verbs, even capturing many of the detailed features of the performance. For the verbs on which the system was not trained, 90% of the regular verbs have the correct performance in forming the past tense and 85% of the irregular verbs do. Correct performance on the irregular verbs is based on system sensitivity to "sub-regularities" in English, such as sing–sung, ring–rung (but bring–brung?). They note that both their model and children exhibit differing past tense forms for the same verb. Rule accounts need to be made probabilistic to account for this.

They point out that because of the superpositional nature of their distributed memory, their system performs automatic generalization. Thus, they claim, the system is not performing rule induction, as in a traditional memory scheme, but neither is it simply storing associations, or rather the associations it is storing are of a more general nature than the root form–past tense association at the phonetic level. Of course, one might argue, the salient features of the phonology have been built into the wickelfeature representation; a more complete solution to the problem would learn the relevant phonological features at the same time as learning the root verb–past tense association.

7.12.A Critique of "Learning the Past Tense"

Pinker and Prince (1988) develop a critique of Rumelhart and McClelland's past tense verb model, and a defense of rule-based models of language acquisition and their use in linguistics in general, which, as a theoretical technique, had reigned almost unchallenged ever since the rise of cognitivism in the 1950s—until connectionism came along. They note that language provides a critical test case for connectionism since linguistic theory has been notoriously rule-laden and reasonably successful in explaining linguistic phenomena.

Pinker and Prince point out that when Rumelhart and McClelland claim that their model does not involve rules, they mean that no rules are explicitly represented in their model. The Rumelhart and McClelland model relies heavily on wickelphones and wickelfeatures to achieve this. Pinker and Prince feel that wickelphones and wickelfeatures are limited as a representation medium. For instance, they point out that "slit" and "silt" have no wickelphones in common in their wickelphone representation; thus a transformation of slit to silt involves a complete replacement of wickelphones. This is not the case in terms of wickelfeatures, but they point out that such a substitution involves just as many changes in wickelfeatures as one that is phonetically much more distant. Yet the wickelfeature model takes clear advantage of similarities between the input and output representations to produce generalization. Pinker and Prince's complaint is that it does not readily support generalizations using the form slit–silt, although such transformations exist in human languages.

They note that the wickelfeature model readily models linguistically impossible phenomena, such as relating a word to its phonetic mirror image, for instance, dumb to mud. This is easy to do in the wickelfeature representation; simply give positive weights to connections between ABC in the input wickelfeatures and CBA in the output.

Pinker and Prince point out that past tense is only one of several processes in English that use the t-d-id regular inflection, as in kicked (t), slugged (d), and patted (id). Other processes, such as the process that makes adjectives from nouns, as in hooked (t), horned (d), and talented (id) use the same inflections. The reason they point this out is to make the point that the inflection is not morphological, but phonological. Phonology is a system that exists outside of morphology; any morphological change is subject to phonological modification.

This is even clearer in the case of the (-s, -z, -iz) alteration (e.g., hawks, dogs, hoses) which is used in no fewer than nine different morphological contexts in English, including plural, possessive, contraction of "is", etc. It can be applied in completely novel circumstances, as in the end of a noun phrase: Pinker and Prince give the example "the man you met's dog". Given the extraordinary productivity of language, this kind of thing can come up in a basically infinite number of ways; the phonological, morphological, and syntactic systems must interact in a complex fashion to attach the possessive in the place. Thus, contrary to what Rumelhart and McClelland's model implies, forming correct inflections is not simply a matter of forming associations between words. Of course, this does not invalidate connectionist models, but just implies that they must be employed as components of a larger system.

Among many other criticisms of details of the model, Pinker and Prince also accuse Rumelhart and McClelland's model of "morphological localism"—that is, for each morphological category there exists a separate system for forming the inflection. In this view, there would have to be one system for each transformation— past tense, possessive, plural, etc.—instead of a purely phonetic system serving the needs of several morphological transformations. This is not a flaw of connectionist models in general, but rather is specific to Rumelhart and McClelland's model. In fact, connectionist models exist that allow interaction between various levels of linguistic analysis, such as Waltz and Pollack's sentence interpretation model (see section 7.4.) Pinker and Prince's criticisms of the Rumelhart and McClelland model can be viewed as a challenge to connectionists to formulate a more linguistically accurate model, although this may involve the representation of explicit rules and reduction of the connectionist model to the status of an implementation theory for complex systems of rules.

7.13.Letter and Word Recognition

Rueckl (1986) developed a connectionist model to account for the mental process of letter and word recognition. His model was motivated by the desire to explain the well-known psychological effect of word repetition. Subjects in psychological experiments are better able to recognize words that they have recently seen. This is also true, Rueckl showed, of pseudo-words, that is, pronounceable non-words such as "zick". Retrieval models (e.g. Forster 1976, McClelland & Rumelhart 1985) account for these phenomena by theorizing that representations for words that are primed (perceived recently) are moved to a more accessible place from long-term memory, or, in the case of the pseudo-words, the representation is constructed during the priming, and it remains more accessible than other items in the long-term memory.

Rueckl's goal was to develop a model which explained these effects more simply. To do this, he turned to a connectionism. He also wanted to come up with a general model of the letter/word recognition process which explains such things as how words and letters are learned over time.

His model is partitioned into a series of modules or layers. The first module produces a retinotopic feature map (RTM) consisting of simple features such as lines, points, angles and curves. The RTM module consists of a two-dimensional representation of sensory input, like that impinging on a human retina. Each unit has a local receptive field which overlaps with the receptive fields of the units near it. There are units for each type of feature at each location. Units have responses that are best for a particular feature (such as a line at a particular orientation) but they also respond to similar features, so that a particular feature causes a pattern of activation in the RTM module. Thus, Rueckl's model is a distributed one.

Rueckl's second module is the object-centered feature map (OFM). The features represented in the RTM module are specified in the coordinate system of the visual fields. In the OFM module, an object's features are represented relative to the object's own center. Features are assumed to have patterns of activity that take up relatively few nodes in the OFM module, so that a number of features can be represented at once with little overlap.

The third level, the object identity representation (OI), consists of patterns of activity corresponding to entire objects, which can be either letters or words, depending on the stimuli given to the system.

The goal of Rueckl's system is to learn to form the same representations in the OFM and OI levels when the same object (letter or word) is presented at the RTM level, regardless of where in the retinal field the object is presented. This learning proceeds by having the system first learn to recognize simple objects, then complex conjunctions of these objects.

The first problem that Rueckl faced was the problem of achieving translation invariance; that is, to take a simple feature and have the system learn to evoke the same pattern of the OFM level, no matter where it was presented on the RTM level. One possible solution is brute-force: first present a single RTM–OFM association, then clamp the OFM pattern while RTM patterns corresponding to other positions of the stimulus are presented, and reinforce associations between each of these RTM patterns and the OFM pattern.

After simple elements are learned, the next task for the system is to learn the RTM–OFM relationship of complex conjunctions of elements. One problem that Rueckl discusses is the possibility that the representations of different simple elements in the conjunction will interfere with one another. One would hope that the representations will be sufficiently sparse so as to make this unlikely, but there is no guarantee of this.

One might argue that this loss of information is acceptable, as long as there is a unique representation for each conjunction, but Rueckl points out that information such as the number of distinct features in the stimulus may be lost; he gives the example of two horizontal lines in the stimulus, one above each other, like an "=". Since, by assumption, both lines would cause the same pattern in the OFM, the OFM would only reflect the presence of one feature, rather than two. Clearly the spatial relational information relating the two features must be retained in some form. Rueckl suggests the solution due to Hinton (1981b). Hinton adds a population of nodes representing reference frames at orientations and positions that sample the space of possible frames in some manner. These nodes serve to gate connections between RTM and OFM. Thus the two horizontal bars would excite different patterns in the OFM.

Rueckl also considers to the problem of classes of objects that are visually distinct. One would like to have the system respond similarly to "A" and "a", even though their visual patterns are quite distinct. In order to handle this, he posits that there is another module, the contextual model (CM), which along with the OFM, gives input to the OI. In order for "a" and "A" to have a similar pattern in the OI, it is sufficient for the CM to give the same input to the OI while both of them are presented. This will allow them to be classified together for certain purposes, while retaining their own distinct visual patterns. This type of representation can account for experiments (McClelland 1976) in which, because of limited stimulus presentation time, subjects are able to report the identity but not the case of a letter stimulus.

Rueckl considers the problem of word identification. While words, like letters, are just conjunctions of features, there is evidence, as common sense might conclude, that what is visually salient about words is the particular sequence of letters involved rather than the global impression that the configuration of features in the word confers.

The prerequisite for word recognition by Rueckl's system is therefore letter recognition; he assumes it has achieved this. Thus the pattern in the OFM caused by a word will be the superposition of the OFM patterns for the constituent letters, containing no information about their order—thus "rat" and "tar" would lead to the same OFM pattern. If this spatial information is to be retained then Hinton's gating scheme mentioned above may be used.

Word identification relies on the following property of the system: hat the input provided to OI by OFM by a particular letter is sufficiently similar, regardless of case, so as to make words in upper and lower case recognizable as the same word. It is also dependent on the gating by reference frames, in order to convey information about the relative position of letters in the word. Both of these are properties of the form of coarse coding, since the information about the relative position of the letters is not represented explicitly, but is a property of the overall representation.

Having elaborated his model, Rueckl is in a position to account for the word-repetition effect. It is understood by positing that the first time a word is presented, the connections between the OFM and OI units that are active during recognition are strengthened. This makes subsequent recognitions easier, because the relaxation process leading to recognition proceeds faster. Thus the word-repetition effect—both in its actual word and pseudo-word versions—emerges as a natural feature of the model. The explanation is less complex than that given by a retrieval model. The major difference between the word and the pseudo-word processes is that the pseudo-word representation constructed is new.

Rueckl considers the problem of how multiple words are perceived at once. The obvious answer is via multiple channels which the brain, with its multitudes of neurons, would be able to provide. The problem with duplicate channels is that word learning, as described above, is a local process occurring in a single channel. Thus, if you want to process words in multiple channels, they system must complicate the learning process.

One system that uses multiple channels is McClelland's Connection Information Distributor (1985), in which learning takes place in a central channel and this information (weights) is distributed to multiple channels for the purpose of parallel recognition. The alternative is to process words and letters serially, attending at different points in time to different elements of the stimulus.

If words are processed sequentially, then one would expect that letters would be too. This would lead you to believe that single letters are recognized faster than whole words, and that short words are recognized faster than long words. In fact, this is not the case, as Rueckl points out: words are recognized faster than single letters, and long words are identified just as fast as short ones are.

Postscript

In the less than ten years since the active revival of neural network research, researchers have shown the applicability of connectionist models to a wide variety of cognitive phenomena. These models have lent themselves naturally to the solution of cognitive problems requiring the integration of multiple constraints, such as object recognition or sentence processing. Several learning algorithms have been proven effective at embodying systems of constraints in a network.

There are several challenges ahead for researchers who want to discover networks that have general-purpose cognitive capabilities. Most researchers agree that this goal is dependent on the embodiment of large amounts of knowledge in a system, and it is best that this knowledge be learned, rather than explicitly wired in. This will require systems with numbers of units that are several orders of magnitude larger than the current system (a typical current system might have 10^2-10^5 units; the brain has about 10^{11}). Learning times, using current algorithms, even with relatively fast computers, for such larger networks, may be prohibitive. The development of special-purpose hardware that implements such algorithms as error back-propagation will ease this problem. Researchers will have to think carefully when designing the topology of their networks, in order not to waste connections. One principle they can use is to give each neuron a receptive field consisting only of nearby neurons; this principle is used by the brain.

Another major challenge to connectionists is to meet the objects given by Fodor and Pylyshyn that neural network models lack the representational power of logic or list-based symbolic computation. One aspect of this challenge is to find a connectionist implementation of the type/token distinction that expresses in a satisfying manner the distinction between a class and one of its members. A related issue is how one might bind variables in a neural network.

Most neural network models—for instance, almost all of those reviewed in this book—are concerned with a single domain of cognition, such as language processing or vision. Part of the reason for this is cultural, in that most researchers tend to be specialists in only one of these areas, and it is difficult to become expert in more than one. Nevertheless, most artificial intelligence researchers would agree that the development of intelligent systems is dependent on building bridges between two or more of these areas, especially between vision and natural language. Future connectionist systems will be highly modular, with sub-networks (modules) devoted to processing different types of information, and with the various modules passing information to one another.

It is still unclear which school in AI, connectionism or symbol-processing, will be the most successful, ultimately. Perhaps an approach that borrows ideas from both schools will succeed. There is the danger that much talent (and research money) may be drawn away from traditional AI in favor of connectionism, and traditional AI (which I do not think has played itself out) may be neglected. If this occurs, it may be unfortunate, because connectionism (given the current level of knowledge of the brain) may be a blind alley. Yet, if it does not produce results, the pendulum may swing back toward traditional AI. It is, however, very likely that connectionism will produce commercial results in both speech recognition and letter recognition, perhaps even of handwriting, within 10 years, if current trends in computing costs continue.

The ready availability of connectionist simulators (such as those available from the University of Rochester, the University of California at Los Angeles, and the George Mason University computer science departments) and inexpensive workstation-based computing has led to an explosion of neural network research. To follow the exciting course of events, one might consider joining the International Neural Network Society (INNS), attending its conferences or those of the AI societies, or reading some of the journals cited in the bibliography. Or one can simply get one of the simulators and start building models; many fruitful learning rules, cognitive domains, and network topologies are, no doubt, still to be explored.

Bibliography

Ackley, D. H. (1987). Stochastic Iterated Genetic Hill-climbing . Ph.D. Thesis, Carnegie-Mellon, Pittsburgh, PA.

Ackley, D. H., Hinton, G. E. & Sejnowksi, T. J. (1985). A Learning Algorithm for Boltzmann Machines. Cognitive Science, 9, 147-169.

Alspector, J. & Allen, R. B. (1987). A Neuromorphic VLSI Learning System. In P. Loseleben (Ed.), Advanced Research in VLSI: Proceedings of the 1987 Stanford Conference Cambridge, Mass.: MIT Press.

Amari, S. (1967). A Theory of Adaptive Pattern Classification. IEEE Transactions on Electronic Computers, EC-16, 299-307.

Amari, S. (1983). Field Theory of Self-Organizing Neural Nets. IEEE Transactions on Systems, Man, and Cybernetics, SMC-13, 741-748.

Anderson, C. (1986a). Learning and Problem Solving with Multilayer Connectionist Systems . Ph.D. Thesis, University of Massachusetts.

Anderson, D. Z. (1986b). Coherent Optical Eigenstate Memory. Optics Letters, 11, 56-58.

Anderson, J. A. (1983). Cognitive and Psychological Computation with Neural Models. IEEE Transactions on Systems, Man, and Cybernetics, 13(September/October), 799-815.

Anzai, Y. & Simon, H. A. (1979). The Theory of Learning by Doing. Psychological Review, 86.

Ash, T. (1989). Dynamic Node Creation in Connectionist Networks (technical report 8901). Cognitive Science Institute, University of California, San Diego.

Axelrod, R. (1987). The Evolution of Strategies in the Iterated Prisoner's Dilemma. In L. Davis (Ed.), Genetic Algorithms and Simulated Annealing Pitman: London.

Bahl, L. R., Jelinek, F. & Mercer, R. L. (1983). A Maximum Likelihood Approach to Continuous Speech Recognition. IEEE Transactions on Pattern Analysis and Machine Intelligence, PAMI-5, 179-190.

Ballard, D. H. (1988). Modular Learning in Neural Networks (technical report preprint). Department of Computer Science, University of Rochester.

Barlow, H. B. (1972). Single Units and Sensation: a Neuron Doctrine for Perceptual Psychology? Perception, 1, 371-394.

Barto, A. G. & Anandan, P. (1985). Pattern Recognizing Stochastic Learning Automata. IEEE Transactions on Systems, Man, and Cybernetics, 15, 360-375.

Barwise, J. & Perry, J. (1983). Situations and Attitudes . Cambridge MA: MIT Press.

Bienenstock, E. L., Cooper, L. N. & Munro, P. W. (1982). Theory for the Development of Neuron Selectivity; Orientation Specificity and Binocular Interaction in Visual Cortex. Journal of Neuroscience, 2, 32-48.

Bookman, L. A. (1988). A Connectionist Scheme for Modelling Context. In G. E. Hinton, T. J. Sejnowski & D. S. Touretzky (Ed.), Proceedings of the 1988 Connectionist Models Summer School San Mateo, CA: Morgan Kaufmann.

Brady, R. M. (1985). Optimization Strategies Gleaned from Biological Evolution. Nature, 317, 804-806.

Burt, P. J. (1984). The Pyramid as a Structure for Efficient Computation. In A. Rosenfeld (Ed.), <u>Multiresolution Image Processing and Analysis</u> Berlin: Springer-Verlag.

Carpenter, G. A. & Grossberg, S. (1987). A Massively Parallel Architecture for a Self-organizing Neural Pattern Recognition Machine. <u>Computer Vision, Graphics, and Image Processing</u>, <u>37</u>, 54-115.

Charniak, E. & Santos, E. (1987). A Connectionist Context-Free Parser Which is not Context-Free, But Then It is not Really Connectionist Either. <u>Proceedings of the Ninth Annual Conference of the Cognitive Science Society</u> (pp. 70-77). Seattle, WA: Erlbaum.

Chomsky, N. (1959). Review of Skinner's *Verbal Behavior*. <u>Language</u>, <u>35</u>, 26-58.

Chomsky, N. (1980). <u>Rules and Representations</u> . New York: Columbia University Press.

Clowes, M. B. (1971). On Seeing Things. <u>Artificial Intelligence</u>, <u>2</u>, 79-116.

Cohen, M. S. (1986). Design of A New Medium for Volume Holographic Information Processing. <u>Applied Optics</u>, <u>14</u>, 2288-94.

Cohen, P. R. & Feigenbaum, E. A. (1982). <u>The Handbook of Artificial Intelligence</u> . Los Altos, CA: William Kaufmann, Inc.

Cooper, L. N., Liberman, F. & Oja, E. (1979). A Theory for the Acquistion and Loss of Neuron Specificity in Visual Cortex. <u>Biological Cybernetics</u>, <u>33</u>, 9-28.

Cottrell, G. W. & Small, S. L. (1983). A Connectionist Scheme for Modelling Word Sense Disambiguation. <u>Cognition and Brain Theory</u>, <u>6</u>(1), 89-120.

Cottrell, G.W, Munro, P. & Zipser, D. (1987). Learning Internal Representations from Gray-Scale Images: An Example of Extensional Programming. <u>Proceedings of the Ninth Annual Conference of the Cognitive Science Society</u>, Seattle, WA: Erlbaum.

Cowan, J. D. & Sharp, D. H. (1988). Neural Nets and Artificial Intelligence. In S. R. Graubard (Ed.), The Artificial Intelligence Debate: false starts, real foundations Cambridge, Mass.: MIT Press.

Derthick, M. A. (1987). Factual and Counterfactual Reasoning by Constructing Plausible Models. Proceedings of the Conference of the American Association for Artificial Intelligence (AAAI) Seattle WA:

Dieterich, J. (1988). Knowledge-intensive Recruitment Learning (technical report TR-88-010). International Computer Science Institute, Berkeley.

Doddington, G. R. & Shalk, T. B. (1981). Speech Recognition: Turning Theory into Practice. IEEE Spectrum, (September), 26-32.

Dolan, C. P. & Dyer, M. G. (1987). Symbolic Schemata, Role Binding, and the Evolution of Structure in Connectionist Memories. Proceedings of the First International Conference on Neural Networks (pp. 287-298). San Diego, CA: IEEE.

Duda, R. O. & Hart, P. E. (1973). Pattern Classification and Scene Analysis . New York: Wiley.

Dyer, C. R. (1982). Pyramid Algorithms and Machines. In K. Preston & L. Uhr (Ed.), Multicomputers and Image Processing New York: Academic Press.

Elman, J. L. (1988). Finding Structure in Time (technical report 8801). Center for Research on Language, University of California, San Diego.

Fanty, M. (1985). Context-Free Parsing in Connectionist Networks (technical report 174). Computer Science Department, University of Rochester.

Feldman, J. A. (1986). Neural Representation of Conceptual Knowledge (technical report TR189). Department of Computer Science, University of Rochester.

Feldman, J. A. & Ballard, D. H. (1982). Connectionist Models and Their Properties. Cognitive Science, 6, 205-264.

Fennel, R. D. & Lesser, V. R. (1977). Parallelism in AI Problem-solving: A Case Study of HEARSAY-II. IEEE Transactions on Computers, C-26, 98-111.

Fillmore, C. J. (1968). The Case for Case. In E. Bach & R. T. Harms (Ed.), Universals in Linguistic Theory New York: Holt, Rinehart, and Winston.

Fletcher, R. (1980). Practical Methods of Optimization . New York: Wiley.

Fodor, J. A. (1981). Representations: Philosophical Essays on the Foundations of Cognitive Science . Cambridge MA: MIT Press.

Fodor, J. A. & Pylyshyn, Z. W. (1988). Connectionism and Cognitive Architecture: a Critical Analysis. In S. Pinker & J. Mehler (Ed.), Connections and Symbols Cambridge, Mass.: MIT Press.

Forgy, C. L. (1981). OPS5 User's Manual (technical report CMU-CS-78-116). Carnegie-Mellon University.

Forster, K. I. (1976). Accessing the Mental Lexicon. In E. C. T. Walker & R. J. Wales (Ed.), New Approaches to Language Mechanism Amsterdam: North Holland.

Francis, W. N. & Kucera, H. (1979). Manual of Information to Accompany a Standard Corpus of Present-Day American English for Use with Digital Computers Technical report, Brown University.

Fukushima, K. (1975). Cognitron: a self-organizing multilayered neural network. Biological Cybernetics, 20, 121-136.

Gallant, S. I. (1988). Connectionist Expert Systems. Communications of the ACM, 31(2), 152-169.

Gardner, H. (1985). The Mind's New Science: a History of the Cognitive Revolution . New York: Basic Books.

Geman, S. & Geman, D. (1984). Stochastic Relaxation, Gibbs Distributions, and the Bayesian Restoration of Images. IEEE Transactions on Pattern Analysis and Machine Intelligence, PAMI-6(721-741),

Graubard, S. R. (1988). The Artificial Intelligence Debate: False Starts, Real Foundations . Cambridge, Mass.: MIT Press.

Greenough, W. T. & Bailey, C. H. (1988). The Anatomy of a Memory: Convergence of Results Across a Diversity of Tests. Trends in Neuroscience, 11, 142-147.

Grossberg, S. (1976). Adaptive Pattern Classification and Universal Recoding I & II. Biological Cybernetics, 23(121-134, 187-202),

Hanna, P. R., Hanna, J. S., Hodges, R. E. & Rudorf, E. H. (1966). Phoneme—Grapheme Correspondences as Cutes to Spelling Improvement (technical report . U.S. Department of Health, Education, and Welfare.

Hanson, S. & Kegl, J. (1987). PARSNIP: A Connectionist Network that Learns Natural Language from Exposure to Natural Language Sentences. Proceedings of the Ninth Annual Conference of the Cognitive Science Society Hillsdale, NJ: Erlbaum.

Hebb, D. O. (1949). The Organization of Behavior . New York: Wiley.

Hewett, C. (1977). Viewing Control Structures as Patterns of Passing Messages. The Artificial Intelligence Journal, 8(232-364),

Hillis, D. (1985). The Connection Machine . Cambridge, MA: MIT Press.

Hinton, G. E. (1981a). Implementing Semantic Networks in Parallel Hardware. In G. E. Hinton & J. A. Anderson (Ed.), Parallel Models of Associative Memory Hillsdale, NJ: Erlbaum.

Hinton, G. E. (1981b). Shape representation in Parallel Systems. Proceedings of the Seventh International Conference on Artificial Intelligence Vancouver, BC, Canada: Erlbaum.

Hinton, G. E. (1986). Learning Distributed Representations of Concepts. <u>Proceedings of the Ninth Annual Conference of the Cognitive Science Society</u> : Erlbaum.

Hinton, G. E. (1989). Connectionist Learning Procedures. <u>Artificial Intelligence</u>, to appear.

Hinton, G. E. & McClelland, J. L. (1987a). <u>Learning Representations by Recirculation</u> (technical report in preparation). Carnegie-Mellon University.

Hinton, G. E., McClelland, J. L. & Rumelhart, D. E. (1986a). Distributed Representations. In D. E. Rumelhart & J. L. McClelland (Ed.), <u>Parallel Distributed Processing: Explorations in the Microstructure of Cognition. Volume 1: Foundations.</u> Cambridge, Mass.: MIT Press.

Hinton, G. E. & Plaut, D. C. (1987b). Using Fast Weights to Deblur Old Memories. <u>Proceedings of the Ninth Annual Conference of the Cognitive Science Society</u> Seattle, WA: Erlbaum.

Hinton, G. E. & Sejnowski, T. J. (1986b). Learning and Relearning in Boltzmann Machines. In D. E. Rumelhart & J. L. McClelland (Ed.), <u>Parallel Distributed Processing: Explorations in the Microstructure of Cognition. Volume 1: Foundations.</u> Cambridge, Mass.: MIT Press.

Holland, J. H. (1975). <u>Adaptation in Natural and Artificial Systems</u> . Ann Arbor, Mich.: Univ. of Michigan Press.

Honavar, V. (1989). <u>Perceptual Development and Learning: from Behavioral, Neurophysiological and Morphological Evidence to Computational Models</u> (technical report 818). Computer Sciences Department, University of Wisconsin.

Honavar, V. & Uhr, L. (1987). <u>Recognition Cones: A Neuronal Architecture for Perception and Learning</u> (technical report 717). University of Wisconsin-Madison, Computer Sciences Dept.

Honavar, V. & Uhr, L. (1988). A Network of Neuron-like Units that Learns to Perceive by Generation as Well as Reweighting of its Links. In G. E. Hinton, T. J. Sejnowski & D. S. Touretzky (Ed.),

Proceedings of the 1988 Connectionist Models Summer School San Mateo, CA: Morgan Kaufmann.

Honavar, V. & Uhr, L. (1989a). Brain-Structured Connectionist Networks that Perceive and Learn. *Connection Science* (to appear)

Honavar, V. & Uhr, L. (1989b). Experimental Results indicate that Generation, Local Receptive Fields and Global Convergence Improve Perceptual Learning in Connectionist Networks. *Proceedings of the International Joint Conference on Artificial Intelligence* : .

Hopcroft, J. E. & Ullman, J. D. (1979). *Introduction to Automata Theory, Languages, and Computation* . Reading, Mass.: Addison-Wesley.

Hopfield, J. J. (1982). Neural Networks and Physical Systems with Emergent Collective Computational Abilities. *Proceedings of the National Academy of Sciences,* 79(April), 2554-2558.

Hopfield, J. J. & Tank, D. (1985). "Neural" Computation of Decisions in Optimization Problems. *Biological Cybernetics,* 52(141-152),

Hopfield, J. J. & Tank, D. W. (1986a). *Disordered Systems and Biological Organization* Berlin: Springer-Verlag.

Hopfield, J. J. & Tank, D. W. (1986b). Computing with Neural Circuits: A Model. *Science,* 233, 625-633.

Hopfield, J. J. & Tank, D. W. (1987). Concentrating Information in Time: Analog Neural Networks with Applications to Speech Recognition Problems. *Proceedings of the IEEE First International Conference on Neural Networks* San Diego, CA: IEEE.

Huffman, D. A. (1971). Impossible Objects as Nonsense Sentences. In E. W. Elcock & D. Michie (Ed.), *Machine Intelligence 8* (pp. 493-509). Edinburgh: Edinburgh University Press.

Hummel, R. A. & Zucker, S. W. (1983). On the Foundations of Relaxation Labeling Processes. *IEEE Transactions on Pattern Analysis and Machine Intelligence,* PAMI-5, 267-287.

Jackendoff, R. (1983). Semantics and Cognition . Cambridge MA: MIT Press.

Jordan, M. I. (1986a). Attractor Dynamics and Parallelism in a Connectionist Sequential Machine. Proceedings of the Proceedings of the Eighth Annual Conference of the Cognitive Science Society : Erlbaum.

Jordan, M. I. (1986b). Serial Order: A Parallel, Distributed Processing Approach (technical report ICS-8604). University of California, San Diego. Institute for Cognitive Science.

Kanade, T. (1980). A Theory of Origami World. Artificial Intelligence, 13, 279-311.

Kasyap, R. L., Blaydon, C. C. & Fu, K. S. (1970). Stochastic Approximation. In K. S. Fu & J. M. Mendel (Ed.), Adaptation, Learning, and Pattern Recognition Systems: theory and applications New York: Academic Press.

Kay, M. (1973). The MIND System. In R. Rustin (Ed.), Natural Language Processing New York: Algorithmics Press.

Kienker, P. K., Sejnowski, T. J., Hinton, G. E. & Schumacher, L. E. (1986). Separating Figure from Ground with a Parallel Network. Perception, 15, 197-216.

Kirkpatrick, S., Gelatt, C. D. & Vecchi, M. P. (1983). Optimization by Simulated Annealing. Science, 220, 671-680.

Knapp, A. & Anderson, J. A. (1984). Theory of Categorization based on Distributed Memory Storage. Journal of Experimental Psychology: Learning, Memory, and Cognition, 10, 616-637.

Kohonen, T. (1988). Self-Organization and Assocative Memory . Berlin: Springer-Verlag.

Kruschke, J. K. (1988). Creating Local and Distributed Bottlenecks in Hidden Layers of Back-Propagation Networks. Proceedings of the 1988 Connectionist Summer School Carnegie-Mellon University, Pittsburgh PA: Morgan Kaufmann.

Lakoff, G. (1987). Women, Fire, and Dangerous Things . Chicago: University of Chicago Press.

Lakoff, G. (1988). A Suggestion for a Linguistics with Connectionist Foundations. In G. E. Hinton, T. J. Sejnowski & D. S. Touretzky (Ed.), Proceedings of the 1988 Connectionist Models Summer School San Mateo, CA: Morgan Kaufmann.

Lang, K. (1987). Connectionist Speech Recognition. Thesis Proposal, Carnegie-Mellon University:

Langacker, R. (1987). Foundations of Cognitive Grammar . Stanford: Stanford University Press.

Langley, P. (1985). Learning to Search: from Weak Methods to Domain-specific Heuristics. Cognitive Science, 9, 217-260.

Le Cun, Y. (1987). Modèles Connexionnistes le l'Apprentissage . Ph.D. Thesis, Université Pierre et Marie Curie, Paris.

Li, T. & Chun, H. W. (1987). A Massively Parallel Network-based Natural Language Parsing System. Proceedings of the The Second International Conference on Computers and Applications.

Linsker, R. (1986a). From Basic Network Principles to Neural Architecture: Emergence of Orientation Columns. Proceedings of the National Academy of Sciences USA, 83, 8779-8783.

Linsker, R. (1986b). From Basic Network Principles to Neural Architecture: Emergence of Orientation-selection Cells. Proceedings of the National Academy of Sciences USA, 83, 8390-8394.

Linsker, R. (1986c). From Basic Network Principles to Neural Architecture: Emergence of Spatial Opponent Cells. Proceedings of the National Academy of Sciences USA, 83,7508-7512.

Linsker, R. (1987). Development of Feature-analyzing Cells and Their Columnar Organization in a Layered Self-adaptive Network. In R. Cotterill (Ed.), Computer Simulation in Brain Science Cambridge University Press.

Lippmann, R. P. (1987). An Introduction to Computing with Neural Nets. IEEE ASSP Magazine, 4(2), 4ff.

Lippmann, R. P. & Gold, B. (1987). Neural-Net Classifiers Useful for Speech Recognition. Proceedings of the First International Conference on Neural Networks , San Diego: IEEE.

Mackworth, A. K. (1977). Consistancy in Networks of Relations. Artificial Intelligence, 8,99-118.

Marr, D. (1978). Representing Visual Information. In A. R. Hanson & E. M. Riseman (Ed.), Computer Vision Systems (pp. 61-80). New York: Academic Press.

McClelland, J. L. (1976). Preliminary Letter Identification in the Perception of Words and Nonwords. Journal of Experimental Psychology: Human Perception and Performance, 4, 80-91.

McClelland, J. L. (1985). Putting Knowledge in its Place: A Scheme for Programming Parallel Processing Structures on the Fly. Cognitive Science, 9, 113-146.

McClelland, J. L. & Elman, J. L. (1986a). Interactive Processes in Speech Perception: The TRACE model. In D. E. Rumelhart & J. L. McClelland (Ed.), Parallel Distributed Processing: Explorations in the Microstructure of Cognition. Volume 1: Foundations. Cambridge, Mass.: MIT Press.

McClelland, J. L. & Kawamoto, A. H. (1986b). Mechanisms of Sentence Processing: Assigning Roles to Constituents of Sentences. In D. E. Rumelhart & J. L. McClelland (Ed.), Parallel Distributed Processing: Explorations in the Microstructure of Cognition. Volume 1: Foundations. Cambridge, Mass.: MIT Press.

McClelland, J. L. & Rumelhart, D. E. (1985). An Interactive Activation Model of Context Effects in Letter Perception: Part 1. Psychological Review, 88, 375-407.

McCloskey, M. & Cohen, N. J. (1987). The Sequential Learning Problem in Connectionist Models: Paper read at the meetings of the Psychonomic Society, Washington, November.

McCulloch, W. S. & Pitts, W. H. (1943). A Logical Calculus of the Ideas Immanent in Nervous Activity. Bulletin of Mathematical Biophysics, 5, 115-133.

Metropolis, N., Rosenbluth, A., Rosenbluth, M., Teller, A. & Teller, E. (1953) Equation of State Calculations for Fast Computing Machines. Journal of Chemical Physics, 6, 1087ff.

Mikkulainen, R. & Dyer, M. (1988). Encoding Input/Output Representations in Connectionist Cognitive Systems. Proceedings of the 1988 Connectionist Models Summer School Carnegie-Mellon University: Morgan Kaufmann.

Minsky, M. (1975). A Framework for Representing Knowledge. In P. Winston (Ed.), The Psychology of Computer Vision New York: McGraw-Hill.

Minsky, M. & Papert, S. (1969). Perceptrons: An Introduction to Computational Geometry . Cambridge, Massachusetts: The MIT Press.

Minsky, M. L. (1977). Plain Talk about Neurodevelopmental Epistemology. Proceedings of the 5th International Joint Conference on Artificial Intelligence, 1083-1092 .

Mjolsness, E., Sharp, D. H. & Alpert, B. K. (1988). Scaling, Machine Learning, and Genetic Neural Nets (technical report YALEU/DCS/TR-613, Yale; also technical report LA-UR-88-142, Los Alamos.)

Mjolsness, E. & Sharp, D. N. (1986). A Preliminary Analysis of Recursively Generated Networks. In J. S. Denker (Ed.), Proceedings of the AIP Conference on Neural Networks for Computing.

Narendra, K. S. & Thathachar, M. A. L. (1974). Learning Automata—A Survey. IEEE Transations on Systems, Man, and Cybernetics, 4(July), 323-334.

Newell, A. (1980). Physical Symbol Systems. Cognitive Science, 4, 135-183.

Oden, G. C. (1988a). Fuzzy Prop: A Symbolic Superstrate for Connectionist Models. <u>Proceedings of the Second IEEE International Conference on Neural Networks</u> San Diego, CA:IEEE .

Oden, G. C. (1988b). <u>Why the Difference Between Connectionism and Anything Else is More Than You Might Think but Less Than You Might Hope</u> (technical report, University of Wisconsin, Dept. of Psychology.)

Oden, G. C. & Rueckl, J. G. (1986). Taking Language by the Hand: Reading Handwritten Words. <u>Proceedings of the Paper presented at the Twenty-seventh Annual Meeting of the Psychonomics Society</u> New Orleans, LA.

Parker, D. B. (1985). <u>Learning-logic</u> (technical report TR-47). Sloan School of Management, MIT.

Parker, D. B. (1987). <u>Second order Back-propagation: An Optimal Adaptive Algorithm for any Adaptive Network</u> (Unpublished Manuscript)

Patil, R. S. (1987). A Case Study on Evolution of System Building Expertise: Medical Diagnosis. In W. E. L. Grimson & R. S. Patil (Ed.), <u>AI in the 1980s and Beyond</u> Cambridge MA: MIT Press.

Pinker, S. (1984). <u>Language Learnability and Language Development</u> . Cambridge, MA: Harvard University Press.

Pinker, S. & Prince, A. (1988). On Language and Connectionism: Analysis of a Parallel Distributed Processing Model of Language Acquisition. In S. Pinker & J. Mehler (Ed.), <u>Connections and Symbols</u> Cambridge, Mass.: MIT Press.

Plaut, D. C. & Hinton, G. E. (1987). Learning Sets of Filters using Back-propagation. <u>Computer Speech and Language</u>, 2.

Posner, M. I. (1973). <u>Cognition: An introduction</u> . Glenview, IL: Scott, Foresman.

Posner, M. I. & Keele, S. W. (1968a). On the Genesis of Abstact Ideas. <u>Journal of Experimental Psychology</u>, <u>83</u>, 353-363.

Posner, M. I. & Keele, S. W. (1968b). Retention of Abstact Ideas. Journal of Experimental Psychology, 83, 304-308.

Pribram, K. (1971). Languages of the Brain . Englewood Cliffs, NJ: Prentice-Hall.

Pylyshyn, Z. W. (1984). Computation and Cognition: Toward a Foundation for Cognitive Science . Cambridge MA: MIT Press.

Rabiner, L. R. & Juang, B. H. (1986). An Introduction to Hidden Markov Models. IEEE Acoustics, Speech and Signal Processing Magazine, 3, 4-16.

Randell, B., Lee, P. A. & Treleaven, P. C. (1978). Reliability Issues in Computer System Design. Computing Surveys, 10(2), 123-165.

Reber, A. S. (1967). Implicit Learning of Artifical Grammars. Journal of Verbal Learning and Verbal Behavior, 5, 855-863.

Reeke, G. N. & Edelman, G. M. (1988). Real Brains and Artificial Intelligence. In S. R. Graubard (Ed.), The Artificial Intelligence Debate: False Starts, Real Foundations Cambridge, Mass.: MIT Press.

Reggia, J. A., Marsland, P. M. & Berndt, R. S. (1988). Competitive Dynamics in a Dual-route Connectionist Model of Print-to-sound Transformation. Complex Systems, 2, 509-547.

Regier, T. (1988). Recognizing Image-Schemas Using Programmable Networks. In G. E. Hinton, T. J. Sejnowski & D. S. Touretzky (Ed.), Proceedings of the 1988 Connectionist Models Summer School San Mateo, CA: Morgan Kaufmann.

Rosenberg, C. R. (1987). Revealing the Structure of NETtalk's Internal Representations. Proceedings of the Ninth Annual Conference of the Cognitive Science Society (pp. 537-554). Seattle, WA: Erlbaum.

Rosenblatt, F. (1961). Principles of Neurodynamics: Perceptrons and the Theory of Brain Mechanisms . Washington DC: Spartan Books.

Rosenbloom, P. S. & Newell, A. (1986). The Chunking of Goal Hierarchies: A Generalized Model of Practice. In R. S. Michalski, J. G. Carbonell & T. M. Mitchell (Ed.), Machine Learning: An Artificial Intelligence Approach, Vol. II Los Altos, CA: Morgan Kaufmann.

Rosenfeld, A. & Kak, A. C. (1976). Digital Picture Processing . New York: Academic Press.

Rosenfeld, R. & Touretzky, D. (1988). Coarse-Coded Symbol Memories and their Properties. Complex Systems.

Rueckl, J. G. (1986). A Distributed Connectionist Model of Letter and Word Identification . Ph.D. Thesis, University of Wisconsin.

Rueckl, J. G., Cave, K. R. & Kosslyn, S. M. (1988). Why are "What" and "Where" Processed by Separate Cortical Visual Systems? A Computational Investigation. Journal of Cognitive Neuroscience.

Rumelhart, D. & McClelland, J. (1986a). On Learning the Past Tenses of English Verbs. In J. McClelland & D. Rumelhart (Ed.), Parallel Distributed Processing: Explorations in the Microstructure of Cognition; Vol. 2: Psychological and Biological Models Cambridge, Mass.: MIT Press.

Rumelhart, D. & McClelland, J. (1986b). Parallel Distributed Processing: Explorations in the Microstructure of Cognition; Vol. 1: Foundations. Vol. 2: Psychological and Biological Models. Cambridge, Mass.: MIT Press.

Rumelhart, D. & Zipser, D. (1985). Feature Discovery by Competitive Learning. Cognitive Science, 9, 75-112.

Rumelhart, D. E., Hinton, G. E. & Williams, R. J. (1986c). Learning Internal Representations by Back-propagating Errors. Nature, 323(533-536),

Rumelhart, D. E., Hinton, G. E. & Williams, R. J. (1986d). Learning Internal Representations by Error Propagation. In D. E. Rumelhart & J. L. McClelland (Ed.), Parallel Distributed Processing: explorations in the microstructure of cognition; vol. 1: Foundations Cambridge, Massachusetts: The MIT Press.

Rumelhart, D. E. & McClelland, J. L. (1986e). PDP Models and General Issues in Cognitive Science. In D. E. Rumelhart & J. L. McClelland (Ed.), Parallel Distributed Processing: Vol. 1: Foundations Cambridge, Mass.: MIT Press.

Rumelhart, D. E., Smolensky, P., McClelland, J. L. & Hinton, G. E. (1986f). Schemata and Sequential Thought Processes in PDP Models. In J. L. McClelland & D. E. Rumelhart (Ed.), Parallel Distributed Processing: Explorations in the microstructure of cognition: vol. 2: Psychological and Biological Models Cambridge, Mass.: MIT Press.

Sabbah, D. (1985). Computing with Connections in Visual Recognition of Origami Objects. Cognitive Science, 9, 25-50.

Saito, K. & Nakano, R. (1988). Medical Diagnostic Expert System Based on PDP model. Proceedings of the IEEE International Conference on Neural Networks, San Diego: IEEE.

Samuel, A. L. (1963). Some Studies in Machine Learning Using the Game of Checkers. In E. A. Feigenbaum & J. Feldman (Ed.), Computers and Thought New York: McGraw-Hill.

Sandon, P. A. & Uhr, L. M. (1988). A Local Interaction Heuristic for Adaptive Networks. Proceedings of the IEEE International Conference on Neural Networks San Diego: IEEE.

Sankoof, D. & Kruskal,J.B. (Ed.) (1983). Time Warps, String Edits, and Macromolecules : the Theory and Practice of Sequence Comparison. Reading, MA: Addison-Wesley.

Schank, R. C. & Abelson, R. P. (1977). Scripts, Plans, Goals, and Understanding . Hillsdale, NJ: Erlbaum.

Schwartz, J. T. (1988). The New Connectionism: Developing relationships between Neuroscience and Artificial Intelligence. In S. R. Graubard (Ed.), The Artificial Intelligence Debate: False Starts, Real Foundations Cambridge, Mass.: MIT Press.

Sejnowski, T. J. & Rosenberg, C. (1986). NETtalk: A Parallel Network that Learns to Read Aloud (technical report JHU-EECS-86-01). Johns Hopkins University.

Sejnowski, T. J. & Rosenberg, C. (1987). Parallel Networks that Learn to Pronounce English Text. Complex Systems, 1(145-168),

Selman, B. & Hirst, G. (1987). Parsing as an Energy Minimization Problem. In L. Davis (Ed.), Genetic Algorithms and Simulated Annealing Pitman: London.

Servan-Schreiber, D., Cleeremans, A. & McClelland, J. L. (1988). Encoding Sequential Structure in Simple Recurrent Networks (technical report CMU-CS-88-183). Carnegie-Mellon University.

Shastri, L. (1988). A Connectionist Approach to Knowledge Representation and Limited Inference. Cognitive Science, 12, 331-392.

Shepard, R. N. (1962). The Analysis of Proximities: Multi-dimensional Scaling with an Unknown Distance Function, I & II. Psychometrika, 27, 125-40, 219-46.

Smolensky, P. (1986). Information Processing in Dynamical Systems: Foundations of Harmony Theory. In J. McClelland & D. Rumelhart (Ed.), Parallel Distributed Processing: Explorations in the Microstructure of Cognition; vol. 1: Foundations Cambridge, Mass.: MIT Press.

Smolensky, P. (1988). On the Proper Treatment of Connectionism. Behavioral and Brain Sciences, 11, 1-23.

Steinbuch, K. (1963). Automat und Mensch . Berlin: Springer.

Sutton, R. S. (1984). Temporal Aspects of Credit Assignment in Reinforcement Learning . Ph.D. Thesis, University of Massachusetts.

Sutton, R. S. (1988). Learning to Predict by the Methods of Temporal Differences. Machine Learning, 3, 9-44.

Tanimoto, S. L. (1978). Regular Hierarchical Image and Processing Structures in Machine Vision. In A. R. Hanson & E. M. Riseman (Ed.), Computer Vision Systems New York: Academic Press.

Taylor, W. K. (1956). Electrical Simulation of Some Nervous System Functional Activity. In E. C. Cherry (Ed.), Information Theory London: Butterworths.

Touretzky, D. S. (1986). BoltzCONS: Reconciling Connectionism with the Recursive Structure of Stacks and Trees. Proceedings of the 8th Annual Conference of the Cognitive Science Society , 155-64.

Touretzky, D. S. (1987). Representing Conceptual Structures in a Neural Network. Proceedings of the IEEE First International Conference on Neural Networks San Diego: IEEE.

Touretzky, D. S. (1988). Connectionism and PP Attachment. In D. Touretzky, G. Hinton & T. Sejnowski (Ed.), Proceedings of the 1988 Connectionist Models Summer School (pp. 325-332). Carnegie-Mellon University: Morgan Kaufmann.

Touretzky, D. S. (1989a). Connectionism and Compositional Semantics (technical report CMU-CS-89-147). Computer Science Department, Carnegie-Mellon University.

Touretzky, D. S. (1989b). Rules and Maps in Connectionist Symbol Processing (technical report CMU-CS-89-158). Computer Science Department, Carnegie-Mellon University.

Touretzky, D. S. (1989c). Towards a Connectionist Phonology: the "Many Maps" Approach to Sequence Manipulation (technical report CMU-CS-89-158). Computer Science Department, Carnegie-Mellon University.

Touretzky, D. S. & Hinton, G. E. (1985). Symbols Among the Neurons: Details of a Connectionist Inference Architecture. Proceedings of the International Joint Conference on Artificial Intelligence,Los Angeles.

Touretzky, D. S. & Hinton, G. E. (1988). A Distributed Connectionist Production System. Cognitive Science, 12(3), 423-466.

Uhr, L. (1972). Layered Recognition Cone Networks that Preprocess, Classify, and Describe. IEEE Transactions on Computers, 21, 758-768.

Uhr, L. (1983). Pyramid Multi-computer Structures, and Augmented Pyramids. In M. J. B. Duff (Ed.), Computing Structures for Image Processing London: Academic Press.

Uhr, L. (1987). Highly parallel, hierarchical, recognition cone perceptual structures. In L. Uhr (Ed.), Parallel Computer Vision New York: Academic Press.

Ullman, S. (1984). Visual Routines. Cognition, 18, 97-159.

Utgoff, P. E. (1986). Shift of Bias for Inductive Concept Learning. In R. S. Michalski, J. G. Carbonell & T. M. Mitchell (Ed.), Machine Learning: An Artificial Intelligence Approach Los Altos, CA: Morgan Kaufmann.

Valiant, L. G. (1984). A Theory of the Learnable. Communications of the ACM, 27, 1134-1142.

Von der Molsburg, C. (1973). Self-organization of Orientation-sensitive Cells in Striate Cortex. Kybernetik, 14(85-100),

Von Neumann, J. (1956). Probabilistic Logics and the Synthesis of Reliable Organisms from Unreliable Components. In C. E. Shannon & J. McCarthy (Ed.), Automata Studies Princeton, N.J.: Princeton University Press.

Waltz, D. (1975). Generating Semantic Descriptions from Drawings of Scenes with Shadows. In P. Winston (Ed.), The Psychology of Computer Vision (pp. 19-92). New York: McGraw-Hill.

Waltz, D. L. & Pollack, J. B. (1985). Massively Parallel Parsing: A Strongly Interactive Model of Natural Language Interpretation. Cognitive Science, 9, 51-74.

Watrous, R. L. & Shastri, L. (1987). Learning Phonetic Features using Connectionist Networks: An Experiment in Speech Recognition. Proceedings of the First International Conference on Neural Networks San Diego: IEEE.

Werbos, P. J. (1974). Beyond Regression: New Tools for Prediction and Analysis in the Behavioral Sciences . Ph.D. Thesis, Harvard University.

Wickelgren, W. A. (1969). Context-sensitive Coding, Associative Memory, and Serial Order in (Speech) Behavior. Psychological Review, 76(44-60),

Widrow, B. (1962). Generalization and Information Storage in Networks of Adaline Neurons. In M. C. Yovits, G. T. Jacobi & G. D. Goldstein (Ed.), Self-Organizing Systems 1962 Washington DC: Spartan Books.

Widrow, B., Gupta, N. K. & Maitra, S. (1973). Punish/reward: Learning with a Critic in Adaptive Threshold Systems. IEEE Transactions on Systems, Man, and Cybernetics, 5, 455-465.

Widrow, B. & Hoff, M. E. (1960). Adaptive Switching Circuits. IRE WESCON Conv. Record, Part 4., , 96-104.

Widrow, B. & Stearns, S. D. (1985). Adaptive Signal Processing . Prentice-Hall.

Wilensky, R. (1986). Common LISPcraft . New York: W.W. Norton.

Willshaw, D. (1981). Holography, Associative Memory, and Inductive Generalization. In G. E. Hinton & J. A. Anderson (Ed.), Parallel Models of Associative Memory Hillsdale, N.J.: Erlbaum.

Willshaw, D. J., Buneman, O. P. & Longuet-Higgins, H. C. (1969). Non-holographic Associative Memory. Nature, 222,

Winograd, T. (1983). Language as a Cognitive Process . Reading, Mass.: Addison-Wesley.

Zadeh, L. A. (1973). Outline of a New Approach to the Analysis of Complex Systems and Decision Processes. IEEE Transactions on Systems, Man and Cybernetics SMC-3, (January), 22-44.

Zucker, S., Hummel, R. & Rosenfeld, A. (1977). An Application of Relaxation Labeling to Line and Curve Enhancement. IEEE Transactions on Computers, C-26(4), 394-403.

Index